POWER
AND
POLITICS

POWER
AND
POLITICS

*Federal Higher Education
Policy Making in the 1990s*

Michael D. Parsons

State University of New York Press

Published by State University of New York Press, Albany

© 1997 State University of New York

Printed in the United States of America

For information, address the State University of New York Press,
State University Plaza, Albany, NY 12246

Production design by David Ford
Marketing by Nancy Farrell

Library of Congress Cataloging-in-Publication Data

Parson, Michael D. (Michael David)
     Power and politics : federal higher education policymaking in the
1990s / Michael D. Parsons.
         p.   cm.
     Includes bibliographical references and index.
     ISBN 0-7914-3423-0 (alk. paper). — ISBN 0-7914-3424-9 (pbk. :
alk. paper)
     1. Higher education and state—United States.   2. Politics and
education—United States.   3. Power (Social sciences)—United
States.   I. Title.
LC173.P37   1997
379.73--dc20   96-43399
                                                                            CIP

10 9 8 7 6 5 4 3 2 1

CONTENTS

ACKNOWLEDGMENTS

The author gratefully acknowledges permission to quote from the following works:

Cooper, K. (1992, February 4). Hill Chairman wants to reshape student aid. *The New York Times*, A9. Reprinted with the permission of *The New York Times*.

DeLoughry, T. J. (1991, March 27). Preparation pays off as students impress lawmakers with testimony on aid. *The Chronicle of Higher Education*, pp. A23, A24. Reprinted with the permission of *The Chronicle of Higher Education*.

Finn, Jr., C. E. (1980, September). The future of education's liberal consensus. *Change*, 25–30. Reprinted with the permission of The Helen Dwight Reid Educational Foundation. Published by Heldref Publications, 1319 18th Street, NW, Washington, D.C. 20036-1802. Copyright 1980.

Johnstone, D. B., Evans, S. V., & Jerue, R. T. (1990). Reauthorization: What's important, what's not. *Educational Record, 71*, 29–33. Reprinted with the permission of the American Council on Education.

McCool, D. (1989). Subgovernments and the impact of policy fragmentation and accommodation. *Policy Studies Review, 8*, 264–87. Reprinted with the permission of the *Policy Studies Review*.

Moynihan, D. P. (1971). On universal higher education. In W. T. Furniss (Ed.), *Higher education for everybody: Issues and implications* (pp. 233–54). Washington, D.C.: American Council on Education. © 1971 American Council on Education. Reprinted with permission.

Ozer, K. A. (1986). Congress and the politics of financial aid: A sudent view. *Academe, 72*, 25–27. Reprinted with the permission of the American Association of University Professors.

Zook, J. (1994, February 2). Key chairman to retire. *The Chronicle of Higher Education*, pp. A21, A24. Reprinted with the permission of *The Chronicle of Higher Education*.

PREFACE:
Power and Politics

The study that follows started in the summer of 1990 when Professor Don Hossler of the Indiana University School of Education invited a group of doctoral students to his home to discuss the formation of a research team to track the upcoming reauthorization of the Higher Education Act (HEA). The invitation seemed like an ideal opportunity to develop new research skills, work with a research team and possibly assist team members who wanted to develop a project around some aspect of the reauthorization process. As the team evolved, with different members taking on different tasks, I took on the task of tracking interactions between the White House, the Congress, and the higher education associations. What started as a social and learning experience quickly evolved into a research project as the contradiction between the rather limited power of the higher education associations and the remarkable growth of programs authorized by HEA became too intriguing to ignore. The questions raised by the apparent contradiction between power and policy outcomes moved the project to the center of my research agenda where it has remained during the 1990s.

Conventional measures and assessments of power tell us that the higher education associations are not powerful policy actors. The American Council on Education (ACE) cannot rally the electorate to oust a member of Congress who disagreed with ACE on a key issue or failed to give his/her vote to ACE on an important bill. The National Association of State Universities and Land-Grant Colleges (NASULGC) does not give large campaign gifts to its friends or finance election eve media blitzes against its opponents. Until recently, no higher education association made campaign contributions and even now contributions are expressions of goodwill far too small to make an impact on today's multimillion dollar election campaigns. The American Association of State Colleges and Universities (AASCU) cannot deliver congressional votes on key education issues. Finally none of the associations can create or produce the type of letter writing or call-in campaigns associated with groups such as the American Association of Retired Persons (AARP) or the National Rifle Association (NRA). The last two acronyms are well known to Americans who watch the news or read a newspaper but the same people have probably never heard of the higher education associations represented by the acronyms AACJC, AAU, and NAICU.

Despite the lack of power as measured by conventional standards, the higher education associations have apparently succeeded in convincing Congress to dramatically expand the scope and size of federal student aid programs. A College Board (1990) analysis of trends in student aid found that aid grew by 24 percent in the 1980s even though the Reagan administration consistently called for decreases in federal student aid spending. In real dollars, spending in 1989–90 was forty times greater than it had been in 1963–64, the year just prior to the passage of HEA. While the higher education associations cannot take full credit for this remarkable growth, it does raise the question of the meaning of power in the higher education policy arena. How is it that groups that are not powerful by conventional definitions of power still succeed in having their policy agendas adopted and implemented?

The literature on higher education policymaking largely ignores the question of power. This may be due, in part, to the problems surrounding the use of power as a research concept. One of the problems associated with power is the difficulty in defining power in operational terms. Everyone seems to intuitively understand the meaning of power but cannot agree on what power means when it comes time to provide a precise definition. While many have tried, none have been able to offer a definition of power that applies at all times and in all places. A related problem is that definitions and theories of power tend to determine what researchers will discover by telling them what to look for prior to the actual research. Power is not discovered through rigorous, disciplined, objective research but rather is a function of the methodology and theory selected to guide the inquiry. Given that these are but a few of the problems associated with the study of power, it is not surprising that researchers have elected to focus on other higher education policy issues leaving power to the implicit understanding and interpretation of readers.

At the same time, the intractable nature of the problem of power makes it intellectually seductive. The contradiction between conventional notions of power and actual outcomes in the higher education policy arena makes the question of power irresistible. The problem facing power researchers is one of reconstructing and reclaiming power so that it can be used as an analytical and explanatory concept in policy analysis and research. This ambitious goal is at the heart of the study that follows. In reconstructing and reclaiming power, the apparent contradiction between power and outcomes in the higher education policy arena can also be resolved.

OVERVIEW OF THE STUDY

Chapter 1 begins the study with a rather detailed discussion of the political philosophy that implicitly frames the way we research, analyze, and think about power. These implicit notions of power play an important role in policy analysis and research but are seldom brought to the forefront for critical analysis and debate. This is especially true in educational policy analysis and research (Slaughter, 1990). As Terence Ball (1992) has suggested, the metaphors of political philosophers "have a way of becoming behavioral scientists' models" (p. 15). Ball (1992) notes "that the rule of metaphor is likely to be most powerful when it is least" (p. 15). To avoid becoming fatally entangled in unspoken metaphors, it is necessary to identify, expose and criticize those metaphors thus preparing the way for the "reconstruction of power" (Ball, 1992, p. 15).

Chapter 1 begins the process of reconstructing and reclaiming the concept of power for use in policy analysis and research. Reconstructing power means understanding it as the thread that holds collective action together. The precise definition or meaning of power emerges from the study of collective action and is potentially different from one social context to the another. Once power has been reconstructed, it can be reclaimed. That is to say power can become a concept that helps social scientists explicate collective action. Several steps are required to achieve this rather ambitious goal. First it is necessary to review the work of Thomas Hobbes and other early political philosophers in order to understand the origin and lineage of the debates on power. After this, the "faces of power" debates that have dominated discourse on power since the 1950s are considered. Following this discussion, interpretivist theorists are presented as an alternative to positivist conceptions of power. Particular attention is paid to the development of communicative action interpretations of power.

Making explicit what had been implicit is only the first step in reconstructing and reclaiming power. To complete the process, a research methodology that avoids the shortcomings of earlier approaches is needed to frame and guide the project. The problems associated with the study of power suggests that a combination of cultural, historical, political, and sociological methods be used, with the common thread being interpretation. The starting point for this research design is Michel Callon and Bruno Latour's (1981) sociology of translation. In using this as a starting point one neither accepts or rejects extant theories of power. Instead, one is acknowledging that a theory or concept can reach "the point where it obscures a good deal more than it reveals" (Geertz, 1973, p. 4). Use of the methodological framework suggested by Callon and Latour presents one with a clearer field of vision unimpeded by a priori interpretations or theories of power.

Callon and Latour are not the first to suggest that power must be understood by interpreting it in the historical and social context in which it is situated. What makes their work of particular interest is that they have developed a clearly stated methodological framework that can be understood and followed by other researchers. Use of the sociology of translation means that the definition and meaning of power emerges from an interpretation of the social situation being studied and is limited to that historical and social setting. Such an approach seems simple enough, but it requires methods and rules that prohibit the researcher from prematurely arriving at a definition of power and then forcing that definition on the social setting being studied. Predetermination of the meaning of power has been and is a problem with methodologies commonly selected to guide power research. In order to avoid this problem, the three methodological principles of the sociology of translation-agnosticism, generalized symmetry and free association-require that any interpretation of the meaning of power be delayed until after the historical and social context is fully developed and presented. It is only then that power can be interpreted. Once power is interpreted, as it is in chapter 5, then a new framework emerges to guide the study.

The three chapters that immediately follow chapter 1 provide the historical and social context of federal higher education policy making and define the higher education policy arena. The historical context of federal higher education policy making is discussed in chapter 2. The historical sketch begins with the Northwest Ordinance of 1787 and ends with the initial discussions of the Higher Education Amendments of 1992. An important part of the historical background and context are a series of dynamic tensions and conflicts that have marked the debate over the federal role in higher education. The resolution of these conflicts and tensions established contested principles that continue to shape and guide the federal interest in higher education today. These principles are identified in chapter 2 and revisited in later chapters.

The task of constructing a new approach to defining and describing the social relations that form policy arenas is undertaken in chapter 3. The intent is to create an approach that captures the dynamic, contingent nature of the higher education policy arena while maintaining the flexibility to adjust to changes in the arena. In addition, the approach will serve as a framework for policy analysis and explanation. The approach is a definition that relies not on conventional geometric shapes or static maps of policy arenas but on the use of subgovernment characteristics and the concept of community. The concept of community, first introduced in chapter 1, is more fully developed in chapter 3 and its development continues through the next two chapters. The resulting definition and framework are not only responsive to change but also can be used to explain change.

The broad outlines of the social context of higher education policy making first presented in chapter 3 are completed in chapter 4. The outline is completed by filling in the details that collectively form the social setting for policy making in the higher education policy arena. Like a pointillist, a whole picture is created from a collection of dots. Once the picture is completed, the historical and social context required by the sociology of translation is also complete and the question of power can be addressed.

In considering the meaning of power in chapter 5, it is clear that any number of extant theories of power can be matched with parts of the historical and social context of the policy arena to make a case for that theory as the defining theory of power. While a case can be made for any number of theories, no one theory matches exactly what was found in the case study of the higher education policy arena. This may be because the developers and proponents of these theories were seeking to develop an overarching theory that explains power at all times and in all places. As such, they lose the ability to explain and define power in specific settings. The interpretation of power offered in chapter 5 emerges from the historical and social context of the higher education policy arena and is applicable only to that policy arena. While it may be applicable to other settings, it must be tested in those arenas before broader claims can be made.

The interpretation of power presented in chapter 5 follows from earlier concepts of power in communication communities but goes beyond the work of Hannah Arendt, John Dewey, and Jürgen Habermas to search for the foundations of power. Power, defined in terms of the ability of policy actors to address problems, rests on three broad foundations. These foundations interact to give form, shape, and meaning to power. One foundation of power is formed by society's defining institutions and structures. These visible structures of power are the products of decisions made in earlier policy arenas. A second foundation is formed by the personal and social relationships of the community. This includes the explicit rules that govern relationships among policy actors and programs, as well as, the personal relationships that develop between policy actors. The third foundation of power consists of the beliefs and values that policy actors draw on for guidance in making policy decisions and choices. The interaction between foundations generates power, regulates power, and provides the channels and boundaries of power in the communication community that is the higher education policy arena.

Lest the idea of foundations of power present an overly neat or static view, it is important to recognize that problem solving in the policy arena is often a messy business. Structural and institutional foundations crumble, fall, shift and are replaced as policy actors build new institutions and renovate existing ones to meet changing societal needs. Personal and social relationships change as new actors enter the community and new rules are created to govern the relationships of the community. Time and a changing world undermine some beliefs and values, renew others, and generate entirely new community beliefs and values as policy actors seek to make sense of a dynamic world. Always there are interactions as ideas, institutions, and individuals bump, clash, conflict, and mesh creating the need for problem solving.

By historical standards, chapter 5 would have marked the end of the study. After most HEA reauthorizations, Congress and the administration have been content to tinker with HEA's making technical changes and adjustments to bring programs and practices in line with the intent of the legislation. Using history as a guide, one would not expect any major changes to the occur until at least 1997 and possibly as late as 1999. Post-1992 events did not conform to historical trends or expectations. The newly elected Clinton administration arrived in Washington with plans to enact direct lending, national service, and student aid reform. While the Clinton administration was successful in achieving much of its student aid agenda, the 1994 midterm elections carried the Republican Party to power in both the House and the Senate. With victory came plans to repeal the Clinton student aid agenda and to reopen the contested principles and assumptions that had guided the higher education policy arena in the post–World War II era. The definition of the higher education policy arena and the interpretation of power that had been so recently reached were already crumbling.

Chapter 6 brings the higher education policy arena into the mid-- 1990s. The first part of the chapter examines the Clinton administration's efforts to enact direct lending and a national service program. This is followed by a discussion of the self-proclaimed "Republican revolution" and its impact on the policy arena. The chapter provides a social context for the reinterpretation of power.

Chapter 7 assesses changes in the policy arena as it moves towards the next century. Given the rapid changes in the arena, does it still function as a communication community characterized by common practices, shared memory, discourse, and emotional and intellectual bonds? The last two years have seen changes in the higher education arena that bring into question its ability to survive as a communication community and forces a reconsideration of the type of community, if any, that exists. Without ties to bind the community and a basis for communication, the community unravels. It may continue as some type of community, but it is no longer a communication community. The foundations of power framework are used to analyze changes in the arena. Part of this assessment includes an examination of the beliefs of the arena in action. Earlier chapters looked at the espoused beliefs of the arena but did not fully examine whether the beliefs were reflected in the policy actions and decisions of the arena. In advancing some interests while punishing others, has the arena been true to its beliefs? Finally, the meaning of power in the late 1990s is considered.

A NOTE ON METHODS

The use of the sociology of translation brings with it the requirement that collective action be studied within the boundaries of its social and historical setting. The historical setting can be analyzed through documents but the social setting demands that the researcher be present in the arena. One must go to the policy actors to interview, listen, observe, and study where they work and interact. In the case of the higher education policy arena, this meant traveling to Washington, D.C., to interview congressional staff members, higher education association representatives, higher education lobbyists, university representatives, and other members of the higher education policy arena.

All of the interviews were semistructured starting with a set of questions that the team wanted each respondent or category of respondents to answer and then moving to questions suggested by their responses. The respondents' demanding schedules meant that most had no more than one hour to share with the researcher for the interview. Fortunately, key respondents agreed to repeat interviews and telephone interviews. The majority of the respondents agreed to have the interview audiotaped, but several objected, and no effort was made to convince them to allow taping. The feeling was that this would only inhibit the respondent, probably would not produce an agreement to tape the interview and might even bring the interview to a premature end. In those interviews, extensive notes were taken and interviewers attempted to reconstruct the interview from the notes and debriefings. The taped interviews were transcribed and shared among team members.

While the interviews produced a wealth of information, their use in the study is problematic. The principal problem is that while nearly all of the policy actors who were approached about participating in the study agreed to an interview, and many agreed to being audiotaped, several actors did not want to be identified by name. This was a reasonable request given the sensitive positions many of the respondents hold and the potential for damaging social relations that have been carefully developed over the years. When these research respondents are quoted, they are identified by type of organization or position as well as by date of the interview, but not by name. This may be objectionable to some but it gives a sense of who is making the comment and as well as when it was made. Finally, publicly available quotes have been used with the attributed and unattributed interview quotes to add to the context and texture of the project.

1

The Problem of Power

The continuing debate over the problem of power highlights the fact that power remains an essentially contested concept (Lukes, 1974). This is not surprising given that "social science is essentially contestable" with "every conclusion open to argument" (Alexander, 1987, p. 25). Social science concepts such as power are often "inchoate, tacit and imperfectly articulated, they require interpretation to make them manifest. And because they are made manifest by interpretation, any particular interpretation is contestable" (Gibbons, 1987, p. 2). The contest over the meaning of power is a relatively recent event, with students of power apparently having operated with an implicit understanding of the concept until the post-World War II era (Riker, 1964). In the social sciences, the concept of power did not gain wide currency until the 1930s and 1940s (Gillam, 1971). As power's use as an analytical concept increased, social scientists undertook a search for an explicit, universal definition of power. The quest for a universal, operational definition of power touched off a debate that still rages across the social sciences. It is a problem that social scientists have been unable to solve.

While the debate continues, power has lost considerable appeal as an explanatory concept within academic circles. John R. Champlin (1971) suggests that "the term has fallen into comparative disfavor" (p. 2) because of the difficulty associated with defining power. The project of producing a universal definition of power has attracted researcher after researcher, but none has been equal to the task (McClelland, 1971). Not even Hans J. Morgenthau (1971), who claimed that "the distinctive, unifying element of politics is the struggle for power" (p. 30) was able to solve this puzzle. The failure to resolve this problem means that while power has remained "an arousing and poetic symbol," it has been "diminished from a commanding theoretical resource to a very modest abstraction for which an occasional legitimate use can be found in theory and research" (McClelland, 1971, p. 60).

The timing of power's entry into the social science lexicon may explain its rise and fall as an explanatory concept. When the modern concept of power was adopted from the mechanical sciences, the orientation of the social sciences was firmly positivistic (Joseph, 1988). The language of positivism and the logic of scientific discovery required that concepts be operationally defined and objectively measured. Herbert Simon (1957), one of the first to revive the Hobbesian concept of power in the 1950s, found that he was "unable . . . to arrive at a satisfactory solution" (p. 5) to the task of giving power an operational definition. Robert Dahl (1957, 1958, 1961, 1968) took up the challenge and sparked the lively "faces of power" debates but was no more successful than Simon had been in producing an uncontested, unproblematic definition of power. Power could not meet the demands of a positivist social science.

The purpose of this chapter is to begin the process of reconstructing and reclaiming the concept of power for use in policy analysis and research. Reconstructing power means understanding it as the thread that holds collective action together. The precise definition or meaning of power emerges from the study of collective action and is potentially different from one social context to the another. Once power has been reconstructed, it can be reclaimed. That is to say that power can become an explanatory concept that helps social scientists explicate collective action.

Several steps are required to achieve this rather ambitious goal. First, it is necessary to review the work of Thomas Hobbes and other early political philosophers in order to understand the origin and lineage of the debates on power. After this, the "faces of power" debates that have dominated much of the discourse on power since the 1950s are considered. Following this discussion, interpretivist theorists are presented as an alternative to positivistic conceptions of power. Finally, the sociology of translation is offered as a methodology that can solve the problem of power while avoiding the pitfalls of earlier approaches. It is through the use of this methodology that power can be reconstructed and reclaimed as a research concept.

LEGISLATORS AND INTERPRETERS

Drawing on the work of Zygmunt Bauman (1987), Stewart Clegg (1989) has classified power theorists as legislators and interpreters. Legislators discuss, debate, theorize, and research the question of "What is power?" Regardless of the exact answer, power is always legislated by some sovereignty. While the source of sovereign power (e.g., the people, the consumer, the law, or the constitution) may differ from theorist to theorist, the focus on what power is remains the central concern. Questions of how and why the sovereign rules are relegated to the periphery or simply not asked. Interpreters focus on the questions of how power is obtained, what power does, and how power is maintained.

Legislators

Under Clegg's classification scheme, Hobbes can be seen as the first legislator and as the intellectual fountainhead of legislative theories of power. Modern legislative theorists continue the "mechanical, causal, and atomistic concept of power" (Clegg, 1989, p. 27) first articulated by Hobbes. While his original intent may not have been this grand, Hobbes's project certainly was not a modest endeavor that grew in stature only as it was recognized by future generations. From the beginning, Hobbes intended to reconstruct political theory as it then existed and to lay the theoretical foundation for modern state power.

In laying this new foundation, Hobbes had to first destroy the foundation that had been built on the work of Aristotle. For Aristotle, sovereign power in any state had to be based on the will of the people and that sovereignty was expressed through the law and the constitution. In the *Leviathan*, Hobbes (1651/1991) charged "that scare any thing can be more absurdly said in naturall Philosophy, than that which now is called *Aristotle's Metaphysiques*; nor more repugnant to Government than much that hee hath said in his *Politiques*; nor more ignorantly, than a great part of his *Ethiques*" (pp. 461-62). Of course, it was not enough to heap insult on Aristotle, Hobbes had to present an alternative formulation to challenge and replace Aristotle's sovereignty of laws. The true sovereign, claimed Hobbes, consisted not of words on paper, but of the state backed by the arms and swords of men.

Defining the new foundation is not the same as having it accepted. Lest anyone cling to the old order or suggest alternatives to the new order, Hobbes (1651/1991) warned that any deviation from his formulation would produce a world in which

> there is no place for Industry; because the fruit thereof is uncertain: and consequently no Culture of the Earth; no Navigation, nor use of the commodities that may be imported by Sea; no commodious Building; no Instruments of moving, and removing such things as require much force; no Knowledge

of the face of the Earth; no account of Time; no Arts; no Letters; no Society; and which is worst of all, continuall feare and danger of violent death; And the life of man, solitary, poore, nasty, brutish, and short. (p. 89)

Finally, in addition to making alternatives seem irrational and frightening, Hobbes sought to give his new conception of sovereignty legitimacy by cloaking it in the language of the new science. Power ceased to be some religious or metaphysical force that could not be understood, shaped, or controlled by humans. Power became a simple matter of mechanics in which one agent pushed (cause) another agent to act (effect). Political power was a matter of agents acting on one another in "a perpetuall and restlesse desire of Power after power, that ceaseth onely in Death" (Hobbes, 1651/1991, p. 70).

Hobbes's mechanical, causal concept of power was taken up and refined first by John Locke (1689/1959) and then later by David Hume (1748/1920). Locke also used the language of cause and effect, adding the metaphor of the billiard table to demonstrate the principles of active and passive power. Active agents on the table, moving balls, strike passive patients, stationary balls, causing them to move. Power is cause and effect with active agents demonstrating their power through effects on passive patients. Taking this idea beyond Hobbes, Locke claimed that power produced observable change and movement among the agents. Power, like natural phenomena, could be observed and measured. This was the only way that one could scientifically study and prove the existence of power.

While Hume used tennis balls to illustrate his views on power, he maintained the concept of power as a mechanical push and pull, cause and effect, that could be observed and measured. Hume added scientific rigor to the study of power by insisting that it should be possible to observe the events producing the cause and effect that constituted power. From repeated observations of the events producing cause and effect, Hume believed that lawlike generalizations about power could be produced.

The Hobbes, Locke, and Hume discourse on sovereignty and power was so forceful that it virtually eliminated any alternative approaches to the question of power. By cloaking discourse on power in the language of science, they represented power as a legitimate, if sometimes arbitrary, force of nature. Rival concepts of power had to either continue along the same conceptual path of cause and effect, or risk being labeled irrational and unscientific. The social sciences' adoption of the natural sciences as a model for inquiry only reinforced the dominance of Hobbes, Locke, and Hume. Even Karl Marx, who challenged the legitimacy of the standing economic order, defined power in positivistic terms of cause and effect. The meaning of power became a matter of implicit understanding even as its philosophical origins were forgotten. This helps explain how students of power were able to operate with an implicit understanding of the meaning of power for three centuries after Hobbes first offered his views on the state and power without fully understanding the origin of that meaning or how it shaped the discourse on power.

The Faces of Power

The implicit meaning of power that evolved from the work of the British political philosophers held such a strong grip on students of power that the problem of power was removed from the mainstream of intellectual discourse until the 1950s. The faces of power debates represents a reopening and a continuation of legislative theory. Ironically, the participants used many of the same types of metaphors as the early political philosophers, but without any apparent awareness of their origin. Power became an exercise in cause and effect that in the new language of the behavioral sciences could be observed, measured, and predicted.

Floyd Hunter's (1953) study of the community power structure of Atlanta, Georgia, is most often cited as the study that reopened the problem of power for discussion and debate in the intellectual community. Concerned with the question of whether or not representational democracy was giving way to local community power elites, Hunter developed a reputational methodology that became the model for subsequent studies of community power structures. In simplified form, Hunter asked people chosen as judges to list the most influential people in the community and then determined whether or not the combined listings produced an elite. What Hunter found was a shift in power from the people to an elite heavily weighted towards business.

If Hunter reopened the debate over power, then C. Wright Mills (1956) exploded the issue with the publication of *The Power Elite*. Naming names, identifying positions, and revealing what he saw as a system of interlocking institutions, Mills (1956) defined the power elite as

> men whose positions enable them to transcend the ordinary environments of ordinary men and women. . . . For they are

in command of the major hierarchies and organizations of modern society. They rule the big corporations. They run the machinery of state and claim its prerogatives. They direct the military establishment. They occupy the strategic command posts of the social structure, in which are now centered the effective means of the power and the wealth and the celebrity which they enjoy. (pp. 3–4)

Robert Dahl (1957, 1958) responded to power elite theorists and in the process launched the faces of power debate that continues to dominate much of the discourse on the meaning of power. Dahl's response to power elite theorists, and to Mills in particular, was remarkably reminiscent of Hobbes' approach. First, Dahl (1958) sought to discredit the work of power elite theorists claiming that their "hypothesis has one very great advantage over many alternative explanations: It can be cast in a form that makes it virtually impossible to disprove" (p. 463). Even worse, the theory was charged with being "quasi-metaphysical" (Dahl, 1958, p. 463). Last, Dahl (1958) sought to dismiss the power elitists by charging that "a theory that cannot even in principle be controverted by empirical evidence is not a scientific theory" (p. 463).

The last point became the basis of a withering attack on Mills and other power elite theorists. Operating from a positivist perspective, Dahl brought Mills to task for failing to define a ruling elite that could be observed, measured, and analyzed. Since Mills had failed to do this, Dahl provided a definition based on Mills' work, and then presented a method for testing the power elite theory. In sum, Dahl (1958) claimed that the power elite hypothesis could be tested if, and only if:

1. The hypothetical ruling elite is a well-defined group.
2. There is a fair sample of cases involving key political decisions in which the preferences of the hypothetical ruling elite run counter to those of any other likely group that might be suggested.
3. In such cases, the preferences of the elite regularly prevail. (p. 466)

Like Hobbes, Dahl also understood that it was not enough to discredit and dismiss rival theorists. As an alternative to power elite theorists, Dahl had to offer a new theory of power. The new theory had to make other theories appear irrational, if not unthinkable. To accomplish this goal, Dahl (1968) followed Simon's lead in grounding power in the language of mechanics to shape the discourse on power and firmly anchor it in the positivist paradigm.

In place of Mills's rather vague conception of power, Dahl presented a precise operational definition. Continuing the mechanical metaphors of Hobbes, Locke, and Hume, Dahl (1957) defined his intuitive idea of power as "something like this: A has power over B to the extent that he can get B to do something that B would not otherwise do" (pp. 202-3). Implicit in Dahl's (1957) definition was the understanding that "power is a relation, and that it is a relation among people" (p. 203). Finally, Dahl noted that questions of the base, means, amount, and scope of power had to be addressed in any comprehensive study of power.

Dahl's critique of the power elite and his pluralist model of power dominated the field of power research and analysis well into the 1960s. By successfully framing the criteria and tests that competing theorists had to meet, Dahl limited the range of alternatives to the pluralist model and to refinements of that model. For example, Newton (1969) mounted a strong attack on *Who Governs?* (Dahl, 1961), but accepted Dahl's definition of power. In many ways, it can be argued that while Newton arrives at quite different conclusions about who held power, it is Dahl's methodology that guides the inquiry. The use of this methodology explains why Newton and other challengers to Dahl could see but one face or dimension of power.

Peter Bachrach and Morton Baratz (1962), in a stinging critique of Dahl, argued that power has two faces. Dahl was correct in describing the one face of power, but his project was seriously flawed because of his inability or unwillingness to examine the second face of power. The other, less visible, face of power is the extent to which "a person or group—consciously or unconsciously—creates or reinforces barriers to the public airing of policy conflicts" (Bachrach & Baratz, 1962, p. 949). Specifically, two individuals or groups must have a conflict of interests; B must accept A's position, and A must have some sanction to use against B should B fail to comply (Bachrach & Baratz, 1970). This second face of power was described as a non–decision-making process.

Non–decision making, or the second face of power, built on and refined Dahl's theory in several important ways. The most obvious improvement was that it allowed researchers to account for power that might be hidden or exercised covertly in ways that could not be directly observed or measured. A second improvement was the use of E. E. Schattschneider's (1960) concept of the "mobilization of bias" to expand the definition of power beyond individuals to include structural relationships. Last, Bachrach and Baratz went beyond Dahl by boldly claiming that power must be interpreted as well as observed and measured.

Anticipating the criticism that their theory would provoke, Bachrach and Baratz (1962) rejected "in advance as unimpressive the possible criticism that this approach to the study of power is likely to prove fruitless because it goes beyond an investigation of what is objectively measurable" (p. 952). Rejecting criticism does not forestall it; non-decision making was vigorously attacked by those who followed Dahl and those who subscribed to the belief that power existed only to the extent that it could be observed and measured. Nelson Polsby (1980) summarized this line of criticism with the questions: "How to study this second face of power? To what manifestations of social reality might the mobilization of bias refer? Are phenomena of this sort amenable to empirical investigation?" (p. 190). The criticism took its toll on Bachrach and Baratz (1970), who moved from defiance to compliance with the admission that "although absence of conflict may be a non-event, a decision which results in prevention of conflict is very much an event—and an observable one, to boot" (p. 46).

While Bachrach and Baratz ceded to the pressures of the positivist paradigm, Steven Lukes (1974) sought to reinforce non–decision-making theory as a legitimate dimension of power and to move beyond it to a third face or dimension of power. In describing this third face of power, Lukes explicitly linked his view of power to the definitions of power produced by Dahl and by Bachrach and Baratz. As Lukes (1974) states the connection, all three "can be seen as alternative interpretations and applications of one and the same underlying concept of power, according to which A exercises power over B when A affects B in a manner contrary to B's interests" (p. 27).

Although Lukes continues the causal definition of power that dates from Hobbes, his introduction of the concept of interests distinguishes him from his theoretical predecessors. According to Lukes, interests in the first two faces of power are subjective interests and the concept of interests is not fully developed in either of the faces. Subjective interests are somewhat akin to the Marxist concept of false consciousness. People are operating under an illusion of their real interests. In his radical view of power, Lukes (1974) brings objective interests to the forefront to provide "a license for the making of normative judgments of a moral and political character" (p. 34). Lukes does not reference a model of objective interests but seems to have in mind a model like Jürgen Habermas's (1979) ideal speech situation, that is, when people know what their real interests are and are unconstrained in their participation in the discourse over those interests.

With this understanding of the concept of interests, one can begin to visualize the three faces of power. The first face is a primitive face in which A openly forces B to do something against his/her will. The second face is more sophisticated in that B does not act because she/he thinks or knows that A does not want him/her to act, or because A creates barriers that limit B. In the third face of power, A has power over B's formation of interests so that B is unable to act on his/her real interests. Lukes (1978) summarizes the third face of power with the question, "Is not the supreme exercise of power to avert conflict and grievance by influencing, shaping, and determining the perceptions and preferences of others?" (p. 669).

The third face of power stretched the causal definition of power to its limits without renouncing the positivist paradigm. Lukes avoids this break by offering an observer who can determine the objective interests of the subjects when the subjects are not fully aware of their own best interests. In ideal situations, the subjects are able to determine their own objective interests. Lukes, after stretching the causal definition of power to its limits, accepts Hobbes's causal definition of power and safely returns to Locke's view that power must be observable.

The emphasis here on the faces of power debates should not obscure the fact that other attempts were being made to define power during the same time period, For example, Nicos Poulantzas (1986) defined power as "the capacity of a social class to realize its objective interests" (p. 144). For Marxists and Neo-Marxists, sovereignty was exercised by the ruling elite through the class system. Talcott Parsons (1951,1963,1967) approached power in a manner similar to Hobbes and Dahl but sought to fit the concept of power into his general theory of action. It seemed that no one was "able to eschew the model of Leviathan in the study of power" (Foucault, 1986, p. 237) and everyone was looking for a singular, universal definition of power.

C. Wright Mills (1959) termed this search for universal concepts and theories the search for "Grand Theory." Grand Theory deals "in conceptions intended to be of use in classifying all social relations and providing insight into their supposedly invariant features" (Mills, 1959, p. 23). Grand theorists work with generalities at a level of abstraction that renders their work virtually meaningless for other researchers and for the public. The result is "an elaborate and arid formalism" that robs ideas of any historical and social context (Mills, 1959, p. 23).

The search for a Grand Theory of power produced numerous cul-de-sacs, but no grand highways leading to greater understanding and knowledge of power. Put another way, the search for a universal definition of power produced any number of useful concepts, but these were limited to certain settings or contexts. This would seem to be a helpful contribution to the understanding of power, but these concepts were abandoned as researchers renewed their quest for a definition or concept of power that was true at all times and in all places. It fell to interpretivist theorists, working in a different research tradition, "to cut off the King's head" (Foucault, 1980, p. 121) and advance the discourse on power beyond cause and effect definitions.

Interpreters

In contrast to legislators who are concerned with the question of "What is power?," interpreters are concerned with how power is obtained, what power does, and how it is maintained. Interpretivist theorists focus on "strategies, deals, negotiation, fraud and conflict" (Clegg, 1989, p. 30). Interpreters, whose lineage runs back to Niccolo Machiavelli (1513/1977), are not concerned with legislating the definition of power, but rather with translating the meaning of power as it appears in different social contexts. This means that interpretivist theorists do not focus on issues of agency, causality, or motion that are so important to legislative theorists. Instead, like Machiavelli, they tend to use an "ethnographic research method for uncovering the rules of the game" (Clegg, 1989, p. 31).

What separates the intellectual descendants of Hobbes and Machiavelli is more than a concern with particular questions or methods to follow in the study of power. What truly separates legislators and interpreters is the choice of metaphors that Hobbes and Machiavelli originally used to drive their work and which continue to drive the work of their intellectual heirs. As discussed above, Hobbes used the language and metaphors of the mechanical sciences to describe and define power. Machiavelli (1513/1977), in contrast, took the language and metaphors of armies and war as can be seen in this quotation from *The Prince*:

A prince, therefore, should have no other object, no other thought, no other subject of study, than war, its rules and disciplines; this is the only art for a man who commands, and it is of such value [*virtu*] that it not only keeps born princes in place, but often raises men from private citizens to princely fortune. On the other hand, it is clear that when princes have thought more about the refinements of life than about war, they have lost their positions. The quickest way to lose a state is to neglect this art; the quickest way to get one is to study it. (p. 42)

The differences in language and metaphors produces entirely different epistemological and ontological approaches to the question of power. For interpreters, power is a socially constructed reality: thus there is not a single foundation from which all interpreters build their theories of power. The lack of a common foundation means that interpretivist theorists are not bound by a common thread in the way that legislators are bound by the question of "What is power?" Since there is no one single meaning and definition of power, interpretivists are not linked by a common research methodology. This makes it much more difficult to summarize and group interpretivists because different schools and individuals have developed their own distinct approaches to the study of power with the only commonality being interpretation.

Rather than attempt to provide a summary paragraph or two on the different individuals and various schools of thought that represent the interpretivist tradition from Machiavelli to the present, this section will trace the development of just one interpretive approach to power: the communications concept. This approach is presented as an example of interpretivist theory for two reasons. First, it is possible to trace the historical development of the communications concept in a way that parallels the above description of the faces of power debate, thus enabling the reader to compare the development of ideas grounded in two rather different research traditions. Second, communications was recognized as an issue in the early mechanical conceptions of power but was ignored because the mechanical sciences model did not have to deal with the problem of communications between objects and political philosophers had no conceptual tools to account for the problem of communications between humans in their definitions of power.

The precursor of modern communicative action theory is found in the work of John Dewey. In *The Public and Its Problems*, Dewey (1927/1988) implies, but does not fully develop, the concept of a communication community. The details of Dewey's communication community must be teased out by the reader. Dewey's theory of a communication community starts with, rather than ends in, the process of collective action. The product of collective action, regardless of how well it is conceived and planned, produces unintended or unanticipated consequences for the public. As these consequences become apparent, the institutions responsible for implementing the public will and the public interact to produce a new decision. Of paramount importance in this process is communication between individuals and institutions who are either affected by a decision or are concerned with the consequences of any new decision.

Dewey's trust in the communication community reveals a political philosophy that is radically different from both Hobbes and Machiavelli. Instead of seeing a natural antagonism between the public and the state, Dewey sees a community bonded together by communication. The public, a true democratic public, emerges from the communication required by group problem solving. The same is true of democratic governments that exist as a function of the collective action process. Communication for problem solving, not force of arms, becomes the mechanism for social order in the communication community.

As sketched by Dewey, the communication community is a lively, free-wheeling society, but one that also places a heavy moral and political responsibility on its citizens. Individuals must be aware of community issues, the consequences of collective actions, the needs of society, and must make decisions based on the needs of the community without the possibility of passing the burden for decision making on to some higher authority or outside agent. In the communication community, power as domination is replaced by power as problem solving, thus the public must take responsibility for solving its problems. If the public fails to take responsibility, there is no external system of social control, and the internal system of social order begins to unravel.

Dewey (1927/1988) claimed that the communication community would "have its consummation when free social inquiry is indissolubly wedded to the art of full and moving communication" (p. 184) but recognized that certain prerequisites were necessary for consummation to occur. One of the prerequisites was a common language that could be used and understood by all of the community. Language by itself was not enough to foster fully understood communications. The public also needed widely understood signs and symbols to convey shared meanings. In addition, groups needed to interact in cooperative activities because "the pulls and responses of different groups reenforce one another and their values accord" (Dewey, 1927/1988, p. 148). The shared activities also produce emotional, intellectual, and moral bonds that help bind the community. To the extent that these prerequisites are met, a community evolves that is capable of transforming the power of domination into the power of problem solving.

One of the criticisms of Dewey was that he tended to present concepts and theories only to leave them underdeveloped as he raced on to new ideas. Unfortunately, this is true of the communication community introduced in *The Public and Its Problems*. After its publication in 1927, Dewey moved on to other ideas leaving the details of a fully developed communication community for other thinkers and writers. It was not until the 1960s that the theory of communicative power was addressed again.

Hannah Arendt was the next person to take up the concept of communicative power. While she does not cite Dewey, her work, rests on a similar theoretical foundation. Arendt's (1968,1969,1986) theory of communicative power developed out of her concern with violence. Arendt (1969) increasingly came to see "the events and debates of the last few years as seen against the background of the twentieth century, which has become indeed, as Lenin predicted, a century of wars and revolutions, hence a century of . . . violence" (p. 3). The increasing level of violence in political life reached the point that it was "taken for granted and therefore neglected" (Arendt, 1969, p. 8) by social scientists. Perhaps worst of all, political theorists had come to view power and violence as concomitant. C. Wright Mills (1956) claim that "all politics is a struggle for power; the ultimate kind of power is violence" (p. 171) is a primary example of what Arendt had in mind when she accused political theorists of uncritically accepting the wedding of violence and power.

The intent of Arendt's project was to separate violence and power and to produce a new concept of power that was not based on domination. Traditional political theory traces the roots of power back to the absolute power of kings and even back to Greek antiquity in defining power in terms of domination. Arendt (1969) sought to draw on "another tradition and another vocabulary no less old and time-honored" (p. 40). The Athenian city-state and the Romans both developed concepts of governments that rested "on the power of the people" (Arendt, 1969, p. 40). The state and all political institutions rested on the power of the people and "they petrify and decay as soon as the living power of the people ceases to uphold them" (Arendt, 1969, p. 41). Violence could be used to hold a government in place, but power could only come from the consent of the governed.

While Arendt did not discuss the role of metaphors in shaping visions of power, she understand the role of language and the need to create a new vocabulary for her discourse on power. Of primary concern was the need to produce distinct, separate definitions for power, strength, force, authority, and violence to avoid the inherent tendency of political theorists to "reduce public affairs to the business of dominion" (Arendt, 1969, p. 44). While all of the definitions are worth considering, only Arendt's (1969) definitions of power and violence are repeated here:

> *Power* corresponds to the human ability not just to act but to act in concert. Power is never the property of an individual; it belongs to a group and remains in existence only so long as the group keeps together. (p. 44)

> *Violence*, finally, as I have said, is distinguished by its instrumental character. Phenomenologically, it is close to strength, since the implements of violence, like all other tools, are designed and used for the purpose of multiplying natural strength until, in the last stage of their development, they can substitute for it. (p. 46)

By carefully defining the language used to discuss power, Arendt sought to give legitimacy to certain types of social behavior while making still other types of behavior socially unacceptable. Arendt's interest in legitimation parallels Talcott Parsons' (1963) concern with the legitimacy of the possession and use of power in a social system. To solve the problem of what is and what is not legitimate power, Parsons took his cue from economic theory. Power, like money in an economic system, was considered a circulating medium that was generated by the political system. Power was legitimate only so long as it was accepted by members of a society and the leaders of the society had a mandate from the members to act in their behalf. Arendt (1986) took her cue from natural law to arrive at the social contract as the mechanism for giving legitimacy to power. Power is legitimate only as long, and only so long, as it comes from the governed and is expressed in a social contract or agreement. Neither resolution of the problem allows a legitimate role for violence, but both resolutions permit the use of force in fulfilling the goals of society.

As noted earlier, Arendt and Dewey's work rests on similar theoretical foundations. Both view power as the formation of a common will developed from acting in concert through communicative action rather than as an instrument of domination. For Arendt (1969), power "corresponds to the human ability not just to act but to act in concert" (p. 44), thus paralleling Dewey's focus on collective action. As a condition of acting in concert, both argue that citizens must be free and equal. In Arendt's work it is this freedom that permits the building of communicative action that allows written social contracts to be developed. Power exists only so long as citizens agree to the granting of power, through a written social contract, to an individual or an agency.

Jürgen Habermas (1986) praises Arendt's work for allowing us to disconnect "the concept of power from the teleological model" and to think of power as being "built up in communicative action" (p. 76). At the same time, he criticizes her thesis as being "a bit too smooth" because "it is not a result of well-balanced investigations but issues from a philosophical construction . . . which, when applied to modern societies, leads to absurdities" (Habermas, 1986, pp. 82–83). Specifically, Habermas cites Arendt's failure to account for the strategic competition for political power, the employment of power within the political system, and her reliance on the contract theory of natural law as major flaws in her communications concept of power. Despite this rather strong criticism, Habermas believed that Arendt's communicative action concept was fundamentally sound and used it as the basis for developing his own theory of communicative action.

Habermas's theory of communicative action is part of a larger program of rearticulating the project of critical theory. The premise of communicative action theory is "that language as communicative discourse is *emancipatory*, but also that communicative forms of discourse have a certain priority over other forms of linguistic usage" (Rasmussen, 1990, p. 18). The purpose of the theory of communicative action is to help develop a philosophy of language, in place of a philosophy of consciousness, for use in his project. A philosophy of language can serve as the guardian and basis for the development communicative action. Clearly, a full discussion of the theory of communicative action is beyond our focus, but key aspects of the theory can be presented.

The core idea in Habermas's (1979,1984,1987) theory of communicative action is communicative competence. The achievement of communicative competence depends on the ability and willingness of speakers to state propositional sentences in a way that are cognitively true, without intent to deceive the listener, and in a manner consistent with the normative orientation of the speaker and listener. For example, communicative competence is reached when participants in discussions recognize the differences between true and false statements and accept as true statements those that would be accepted as true statements in the absence of coercion.

As part of his reconstruction of rational society, Habermas (1984) makes certain assumptions that give communicative action priority over all other forms of action. Specifically, Habermas asserts that action takes the form of either strategic action or communicative action. Strategic action is purposive-rational action in which communication is instrumental. Communicative action is noninstrumental in the sense that "a communicatively achieved agreement has a rational basis; it cannot be imposed by either party, whether instrumentally through intervention in the situation directly or strategically through influencing decisions of opponents" (Habermas, 1984, p. 287). Communicative action has priority over, and cannot be reduced to, strategic action because it can be demonstrated "that the use of language with an orientation to reaching an understanding is the *original mode* of language use, upon which indirect understanding, giving something to understand or letting something be understood, and the instrumental use of language in general, are parasitic" (Habermas, 1984, pp. 288–92). Communicative action thus becomes the foundation on which community is constructed.

Habermas (1979, 1987) has used the two types of action as the basis for constructing a two-level concept of society. The economic system and political administration are action spheres characterized by strategic action. Rather than responding to normative values, these spheres are coordinated and driven by money, power, and success without regard for communicative competence. Detached from the action system is the life-world. The life-world is characterized by the drive to reach communicative competence and is coordinated through full, open, and truthful communication. This dualism helps protect communication from the distortions of power.

The division of the world into separate, nonintersecting spheres with different foundations has produced considerable criticism as has the privileging of communicative action over all other forms of action. Axel Honneth (1987) has suggested that Habermas is building his project on a theoretical fiction if he really believes that the two spheres can exist independently. Michel Foucault (1986) has noted that communication and knowledge, far from freeing us, have been servants to disciplinary power and subjection. In Habermasian terms, one would say that the life-world has become the handmaiden of the action system. Despite these and other criticisms, Habermas remains the best known and most respected proponent of communicative action.

In examining his large body of work, it is easy to see how Habermas (1979,1984,1987) builds on Dewey and Arendt in the development of his theory of communicative action. At the core of Habermas's theory is the idea of uncoerced communication between competent participants. Communicative competence rests upon the ability and willingness of participants to speak without the intent to deceive. A communicative community rests on a foundation of trust reinforced by unrestrained communication. Power, the power to dominate, is a barrier to building a communicative community because power interferes with and distorts universal communication, thus it is relegated to a separate sphere.

While, Dewey, Arendt, and Habermas are linked by the common thread of communicative action, it is important to note differences that separate the three theorists. Dewey bases his communication community on praxis. Consistent with his pragmatic philosophy, the community is never complete but is constantly evolving, through collective action, in search of a more perfect community. Power is found in the ability of the community to engage in problem solving. Arendt also sees power as coming from communicative action aimed at reaching agreement. Unlike Dewey, she envisions a more static community in which agreements are reached within the boundaries of a written social contract rather than through praxis. Finally, Habermas, with his explicit rules for defining communicative action, creates an ideal theory to which a community can aspire and against which it can judge its level of communicative competence. Unlike Arendt and Dewey, Habermas does not accept the idea that power can be transformed into a social good that promotes communicative action, but sees power as distorting communications.

In summary, Clegg's system of classifying and categorizing power theorists is useful on many counts, but selecting one approach or theory to guide the study of power remains problematic at best. For legislators, the problem is one of finding a definition of power that applies at all times and in all places. It seems that legislators have given themselves a task that is impossible to fulfill. Indeed, the difficulty associated with defining and studying power has produced a division among political scientists with some claiming that power is no longer a useful concept and others claiming that it must be *the* guiding concept for political science (Falkemark, 1982).

Interpreters have avoided the problem of finding a universal definition of power, but have created a different set of problem by defining power a posteriori. Critics of interpretivist approaches claim that far from interpreting power, interpreters find only the "facts" that fit their theory of power. Other critics note that theories of political power, whether legislative or interpretive, tend to coincide with disciplinary perspectives and worldviews. Political scientists ask how the state influences society and discover that power is pluralistic. Some political scientists find that pluralism is too simple and offer non–decision making as an alternative. In contrast, sociologists generally ask how society influences the state and find a power elite or ruling class. The meaning of power is not a matter of interpretation, but rather a function of the methodology and theory selected to guide the inquiry.

SOCIOLOGY OF TRANSLATION

As one looks at the problem of power, it appears that Dahl's (1957) concern that power research could turn into a "bottomless swamp" (p. 201) has become a reality. It may be possible to avoid this swamp by using an eclectic assortment of research methods to reconstruct and reclaim power for use in policy analysis and research. This suggests some combination of cultural, historical, political, and sociological methods with the common thread being interpretation. The starting point for this design is Michel Callon and Bruno Latour's (1981) sociology of translation. In using this as a starting point one neither accepts or rejects extant theories of power. Instead, one is acknowledging that a theory or concept can reach "the point where it obscures a good deal more than it reveals" (Geertz, 1973, p. 4). Use of the methodological framework suggested by Callon and Latour presents one with a clearer field of vision unimpeded by a priori interpretations or theories of power. The meaning of power must truly emerge from the social and historical context in which it is being studied.

Callon and Latour are not the first to suggest that power must be understood by interpreting it in the social context in which it is situated. What makes their work of particular interest is that they have developed an explicitly stated methodological framework that can be understood and followed by other researchers. The principles that guide the translation model and the "moments" of translation are discussed below.

The sociology of translation developed out of Callon and Latour's concern with the paradox inherent in the problem of power. In summary form, the paradox can stated as follows: "when you simply *have* power—*in potentia*—nothing happens and you are powerless; when you *exert* power—*in actu*—others are performing the action and not you" (Latour, 1986, pp. 264–65). This paradox has been repeated methodologically as social scientists treated power as both cause and effect. Latour (1986) suggests that one way out of this paradox is to think of power as a way to summarize the consequences of collective action. The translation model was designed to "allow social scientists to understand power as a consequence and not as a cause of collective action" (Latour, 1986, p. 269). To understand power, one must understand what holds the collective action together. It is only then that power can be named and defined.

Three methodological principles guide the researcher who elects to use the sociology of translation as a guide to the study of power (Callon, 1986). The first principle is agnosticism. The researcher must be an impartial observer who refrains from privileging any one point of view or censoring any respondent. The second principle is generalized symmetry. This principle requires that the researcher use the same vocabulary and terms when describing and explaining the actors in the study. The third principle is free association. This means that a researcher must not impose an a priori grid of analysis on the actors, but must observe the actors to determine how they "define and associate the different elements by which they build and explain their world, whether it be social or natural" (Callon, 1986, p. 201).

Translation is used to refer to all of "negotiations, intrigues, calculations, acts of persuasion and violence" (Callon & Latour, 1981, p. 279) that actors use to gain the authority to speak for other actors in the political process. It is the process that allows micro-actors to become macro-actors with the authority to speak for other actors and to speak with one voice. The translation process can be divided into four steps or "moments": problematization, interessement, enrollment, and mobilization (Callon, 1986). The steps overlap and mix in a far more complex social interaction than is suggested by the simple linear presentation provided below. Translation is a continuous process and any description is at best a snapshot that quickly ages as the process moves forward in a never-ending reenactment of the translation steps.

Problematization

In the first step in the translation process, the actor attempts to either convince other actors that his/her definition of the problem is the correct definition or that her/his solution is the proper solution for a given problem definition. By accomplishing this, the actor gains the right to speak for other actors. Equally important is the control thus gained over the range of policy options available for responding to public problems.

The implications of problematization extend beyond this to the creation of policy arenas. Policy arenas are created by marking off two distinct boundaries. In the case of the higher education policy arena, the first boundary is the one that divides higher education from other policy issues while the second marks off what can and cannot be problematized within the higher education policy arena. The first boundary was drawn some time ago by Congress and is beyond the focus of this study. By creating education committees and subcommittees in the House and Senate, Congress established a recognized policy territory that is largely off limits to other committees. Within this closed domain, policy actors, over time, have developed a language, a logic, and a coherence that drives the higher education policy formation process.

The second boundary, between what can and cannot be problematized, exists within the confines of the first boundary. Unlike the boundary that separates higher education from other policy arenas, this internal boundary is subject to constant contest and conflict. The ideal solution for policy actors within the arena is to place their problems/solutions into black boxes (Callon & Latour, 1981). Black boxes contain issues that are accepted within the policy arena and are no longer subject to contest. The more black boxes actors control the greater the area of the policy arena they can control. It also means that an actor can safely leave these issues and move to problematize other issues. Of course, no matter how successful an actor might be in organizing black boxes, they seldom remain securely closed because other policy actors are always attempting to open the boxes.

Interessement

An actor's definition of the problem and/or solution is not an adequate step in itself because other actors will attempt to position themselves to control the policy agenda. This means that an actor must make his/her position interesting to actors who have committed to or expressed interest in another problem definition/solution. This is what Callon and Latour call *interessement*. To be successful in this step, an actor must come between two other actors and win the supporting actor over to his/her position. In other words, the actor must win the agents of other actors to her/his position.

Enrollment

The third step builds on the first two steps by seeking to build stable alliances and coalitions around the problem definition/solution. This step, called enrollment, may or may not produce stable alliances and coalitions that last beyond the current policy action. If it does, then the strength of the actor is enhanced, but what is important for the process is that the actors remain enrolled until the policy decision is reached.

Mobilization

The last step in the translation process is mobilization. This consists of the steps, actions, strategies, and so on that are employed to maintain the alliance through the policy decision. If actors can be fixed in the alliance after the policy decision is reached, then the power of the lead actors will be institutionalized.

While Callon and Latour provide a rather complete approach to the study of power, a few additions are required to fill out the eclectic assortment of methods that the problem of power demands. Consistent with Callon and Latour, Theodore J. Lowi (1971) has suggested the use of interpretative case studies in power research as a way to avoid the problem of imposing one theory or interpretation on a study before the actual collection and analysis of data. For Lowi, the meaning of power must emerge from the case being studied. While Lowi offers a schema for categorizing cases after they have been interpreted, he leaves the methods of interpreting the meaning of power within various cases to other researchers.

Some guidance in the interpretation of meaning in social settings can be gained from anthropology. Clifford Geertz (1973) describes finding meaning in cases as a process of picking one's way through "piled-up structures of inference and implication" (p. 7). Analysis of meaning becomes a process of "sorting out structures of signification . . . and determining their social ground and import" (Geertz, 1973, p. 9). Analytic induction provides a method for sorting, summarizing and classifying the qualitative data that results from case studies. Paul F. Lazarsfeld (1972) suggests that four principles be followed in classifying data: articulation is a process of placing the large mass of data into smaller categories so that smaller chunks of data can be analyzed, compared, and related; logical correctness requires that categories be both exhaustive and mutually exclusive; the categories fit the data rather than making the data fit the categories; and concepts and categories should reflect the respondents' definition(s) of the situation. The concepts and categories identified through the induction process become the building blocks for the case study.

By combining these methods with the sociology of translation, it is possible to overcome the methodological problems that have plagued the study of power in the post–World War II era. The combination of methods does not fall into the trap, associated with more narrow disciplinary studies, of predetermining the results of a study through the initial selection of methodology and theory. The approach outlined above also avoids the problem that has bedeviled researchers for nearly half a century, that is, providing a universal definition of power. The failure to provide an operational definition of power will be criticized as a weakness by some readers, but it seems wise to heed Barrington Moore's (1988) warning that "starting off research with a series of carefully drawn definitions . . . is actually pernicious because it may close the mind to crucial evidence" (p. 169). Finally, it is important to note that this approach does not exclude the use of extant theories. Extant theories can be used in two ways. One is as touchstones against which to compare data during the analysis process. The other use is after the case study is completed to compare the actual findings with the outcomes suggested by extant theories.

CONCLUSION: POLICY ARENAS AND POWER

Philosophers, political scientists, sociologists, and other students of power have noted the importance of understanding power in the social content in which it is being studied (Wartenberg, 1992). This means that power cannot be explained as an abstract concept, but must be understood within the larger social context that holds power roles and relationships. The next three chapters provide the historical and social context for the study of power in the higher education policy arena. Chapter 2 sketches the historical background and context for the Higher Education Act of 1992, while chapter 3 provides a more precise definition and picture of the current higher education policy arena. Chapter 4 completes the contextual development with a discussion of the social context of policy making.

The question of how to study power in a policy arena, or in any social context, is problematic at best. The problem of power has become so interesting to students of power that it has them mesmerized and paralyzed. Instead of actually studying power, students of power seem to have locked themselves into a debate over how to study power. The debate has reached the point where it obscures a good deal more than it reveals. How one breaks out of this trance of methodology and moves forward with the study of power is also problematic. Whatever approach one takes, "one has to live with the uncomfortable fact that *no* points of departure are free from difficulties" (Falkmark, 1982, p. 15). The use of Callon and Latour's sociology of translation in combination with additional methods seems to be the most plausible way to move forward with the study of power. While this approach avoids the pitfalls associated with earlier approaches to the study of power, it does not ignore the issues and concerns identified in these approaches, but instead considers them from a different perspective.

While the debate over power, the meaning of power, operational definitions, and approaches to the study of power will continue, the approach outlined above offers an opportunity to reconstruct and reclaim power for use in policy analysis and research. The sociology of translation provides a sturdy framework for the study of power. In this framework, the meaning of power emerges from the study of what holds collective action together in the higher education policy arena. It is from this understanding of what holds collective action together that power is given meaning and definition. Once this is achieved, then power can be reclaimed as an explanatory concept.

Finally, it may be that the claims made in this chapter for power as a research construct are too great for what is a very modest abstraction. Reconstructing power as the undefined thread that holds collective action together and whose meaning must be interpreted from a careful analysis of that action might well be an avoidance of the problem of power rather than a solution. Reclaiming power as an explanatory concept might be a case of a researcher being seduced by an arousing and poetic symbol rather than a disinterested assessment of a research concept. The following chapters provide the reader with an opportunity to make his/her own judgment as the research approach described above is used to interpret and give meaning to power in the higher education policy arena.

2

Historical Context of Federal Higher Education Policy Making

Histories of American higher education tend to highlight or emphasize the defining characteristics of the American higher education
system that distinguish it from other national systems. The most
frequently cited characteristics include: the absence of centralized
control; existence of strong public and private sectors; trustee
authority in the form of a lay board; presidential authority; and
departmental authority (Carnegie Commission, 1975). While these
characteristics are reflective of the American experience, the lack of a
central system and the presence of a private sector are sometimes
expanded to mean that the federal government has been uninvolved
with higher education until recently (Duryea, 1981). A closer examination of history reveals that higher education has been an interest
and concern of the federal government from the first days of the
republic. At the local level, federal concerns were preceded by colonial
officials' interest in educating ministers for the church (Rudolph,
1990). Far from being uninvolved, American governments, federal and
state, have a long history of encouraging, supporting, funding,
regulating, and working with institutions of higher education.

Higher education associations have played a relatively recent role
in higher education policy making. As recently as 1952, the Association of American Universities (AAU) "called for an end to further
government financial assistance, fearing federal control" (Morgan,
1981, p. 73). Despite this early reluctance, higher education associations have become involved with the federal government as part of
what McGeorge Bundy termed "a constructive partnership which
benefits both sides" (quoted in Morgan, 1981, p. 76). After nearly
thirty years of active participation in the partnership, many aspects of
the relationship between higher education associations and federal
higher education policy makers remain unexamined. This is particularly

true of the level of influence or power that associations wield in the policy process. Despite the lack of empirical evidence, higher education associations, at least since the early 1980s, have been credited with being powerful policy actors.

The purpose of this chapter is to provide a historical sketch of the development of the federal interest in higher education from the Northwest Ordinance of 1787 to the Higher Education Amendments of 1992. This will create a background and context for a the detailed discussion of the higher education lobby's influence on Title IV of the Higher Education Amendments of 1992 that follows in the next three chapters. An important aspect of this background and context is a series of dynamic tensions and conflicts that have marked the debate over the federal role in higher education. The resolution of these conflicts and tensions established contested principles that still guide the federal interest in higher education today. These principles are identified below and will be revisited in later chapters. Finally, some scholars have suggested that the higher education lobby formed primarily in response to federal higher education policy initiatives (e.g., Babbidge & Rosenzweig, 1962; Graham, 1984; Rudolph, 1990). This rather interesting thesis is beyond the scope of this study, but the formation of higher education associations in relationship to federal policy actions can and will be noted.

FROM THE NORTHWEST ORDINANCE OF 1787 TO THE COLD WAR OF THE 1950s

The earliest federal expression of interest in higher education can be found in the Northwest Ordinance of 1787. Coming some two years before the Constitution took effect, the Northwest Ordinance reserved one square mile of each township for the creation of public schools. While the intent was to encourage New Englanders to move into what has then the American West, the action established a pattern that was followed in the development of all new territorial lands. In addition, two principles of federal support for higher education were established that would be followed well into the 1900s. One was the principle of federal grants for the support of education. The other was that education would be used as an instrument to achieve other policy objectives.

The first federal land grants for colleges were made in the Northwest territories. In 1787, the federal government entered into a contract with the Ohio Company that provided land for the development of a university (Babbidge & Rosenzweig, 1962). The contractual provision for support of a university was included, in part, due to the lobbying efforts of Manasseh Cutler, a Massachusetts clergyman (Rudolph, 1990). As with the Northwest Ordinance's provision for schools, the intent was not so much the encouragement of education, but rather as an inducement to New Englanders to immigrate to the frontier. Regardless of the intent, Cutler seems to have earned the distinction of being the first lobbyist for higher education in the United States.

Cutler was not alone in his efforts to obtain federal support for higher education. A number of leading citizens and political leaders advanced the idea of federal support for a national university. During debate over the Constitution, it was suggested that the right to create a national university be one of the federal government's enumerated powers (Babbidge & Rosenzweig, 1962). The idea was dropped because it was assumed that the national university would be developed in the federal district, thus no special authority was needed since the Constitution gave sovereignty over the district to the federal government (Babbidge & Rosenzweig, 1962).

George Washington held a special interest in the creation of a national university. In his first message to Congress in 1790, Washington spoke of the need for a national university (Rudolph, 1990). In his last address to the Congress in 1796, Washington again called for the creation of a national university. Unsuccessful in his lifetime, Washington willed fifty shares of stock in the Potomac Canal Company for the purpose of founding a national university (Babbidge & Rosenzweig, 1962). The concept continued to enjoy presidential support until the Andrew Jackson administration, but the idea never gained the Congressional support necessary for it to become a reality.

While the idea of a national university faded, supporters of higher education were successful in getting the federal government to create other institutions of higher education. In 1802, the United States Military Academy at West Point was founded to educate officers for the military (Babbidge & Rosenzweig, 1962). Unable to find the trained officers, leaders, and engineers it needed, the federal government created the first technical institute in the United States. In 1845, the United States Naval Academy was opened to provide technical education for Navy officers. These institutions emphasized engineering and science long before the established higher education institutions enlarged the curriculum to include what were then considered mere vocational topics of study.

The creation of the service academies reflects an implicit principle in the federal action in higher education, namely the tendency to look to higher education only in times of national need or emergency. In the instance of the service academies, the federal government created a new institutional form because the existing higher education system could not meet the need for engineers. When the existing system has been able to respond, then the federal government has used higher education as a policy instrument to meet the particular national need or emergency of the time.

The national university concept and the service academies are consistent with the theme enunciated in President Thomas Jefferson's message to Congress in 1806. Jefferson conceded the "ordinary branches" of education to private enterprise and to the states, but identified the need for a special type of public institution to "complete the circle" of education by providing science and "other rarely called for" but vital fields of knowledge (Babbidge & Rosenzweig, 1962). Not even the great mind of Jefferson could have foreseen the role that the federal government would play in the support of university research in the post–World War II era, but this is an early example of the recognition that the federal government had a role to play in support of higher education. Jefferson himself later helped close the circle with his design for the University of Virginia that "combined an attention to the popular and practical new subjects with an intellectual orientation of university dimensions" (Rudolph, 1990, p. 125).

At least two other events of the early 1800s are worthy of mention before turning to the Morrill Land-Grant Act of 1862. One is the famous Dartmouth College case of 1819. The specific details of the case are too well known to bear repeating, but it is important to mark this as a failed government effort to intervene in higher education. The resulting decision created a public and private sector of higher education, but this was little noticed at the time as states continued to fund private institutions and private groups continued to control public institutions (Brubacher & Rudy, 1976; Rudolph, 1990). The other is the letting of the first federal research contract to the Franklin Institute in 1830 (Babbidge & Rosenzweig, 1962).

The Morrill Land-Grant Act of 1862 is often treated as the touch-stone for federal legislation on higher education (e.g., see King, 1975). For many, the Morrill Act stands as a sentinel marking the starting point of the federal interest in higher education. Of course, policy decisions seldom, if ever, arrive as a fully formed program of action or legislation. Instead, policy decisions tend to bubble up from many ideas, actions, and decisions until finally, a feasible policy proposal is accepted by the polity. This is not to say that Justin Morrill is undeserving of the credit he justifiably earned, but rather to suggest that one must start before 1862 to understand why Congress accepted Morrill's idea in 1862.

After several false starts, a number of ideas and events combined to make the Morrill Act a reality. One was the increasing demand for agricultural sciences and education (Eddy, 1956). Established institutions often promised to meet these demands, but never actually followed through with the delivery of educational courses and programs. By the 1850s, America's farms were being replaced by an agricultural industry and manufacturing was becoming the leading industrial sector. Far from lessening the demands on institutions, this increased the demand and added mechanical sciences as a need.

The national university concept, despite its demise as a viable political idea, continued to have its supporters. Building on this support, Morrill conceived of his agricultural and mechanical colleges in the framework of the national university or service academy model in which national agricultural schools would be built and a limited number of students from each Congressional district would be selected for advanced training (Babbidge & Rosenzweig, 1962). It was only after this idea failed to win support that Morrill turned to the land-grant concept.

Jefferson's notion of completing the circle may also have influenced the formulation and passage of the Morrill Act. When Morrill first introduced the legislation in 1857, he was promoting a type of scientific and technical education that was not being offered in either the public or private colleges (Eddy, 1956). In doing this, he was not asking Congress to go beyond its higher education policy experience. Congress had already created new forms of higher education when it found that the service academies were needed to complete the circle of education. With this combination of ideas and experiences influencing the Congress, Morrill was successful in getting the legislation passed, but President James Buchanan vetoed the bill and Morrill was forced to wait for a more favorable confluence of forces (Rudolph, 1990).

In 1862, Morrill found a more favorable combination of forces and events. With the withdrawal of the South from the Union, Morrill was rid of his most hostile and active political opponents. The concept of the land-grant college also fit well with President Abraham Lincoln's political agenda that saw the creation of an office of agriculture and the signing of the Homestead Act in 1862. Also, not to be discounted, was the Republican Party's desire to win the farm vote (Ross, 1942). In July 1862, Congress passed the Morrill Land-Grant Act and Lincoln signed the legislation into law (Rudolph, 1990).

In passing the Morrill Act, Congress continued to act on the principle that the federal government would use the higher education system to meet national needs for specially trained and educated human resources while recognizing the independence of the individual institutions. In addition, Congress created the principle of nondiscrimination between public and private institutions. Land-grant funds were equally available to both and some states designated private institutions as their land-grant colleges. These principles continue to guide federal higher education policy making to this day.

The federal-higher education interaction created by the Morrill Act also spurred the development of the first higher education association. Unhappy with the federal role in the post–Civil War years, representatives from the land-grant colleges held a convention in Washington, D.C. in 1882 to discuss federal policies and practices toward the institutions (King, 1975). In 1887, they formed the Association of American Agricultural Colleges, which was followed by the founding of the National Association of State Universities in 1895 (Bloland, 1985). In 1963, these two associations combined with the State Universities Association to form the National Association of State Universities and Land-Grant Colleges (NASULGC) (Bloland, 1985).

The same year the American Association of Agricultural Colleges was founded Congress expanded the federal role in higher education with the Hatch Act of 1887. The Act provided funds for the creation of agricultural experimental stations that proved to be valuable for farmers and helped increase support for the land-grant colleges (Ross, 1942). This was followed by the Morrill Act of 1890, which provided for annual appropriations to land-grant colleges. In addition, the act prohibited funding to states that denied black students admission to land-grant colleges unless separate but equal schools were provided for blacks. Not eager to foster racial equality, seventeen states created black land-grant colleges, while de facto segregation continued in many more (Ross, 1942).

The Smith-Lever Act of 1914 cemented the relationship between the land-grant colleges, their extension services, and the federal government (Rudolph, 1990). The evolution of this relationship illustrates both the federal government's philosophy toward higher education and the impact of its ad hoc policy making approach. As noted above, the federal government turned to the higher education system when the national need demanded some type of specialized education and training, or when higher education could be an instrument to achieve some policy objective. At other times, the federal government created policy in response to the pressure of interest groups. With the creation of categorical aid programs, special interest groups formed to defend and expand their programs. As the United States stood on the eve of World War I, national education policy was not guided by a coherent philosophy, but instead was a patchwork quilt of programs, offices, associations, and individuals that formed a loose federal–higher education partnership.

The movement towards involvement in World War I added even more patches to the quilt. On the eve of World War I, the military had available the two service academies, the Army Medical School, and the Army War College to meet its educational needs, but it was clear that more would be needed if the country entered the war in Europe (Babbidge & Rosenzweig, 1962). In 1916, Congress passed the National Defense Act, which created the Reserve Officers Training Corps (ROTC) (King, 1975). By the end of the war, over 500 colleges had ROTC units on campus.

Concerned that they might not be doing their share toward the war effort, fourteen national educational associations formed the Emergency Council on Education to coordinate higher education's support for the war (King, 1975). Following the war, the council renamed itself the American Council on Education (ACE) and expanded its interest (Bloland, 1985). ACE is now the oldest and largest education umbrella organization in Washington, D.C. (Bailey, 1975).

The era between the two world wars was marked by the continuation of existing federal programs and the addition of a few small programs. One of the small, but important, programs was the Public Health Service Fellowships program (Babbidge & Rosenzweig, 1962). Another small program, at least initially, was the student work-study program established in 1935 as part of the National Youth Administration (King, 1975). From 1935 to 1943, over $93 million was spent on a program that served 620,000 college students (Brubacher & Rudy, 1976).

As World War II loomed on the horizon, the federal government repeated its World War I pattern of calling on higher education to help against the threat to the nation. In response, higher education accepted the federal government's agenda and served as an instrument for implementing national programs. One of the programs implemented as part of the federal-higher education war effort was the Engineering, Service and Management War Training Program (Babbidge & Rosenzweig, 1962). Using college and university campuses, the War Training program trained over 1.5 million men and women in skills that would be needed during the war. The Army Specialized Training Program employed some 200 institutions to educate enlisted men and women in areas of special need. Another program gave loans to students in engineering, medicine, pharmacy, and physics. Over 11,000 students used government loans to attend college between 1942 and 1944 (King, 1975).

America's entry into World War II expanded the size and complexity of the patchwork quilt of policies and practices that passed for federal higher education policy. Virtually all branches of the federal government and the military entered into some contract or arrangement with higher education (McGuiness, 1981). To bring some order to this explosion of contracts and grants, the National Defense Research Committee, which later became the Office of Scientific Research and Development, was created to coordinate wartime contracts (Wilson, 1982). The federal role became so large that by the end of World War II some institutions were receiving as much as 50 percent of their income from federal contracts and grants (Brubacher & Rudy, 1976).

The end of the war did not reverse or even slow the flow of federal funds to higher education. The G.I. Bill, designed to reward soldiers and ease the transition to a peacetime economy, made it possible for millions of men and women to attend college (King, 1975). To assist colleges and universities with the influx of new students, the Surplus Property Act of 1944, along with related legislation, made it possible to discount and give millions of dollars worth of equipment and supplies to institutions (Brubacher & Rudy, 1976). The College Housing Loan Program, initiated in 1950, made low-cost, long-term loans available to institutions for the construction of dormitories (Babbidge & Rosenzweig, 1962). The Cold War competition with the USSR helped direct huge sums of federal money to institutions for space research, science, area studies, and language programs (Rosenzweig, 1982). By 1947, half of the income for all of higher education was from federal funds and by 1960 federal dollars purchased seventy percent of all university and college research (Brubacher & Rudy, 1976; Rudolph, 1990).

While the postwar years saw a steady increase in the federal interest in higher education, the National Defense Education Act (NDEA) of 1958 is often cited as a turning point in the federal-higher education partnership. The importance of the NDEA rests not only in its specific provisions, but in "the psychological breakthroughs it embodied. It asserted more forcefully than at any time in nearly a century, a national interest in the quality of education that the states, communities, and private institutions provided" (Sundquist, 1968, p. 179). Before turning to the NDEA, it is important to summarize the principles and characteristics that guided the federal interest in higher education up to the NDEA of 1958.

Until the late 1950s, "one of the most distinctive attributes of America's political culture had been the tenacity with which the United States, unlike most nations, had resisted a national education policy" (Graham, 1984, p. xvii). In place of a coherent national policy stood a series of categorical aid programs that had been devised in response to national needs or crisis, or in response to interest group pressure. Higher education, as an issue, was usually peripheral to the aid program. In using higher education as an instrument, the federal government did not discriminate, that is, private and public institutions were treated equally. Finally, the federal government acted as a benevolent patron allowing higher education extensive freedom and flexibility (Rosenzweig, 1982).

NATIONAL DEFENSE EDUCATION ACT OF 1958

When President Dwight D. Eisenhower faced the press on October 9, 1957, five days after the USSR had placed Sputnik in orbit, Merriman Smith of the United Press started the press conference with, "I ask you, sir, what are we going to do about it?" (quoted in Sundquist, 1968, p. 173). While it was not part of his answer that day, Eisenhower would quickly turn to the school system as both the problem and the solution. The problem was that U.S. schools were not as effective as Soviet schools and that U.S. higher education was not producing the scientists and engineers needed to maintain America's leadership position in the world. The nature of the crisis was such that Eisenhower felt it was time for the federal government to help the education system "meet the broad and increasing demands imposed on it by considerations of basic national security" (quoted in Thomas, 1975, p. 23).

Proponents of federal aid to education had been trying for some ninety years, with limited success, to obtain general aid to education (Munger & Fenno, 1962). The orbiting Sputnik seemed to overshadow race, religion, states' rights, and other obstacles that had blocked previous aid attempts. When Congress convened in January 1958, both Republicans and Democrats offered national defense education bills. Despite the strong sense of national support for such a bill, the sponsors were taking nothing for granted. The linking of education and defense was designed not only as a response to Sputnik, but also to make it more difficult for congressional members to oppose the legislation (Thomas, 1975).

The two bills put forward were remarkably similar in content and approach (Sundquist, 1968). For example, both provided for college scholarships, graduate fellowships, student loans, and state aid. The similarities made it appear that a compromise bill would breeze through Congress and be signed by the president. Many of the groups that traditionally opposed federal aid to education stood aside or offered only token opposition to the proposed legislation. Ironically, it was the student aid provisions that produce the greatest opposition and even more ironic was the fact that it came from the administration, which had originally suggested merit aid. Eisenhower switched positions to oppose the number of scholarships and the fact that not all of the awards were need-based (Sundquist, 1968).

Eisenhower was joined in his opposition to merit scholarships by several members of Congress. The consensus seemed to be that a free college education would undermine the character of the recipient. Representative Walter H. Judd of Minnesota summarized the opposition's view on scholarships with the statement that "any boy or girl bright enough to merit a scholarship is good enough to be able to pay a low-interest loan back without difficulty or hardship in an 11-year period after his graduation. Any boy or girl who is not sufficiently competent to be able to pay back such a loan . . . is not good enough to deserve a free scholarship" (quoted in Sundquist, 1968, p. 178). The proponents of merit aid failed to offer a reasonable rationale for a public investment in a seemingly private good. The human capital investment theory would have been an apt response to the opposition, but it was not yet well known. Without a popular response and facing the opposition of the administration, scholarship proponents were forced to withdraw.

Without the student scholarship provisions, the National Defense Education Act (NDEA) of 1958 passed Congress and was signed into law by Eisenhower on September 2, 1958 (Lu, 1965). NDEA provisions included:

Title II authorized loans to college students with the provision that up to 50 percent of the amount would be "forgiven," at the rate of 10 percent a year for each year that the student taught in public schools

Title III authorized matching grants for public schools and loans to private schools for the purchase of equipment used in teaching science, mathematics, and foreign languages

Title IV authorized 5,500 three-year graduate fellowships for students enrolled in new or expanded programs

Title V provided state education agencies with funds for guidance, counseling, and testing and for guidance and counseling training

Title VI sought to improve foreign-language teaching by authorizing research centers and institutes and teacher-training institutes

Title VII authorized a program for the development of educational utilization of television and related communications media

Title VIII expanded vocational education by providing funds to the states for training skilled technicians in science-related occupations. (Thomas, 1975, p. 24)

As noted above, the NDEA is perhaps most important for "the psychological breakthroughs it embodied." The NDEA demonstrated that it was possible to formulate legislation that avoided the traditional obstacles to federal aid to education. While the proponents of general aid and merit scholarships were disappointed, NDEA opened the way for future legislation.

Finally, despite the breakthrough status accorded NDEA, it continued many of the principles previously established in federal aid to education programs. Education continued to be an instrument for reaching other, primary policy objectives. In this case, education was the means to reach an end, that is, national defense. The structure of NDEA reflects the continuation of categorical aid programs at the expense of a coherent national policy on education. In designing the aid programs, Congress continued to treat public and private institutions as one and the same. Last, Congress continued to select student aid over institutional aid as the best way to help education.

HIGHER EDUCATION ACT OF 1965

The story of the Higher Education Act of 1965 actually starts in the spring of 1964 when President Lyndon Johnson began planning for his next term of office. Sensing what would soon become reality, Johnson anticipated an overwhelming victory over Republican candidate Barry Goldwater and large Democratic majorities in the Eighty-ninth

Congress. Not wanting to miss an historic opportunity, Johnson instructed his staff to organize a number of task forces to work on legislative proposals for immediate presentation to the new Congress. The president wanted to present Congress with a massive social reform program and enabling legislation when it meet in January 1965 (Graham, 1984).

The use of task forces was not a unique political idea. President John F. Kennedy had used education task forces during his abbreviated term. The Kennedy task forces were open to public view and their work was open to public criticism. Kennedy had also placed aid to higher education together with aid to the lower schools to form one legislative proposal for education (Graham, 1984).

Graham (1984) summarizes Kennedy's 1961 legislative efforts under the heading "FIASCO" (p. 22). While this may overstate the case, it probably reflects the frustration and failure the administration must have felt as its education agenda was scuttled in 1961 and again in 1962. After Kennedy's assassination, the Higher Education Facilities Act of 1963 (HEFA), which created a five-year program of matching grants and loans for construction of academic facilities, was passed by Congress and signed into law by President Johnson. The remainder of the Kennedy agenda would be folded into Johnson's Great Society.

After having witnessed the Kennedy defeats firsthand, Johnson created small, secret task forces oriented towards policy formation (Graham, 1984). Each task force blended together practitioners, intellectuals, a White House liaison, and an executive secretary who usually came from the Bureau of the Budget. Altogether, some 135 task forces were formed to help plan the legislative and policy proposals of the Great Society. This device not only allowed the planning of policy initiatives without the hindrance of public criticism, but it also guaranteed tight executive control over policy formulation. Congress would have input, but it would come after the administration had formed the policy, thus forcing Congress to respond on Johnson's terms.

The legislative task force on education was chaired by John W. Gardner, then president of the Carnegie Corporation, William B. Cannon of the Bureau Budget served as executive secretary, and Richard Goodwin acted as White House liaison (Graham, 1984). Task force members included, among others, Clark Kerr, Francis Keppel, David Riesman, Ralph W. Tyler, Stephen J. Wright, and Jerrold R. Zacharias. Their mission was "to think in bold new terms and strike out in new directions" (Graham, 1984, p. 57). By November 10, 1964, the task force was to have its action report ready for the White House. Johnson's plan was to hit Congress with a full package of legislative proposals, rush the bills through committee, and then force a floor vote before he lost his election momentum (Thomas, 1975).

The success of this strategy is now well documented. Through skillful use of his election mandate and well honed legislative skills, Johnson was able to move the Elementary and Secondary Education Act (ESEA) through Congress in less than three months. The ESEA's "five substantive titles managed to fashion artful compromises that dodged the thorny problems of religion and federal control" (Thomas, 1975, p. 29). The compromises successfully directed the legislation between what Senator Lister Hill had once called "the Scylla of race and the Charybdis of religion" (quoted in Sundquist, 1968, p. 176). On April 11, 1965, Johnson signed ESEA in the one-room schoolhouse in Texas that he had attended as a child. With his signature, education moved from the policy periphery to center stage and from being an instrument of policy to being an object of policy.

After the dramatic passage of ESEA, the Higher Education Act (HEA) of 1965 was almost anticlimactic (Thomas, 1975). In contrast to ESEA, HEA was not a major break from past policy experiences. Congress had given aid to higher education on several occasions as an instrument to obtain some national purpose. In addition, most of the opponents to direct aid had been voted out of office in the Democratic landslide of 1964. Republicans still raised their voices in opposition but were too weak to stop, or even slow, HEA. Johnson and "the Congress were working together in harness" (Keppel, 1987, p. 50) and nothing could slow the legislative gallop.

While it is sometimes forgotten, it is worth remembering that HEA, like ESEA, was part of the larger War on Poverty (McGuiness, 1981). As such, HEA was more than just student loans, educational grants, or institutional aid. It was part of a larger plan to use education to fight poverty, to give the disenfranchised access to education, to create educational opportunities where none had existed, and to promote a peaceful transformation to a Great Society. The goal of social equality was a significantly new instrumental use of education by the federal government. In this regard, the Johnson administration seemed to hold a Deweyan belief in the power of education to reform society.

The intent of the legislation and the composition of its constituency are reflected in the HEA's eight titles. Title I attempted to expand the land-grant extension concept to urban universities. This was included as a concession to ACE and to the U.S. Office of Education (USOE) (Graham, 1984). The urban riots of the early 1960s also gave an impetus to the urban land-grant concept. Title II provided money to expand college and university libraries and to train librarians. This was supported by the USOE, the American Library Association, and the Association of Research Libraries as a necessary program to meet the demands of a rapidly expanding college population (Graham, 1985; Keppel, 1987). Title III was designed to aid historically black colleges, but was "drafted in terms that veiled the basic intent of supporting primarily black institutions" (Keppel, 1987, p. 53). While it was presented as aid to developing colleges, Representative Edith Green, Keppel, and Zacharias lobbied for Title III with the clear understanding that it was intended to assist historically black institutions (Graham, 1984; Keppel, 1987). Title IV, with its four-part package of financial aid, is the heart of HEA. The Democrats were finally able to gain student scholarships in the form of Educational Opportunity Grants to institutions. To forestall support for tuition tax credits and to undermine Republican opposition, a guaranteed student-loan program for the middle class was included (Graham, 1984). College work-study and an extension of the NDEA loan program completed the aid programs. Title V established the National Teachers Corps. The Corps was to provide teachers to poverty stricken areas of the U.S. (Thomas, 1975). Title VI created a program of financial assistance for improving undergraduate instruction. Finally, Title VII amended the Higher Education Facilities Act, while Title VIII contained the law's general provisions.

If the passage of HEA was anticlimactic, its impact was certainly dramatic. For the first time in history, Congress had passed a general aid to higher education bill. The national defense link that was so vital to the NDEA was not important in the passage of HEA. The goals of social equality and equal educational opportunity were important aims of the new legislation, but HEA marked the beginning of higher education's emergence as an independent policy issue supported by its own policy arena. HEA tied together a diverse group of constituents—higher education associations, teacher unions, historically black institutions, urban institutions, librarians, civil rights groups— that would fight to defend HEA and to expand "their" programs in the years ahead. The diverse composition of the evolving policy arena was consistent with Johnson's belief that the creation of a program was more important than the size and scope of a program. Once created, programs take on a life of their own and are very difficult to kill.

REAUTHORIZATIONS AND AMENDMENTS

In legislative language, the Higher Education Act of 1965 is an authorizing statute. This means that it defines the purpose of programs under the act and sets the life span at the end of which programs must either be reauthorized or come to an end. Funding levels are also authorized, or recommended, but the actual appropriations are provided by a separate appropriations process. When originally passed, HEA was authorized for two years, thus the first reauthorization was in 1968. HEA was also reauthorized in 1972, 1976, 1980, and 1986. The 1992 reauthorization will be the sixth and possibly last reauthorization before the year 2000.

Typically, the bulk of legislative work on an authorizing statute occurs during the reauthorization, but after passing the HEA Congress seemed impatient and immediately started to tinker with and amend the legislation instead of waiting until reauthorization. Indeed, even the Johnson administration seemed anxious to fine tune its recent legislative work. Joseph Califano, Johnson's domestic advisor, set the Keppel Interagency Task Force on Education to work on devising a plan to expand financial aid to the middle class and to move NDEA loans to an off budget account in the form of an "Educational Development Bank" (Graham, 1984, pp. 114–15). In making its actual proposals to Congress, the administration took a cautious approach, asking for small funding increases, the NDEA changes, and a three-year extension of the HEFA. Congress accepted most of the administration's recommendations in 1966 but refused to restructure the NDEA loan program and actually increased authorization levels (Thomas, 1975).

Congress made an effort at fine tuning the HEA in 1967 when Senator Abraham Ribicoff presented his "perennial call for tuition tax credits" (Graham, 1984, p. 147). Several factors made tuition tax credits politically appealing in 1967. The increase in inflation coupled with the rise in college tuition made the plan attractive to families who were having a difficult time paying for college even with the assistance of the student-aid programs created by HEA. The rise in inflation and interest rates also made it more difficult to obtain loans, as banks moved out of the student loan market and into other more profitable lending markets. Finally, on the eve of an election campaign, the idea looked too attractive, in terms of votes, for members of Congress not to support Ribicoff's call. The Johnson administration was able to stop the bill by locking it in the Senate Finance Committee and in the House Ways and Means Committee, thus preventing a floor vote.

The tuition tax credit fight was merely a minor battle on the way to the 1968 reauthorization. In 1968, Congress would be faced with reauthorizing the HEA, HEFA, NDEA, and the National Foundation for the Arts and Humanities. With the exception of the science programs, virtually every higher education related program was facing renewal. In addition to its legislative focus, Congress' eyes were fixed on the campuses as the increasingly unpopular Vietnam War sparked student protests and campus strikes. The anti-war protests served to make a difficult task even more difficult.

As in 1965, consideration of HEA waited until after ESEA was completed. When consideration of HEA finally got under way, Congress did not address the issues included in the president's legislative package. Instead of asking about the administration's reauthorization proposals, Representative Edith Green's subcommittee immediate began to grill USOE Commissioner Harold Howe on the administration's budget plans for 1969 (Thomas, 1975). Johnson was facing the dilemma of paying for guns and butter, but was unwilling to compromise on either. The administration's proposals for reauthorization trimmed some programs, eliminated none, and called for the creation of several new programs. Johnson eventually got much of what he wanted from Representative Green's subcommittee, but not until after she had clearly communicated her displeasure with the administration's budget proposal.

While Representative Green was criticizing the administration on the education budget, Representative L. H. Wyman was attacking students for disruptive behavior on the campuses (Thomas, 1975). Representative Wyman's concern was formulated into an amendment to withhold financial aid from students who were found to disobey campus regulations or to cause disruptions. The Wyman Amendment was opposed by ACE, which noted that colleges and universities already had this authority and that the amendment might actually provoke more student challenges. The ACE was accurate in its argument, but the House was fixated on the issue of campus unrest. The Wyman Amendment was included in the House bill that went to conference.

In the Senate, Subcommittee Chair Wayne Morse, a vocal critic of the Vietnam War, was outraged at the proposed funding levels for higher education programs. The tone for reauthorization was set when he asked the Bureau of the Budget how it measured "the value of the life of one American boy against the lives of a number of Viet Cong, the education of the boys and girls of this country against the present regime in South Vietnam, and the future of the lives of our boys and girls against national prestige" (quoted in Graham, 1984, p. 191). As with the House, Johnson eventually got much of what he wanted from the Senate, but not until after senators such as Morse made certain that the administration understood their sense of anger and moral outrage over what they saw as the sacrifice of the nation's resources in a meaningless war.

The conference committee was given two bills that agreed on the basics, but not on the particulars of HEA. The major point of controversy involved the Wyman Amendment (Thomas, 1975). The House wanted language on student protests while the Senate saw no need for the inclusion of such language. The final bill reflected a compromise that provided for the   ithdrawal of aid but left enforcement in the hands of the institutions. While the final bill provided funding levels that far exceeded the administration's requests, it did contain most of their new program requests. On October 16, 1968, Johnson signed the Higher Education Amendments of 1968, his fifty-ninth education bill, into law (Graham, 1984).

While the next reauthorization would not take place until 1972, the 1968 reauthorization was the genesis for many of the issues raised in 1972. One of the major issues involved the question of institutional aid versus student financial aid. The question had been discussed for several years but was not resolved in 1968. Instead, the question was deferred for future consideration.

A second issue involved the role of banks and lending agencies in the guaranteed student loan program. The Barr Task Force had recommended several technical changes for the Congress to consider during reauthorization (Thomas, 1975). One change was to pay banks a processing fee for each student loan a bank originated. Another change involved aid to increase the participation of state and private lending agencies in the loan program. Both changes were apparently adopted with little controversy and produced the desired outcome of increased lender participation in the student loan program. The size, condition, and nature of that participation would become an ongoing issue in the years ahead.

Related to the Barr Task Force report was the Rivlin report, prepared by Department of Health Education and Welfare assistant secretary for planning and evaluation, Alice M. Rivlin (Graham, 1984). While it was prepared too late to be part of the 1968 reauthorization process, ideas from the Rivlin report would become important issues during the 1972 reauthorization. Among other things, Rivlin proposed a National Student Loan Bank to be created by the sale of government securities, but to be operated as a private, nonprofit corporation. As with earlier proposals to eliminate the NDEA loan program, this proposal would allow the guaranteed student loan program to be taken off the books, thus giving the appearance of reduced government expenditures.

The last issue that arose in 1968, and reappeared in 1972, was the question of busing children to achieve racially integrated public schools. This was not a HEA issue nor was it attached to HEA in 1968. Instead, the issue was attached to ESEA. In the debated that followed, Representative Green "established herself as a major figure shaping federal educational policy" (Thomas, 1974, p. 85) as she moved ESEA through the House. In 1972, the busing issue would be attached to the HEA, and Representative Green would once again play a major role in the legislative process.

Of course, none of the major policy actors waited until 1972 to begin efforts to influence HEA reauthorization. Robert H. Sullivan, president of the Association of American Colleges (AAC), used his 1969 annual report to propose the creation of two new higher education associations (King, 1975). One would be devoted exclusively to lobbying for higher education legislation. The second organization would serve to educate the public and work to increase support for higher education.

No new organizations were created as a result of Sullivan's recommendations, but AAC itself began to change. The Federation of State Associations of Independent Colleges and Universities (FSAICU), a national coordinating body within AAC, was reorganized in 1971 and became the National Council for Independent Colleges and Universities (NCICU) (Bloland, 1985). FASCIU had originally been organized to answer internal complaints about AAC's emphasis on educational rather than governmental issues (Hunt, 1977). NCICU was an attempt to address internal dissatisfaction over AAC's ability and willingness to speak on federal higher education policy issues.

NCICU was able to address the issue for a time, but there was a continuing sense that a national voice for independent colleges and universities was needed (Hunt, 1977). In 1976, NCICU completed its evolution and became the National Association of Independent Colleges and Universities (NAICU). If there were any doubts about NAICU's purpose, then they were answered when John Phillips, former deputy commissioner of postsecondary education in the USOE, was selected as NAICU's first president. NAICU would be the national voice for the independent sector of higher education.

The budget cuts in the last years of the Johnson administration and in the first year of the new Nixon administration helped give life to a new lobbying coalition called the Emergency Committee for the Full-Funding of Education Programs (Bloland, 1985). Formed in the spring of 1969, the new organization united some eighty education interest groups behind one clear goal: restoring full-funding for all federal education programs. While the effort was unsuccessful, the higher education associations experienced a level and style of lobbying that went beyond their previous experience. It also brought them into contact with groups with whom they had not worked before despite the existence of common goals.

While the associations were getting a new taste of political life, they were not certain that they liked it all that much. One ACE representative summarized the experience with the Full-Funding Committee by saying, "I did have serious misgivings about crawling into bed with so many other interests like the labor unions and the impact aid people. Now I have nothing against labor unions, but I'm just not sure about getting too deeply involved with that kind of coalition" (quoted in King, 1975, p. 70). Like it or not, higher education programs were competing for scarce federal resources and the higher education associations would have to compete or watch their programs deteriorate.

One person in Washington who knew how to compete was Richard M. Nixon. To use a sports analogy, a type that Nixon was fond of using, the new president went on the offense by presenting a full range of legislative proposals in March 1970. Many of the proposals in the March Education Message came from the report of the Friday Education Task Force that had been organized under President Johnson (Moynihan, 1975). Among other things, Nixon proposed universal access to education grants for low-income students, a new Student Loan Association to make loans available for all students, and a National Foundation for Education. In addition, Nixon offered an olive branch to higher education by noting that "I have repeatedly resisted efforts to attach detailed requirements on such matters as student discipline to programs of higher education. In the first place they won't work, and if they did work they would in that very process destroy what they nominally seek to preserve" (quoted in Moynihan, 1975, p. 137).

To drive home the Education Message, Nixon made a nationally televised address to the nation the day the Message was sent to the Congress (Moynihan, 1975). Despite this potent display of presidential offense, the proposals that were to be the Higher Education Amendments of 1970 gained no yardage. The higher education associations dismissed the message on delivery and Congress expressed no interest. The National Foundation for Higher Education was eschewed in favor of continuing the associations' rigid support of institutional aid. With no one to join the debate, a silence fell over the policy arena.

The silence lasted until the fall of 1970 when Daniel P. Moynihan, Nixon's counselor on domestic issues, unloaded on the higher education community in a speech to the ACE at its annual meeting. Speaking with characteristic candor, Moynihan (1971) charged that if there is to be a fundamental reform in relations between national government and higher education, there must be leadership on both sides, there must be negotiations, agreements, oversight, revision. The higher education community is not now organized for any such effort. It has no such men. It seemingly comprehends no such undertakings. (p. 254)

Moynihan was sorely disappointed with the higher education lobby's failure to respond to what he saw as a historic opportunity for higher education to regain control of the federal higher education policy agenda. The Nixon proposals for higher education were similar to the block grant programs of state and local aid. The institutions would be free to spend funds granted by the National Foundation for Higher Education as long as the case for excellence was established. Lest the ACE audience miss his sense of disappointment, Moynihan (1971) stated:

Had we thought categorical aid had distorted the relations of the higher education community to the federal government before the program was announced, in the aftermath we are utterly convinced corrupted would not be too strong a term. No one seemed able to think of the whole subject. Few even seemed able to think of the interests of a single institution. A major presidential initiative that, right or wrong, was at very least the product of some thought and some analysis was greeted by silence on the part of precisely those institutions that were presumably devoted to thought and analysis. (pp. 252–53)

Finally, Moynihan condemned the higher education community's failure to organize and speak for its interests. Comparing the ineffective higher education lobby to the well-organized elementary and secondary school lobby, Moynihan (1971) complained that:

Had there existed a powerful higher education lobby that willy-nilly would push through great increases in existing programs, the sequence of events might be more explicable. (It is worth noting that in the course of five years, the elementary and secondary school interests have created such a lobby in Washington.) But there is no such lobby and the result was predictable; Congress did nothing. (p. 253)

Much of Moynihan's bitter disappointment and anger with the higher education lobby can probably be attributed to the fact that he was one of the chief architects of the Nixon administration legislative proposals (Finn, 1977). It was not only pride of authorship, however, that sparked the tongue-lashing of the ACE audience in the fall of 1970. The foundation was a well-reasoned response to a range of ills that Moynihan and other Nixon staff saw as serious threats to higher education. The White House working group on education viewed the categorical aid programs as distorting and fragmenting higher education while making it dependent on Washington. The members of the working group were also concerned with the lack of reform and innovation in the nation's research institutions. These problems were seen as threats to institutional autonomy and academic freedom by Moynihan and others in the group. The foundation emerged as a structure that could respond to the problems "while strengthening the autonomy of higher education and keeping government out of its internal affairs " (Finn, 1977, p. 65). Moynihan (1975) could not understand higher education's failure to respond to the legislative proposals and why it seemed "almost to prefer the role of victim" (p. 145).

While the higher education associations stood silent, 1971 was rich with policy proposals. The metaphor of a primordial soup might be an apt way to describe the various policy ideas that were floating around. Some were newly born while others had been tossed back into the soup only to reemerge in a new form and still others were on the verge of taking life. The Nixon administration had unveiled its proposals and would certainly return with a legislative package in 1972. The Carnegie Commission and Rivlin reports were promoting the concept of student aid rather than institutional aid as the best way to help students pay for college. In addition, income-contingent loan plans were floating around as was the idea of a student loan bank. In the midst of all of this ferment, the ACE spoke for the major higher education associations when it stated that "the principal unfinished business of the federal government in the field of higher education is the necessity to provide support for general institutional purposes" (quoted in Gladieux & Wolanin, 1976, p. 44).

In 1971, the Nixon administration offered a refined version of its earlier legislative package (Gladieux & Wolanin, 1976). The loan program was expanded to help low-income students better afford private institutions, the proposal to eliminate construction grants and loans was withdrawn, and the career educationcommunity college program was eliminated. The structure and purpose of the National Education Foundation was adjusted, but continued to be the centerpiece of the administration's legislative package. Finally, the administration also proposed the creation of a National Institute of Education.

The administration proposals were virtually dead on arrival. Senator Claiborne Pell, chair of the subcommittee on education, was moving to fashion a reauthorization bill that would address the concerns of equal educational opportunity, the plight of private institutions, and the need to maintain diversity within the higher education system (Gladieux & Wolanin, 1976). One of Pell's key proposals was to create a Basic Educational Opportunity Grant for students. This would provide a floor or foundation of aid that students could depend on as a minimum and then build on from other sources (Gladieux, 1986). With the aid going directly to the student, he/she could then determine which institution to attend.

Other members of the Senate subcommittee also held strong, well-defined ideas about what should be included in the reauthorization bill (Gladieux & Wolanin, 1976). Harrison Williams wanted a community college bill included. Edward Kennedy wanted a program to strengthen American Indian schools while Richard S. Schweiker wanted a program of ethnic heritage studies for all schools. Jacob Javits proposed a state scholarship incentives program as a way to help spur the development of state student aid programs. Finally, Peter Dominick was pushing the concept of a Student Loan Marketing Association.

Although it was his first term as subcommittee chair, Pell displayed a deft touch in bringing together the various ideas of the subcommittee members into a comprehensive bill (Gladieux & Wolanin, 1976). As the senators and their staff members fashioned the final bill, they came to the conclusion "that the Federal government has an obligation to people rather than institutions" and that this meant placing "the decision-making in the hands of the 'consumer' of educational services rather than in the 'conduits' of those services" (Pell, quoted in Gladieux & Wolanin, 1976, p. 110). Pell was so successful in molding a consensus that the full membership of the Senate Labor and Public Welfare Committee joined its subcommittee members as cosponsors of the reauthorization bill, S.659. Not wanting to lose his consensus, Pell pressured senate leaders into scheduling a quick vote on the bill before the Senate left for its August recess. On August 6, 1971, the Senate voted 51–0 to approve S.659.

The formulation and passage of S.659 generated a considerable amount of mutual hostility between members of the Senate Subcommittee on Education and the higher education associations (Gladieux & Wolanin, 1976). The associations had not been involved in the formation of the legislative proposals and for the most part had elected not to participate in the hearings. The American Association of Junior Colleges did testify in support of the Williams bill and the National

Association of State Universities and Land-Grant Colleges testified in support of the status quo recommending an extension of all existing programs. The National Association of Student Financial Aid Administrators also testified in favor of expanding existing programs without any changes and expressed concerns about giving aid directly to students. Finally, a few individuals testified, but those who did were ill-prepared and uninformed (Honey, 1979).

As the hearings progressed, Pell could not contain his anger and disappointment over the higher education associations' interactions with his subcommittee. Speaking to one higher education representative, Pell stated:

> I would be wrong if, as chairman of the Education Subcommittee, I did not, in all fairness, consider all the different ideas and proposals that come to us. I have expressed great disappointment that the higher education community hasn't taken the trouble to reflect on and study our ideas which we think will help solve the problem. (quoted in Gladieux & Wolanin, 1976, p. 95)

In a speech to the American College Public Relations Association, Pell expressed the belief that

> what we have seen up to this point in time is a lack of willingness on the part of the higher education community to look at new ideas. It is the same spirit . . . that has caused the educational community to bristle at the Newman Report or even at the concept of cost accounting in educational institutions. (quoted in Gladieux & Wolanin, 1976, p. 111)

While he might be viewed as a harsh critic, Pell's observations were on target. The higher education associations had staked their entire reauthorization agenda on winning institutional aid. Furthermore, they had bet on Representative Edith Green's ability to translate that agenda into legislation. This was not a risky bet given that Green was more experienced than Pell and had successfully steered earlier education reauthorization bills through Congress. In 1971, Green was supporting institutional aid and there was no reason to think that she would not be as successful with this issue as she had been with earlier issues. Still, in betting on Representative Green, the associations had largely ignored the Senate. As a result, the higher education associations missed an opportunity to win friends and unnecessarily created animosity between themselves and Senator Pell.

In the House, Green worked closely with the higher education associations to develop an acceptable institutional aid formula (Gladieux & Wolanin, 1976). The associations wanted a capitation formula weighted for enrollments at different degree levels with an associate degree carrying the smallest weight and a doctorate the greatest weight. The issue of equal educational opportunity was addressed by including a bonus for enrolling disadvantaged students. Green largely accepted the formula but moved the weight away from doctoral students and expanded the formula to include small private institutions. What had been the association position became, with limited modification, the Green bill.

Unlike Pell, Green did develop her bill in close consultation with the associations. Also, unlike Pell, she developed her bill without consulting other members of the subcommittee (Gladieux & Wolanin, 1976). In addition to the institutional aid formula, the Green bill, H.R. 7248, continued existing programs and increased the discretion of financial aid officers in the awarding of Educational Opportunity Grants. With the exception of institutional aid, the Green bill offered no new programs that could be compared to the policy initiatives of the Nixon administration or of the Senate. With some minor changes, this was the bill that reached the House floor in late October 1971.

Just as H.R. 7248 reached the floor, the busing issue that had been part of the ESEA debate in 1968 flared up again. This time H.R. 7248 was the target of opportunity for the antibusing lobby. Representative Roman Pucinski announced that he would attach the Emergency School Aid Program (ESAP) to the Higher Education Amendments bill (Gladieux & Wolanin, 1976). In short, the purpose of ESAP was to ban all busing. Without a probusing opposition to fight the ESAP amendment and with antibusing leader Green directing the higher education bill, it was hardly surprising that the final House bill included a curb on busing for integration. In early November, the bill passed on a vote of 332-38 and was sent to the Senate.

When the House bill reached the Senate, it was referred to the Labor and Public Welfare Committee (Gladieux & Wolanin, 1976). S. 659 was amended and reported back to the Senate floor. Once on the floor, the Senate leadership offered a milder antibusing amendment that was accepted as part of the final bill. In March 1972, the Senate passed the amended S. 659 by a vote of 88-6 and sent it to the House.

The intent of the Senate action was to create matching sections in the bills, thus making compromise on the language easier. The House, however, was in no mood to compromise and voted to instruct its conferees not to accept the Senate language on busing (Gladieux &

Wolanin, 1976). Comparing the conference committee on HEA that followed with others during his twenty-two years in the House, Representative John Brademas (1987) found that none were as "lengthy, difficult, or fascinating" (p. 35). Carl Perkins was selected to lead the House conferees and Pell was selected to lead the Senate. Perkins acted as chair of the conference committee.

Two actions helped the conferees move towards agreement on a final bill. One was the decision by Perkins to take the first item in the Blue Books (the blue-covered side-by-side of the House and Senate bills) first and then precede through the rest of the items in the order in which they appeared (Gladieux & Wolanin, 1976). This meant that education issues would be dealt with first while the highly emotional busing issue would be dealt with last because it was printed at the end of the Blue Books. This did not totally diffuse the busing issue, but it did produce an atmosphere of agreement and probably contributed to the final language on busing, which proved to be far removed from what the antibusing groups had wanted or expected.

The other action was the silent revolution against Green. Representatives Brademas, Albert Quie, and Ogden Reid were increasingly unhappy with Green's conduct but had yet to make an open break with her (Brademas, 1987). Unaware that her support was wavering, Green compounded her difficulties by attacking Perkins and the other House conferees in a speech on the House floor (Gladieux & Wolanin, 1976). Following Green's speech, Perkins instructed Brademas to resolve the student grant and institutional aid issues with Pell, but to keep the negotiations and any agreement secret from Green (Brademas, 1987). Without knowing it, Green and the associations had lost on the issue of institutional aid. When they did find out, it was too late to reverse the decision or to produce a meaningful compromise.

The conference bill did contain a compromise provision for institutional aid, but it was never funded (Brademas, 1987). The months of debate over the best approach to institutional aid were essentially wasted. The busing issue that had obscured the more important issues addressed by the 1972 amendments was resolved with language that actually made busing easier. When Nixon signed the bill on June 24, 1972, the busing issue was still the focus of public attention, but in time it would become clear that what had resulted from the emotional and lengthy legislative process was nothing less than "a charter for federal policy toward postsecondary education" (Wolanin & Gladieux, 1975, p. 301). As the busing and institutional aid issues faded from memory, Brademas' claim that the Educational Amendments of 1972 were "a landmark in federal support for higher education" (quoted in Wolanin

& Gladieux, 1975, p. 301) seemed less and less like hyperbole and more and more like a reasoned assessment.

The major new program created by the 1972 amendments was the Basic Educational Opportunity Grant (BEOG) that was first proposed by Pell. The intent of the program was to enhance equal educational opportunity by creating a floor or base for student aid. Since BEOGs went directly to students, not to institutions, students were free to select the institution of their choice. Finally, BEOGs expanded equal educational opportunity by including part-time students and students attending accredited vocational-technical and proprietary schools.

Another important new program was the State Student Incentive Grants (SSIG) that had been proposed by Javits. The SSIG program provided seed money for states interested in expanding or creating a state scholarship system. Indirectly, it was a mechanism for assisting students who needed additional support in order to attend private institutions.

The administration's call for higher education reform and innovation was recognized in the creation of the Fund for the Improvement of Postsecondary Education (FIPSE). The FIPSE was charged with encouraging reform and innovation through grants to institutions. To avoid the creation of a permanent relationship between it and an institution, FIPSE was limited to giving seed grants for demonstration projects and educational experiments.

The Student Loan Marketing Association (Sallie Mae) was not a new aid program, but did serve to strengthen existing aid programs. As a government created, private corporation, Sallie Mae would serve as a secondary market for student loans. In turn, this would free lenders to increase the volume of student loans.

Finally, the Education Amendments attempted to introduce some level of rationality and accountability into the higher education system. One way in which this was attempted was the requirement for the creation of state postsecondary education planning commissions, commonly called "1202 Commissions" after the section of the HEA that imposed the requirement, as a condition for receiving grants under the community college and occupational education provisions of the HEA. The 1972 amendments also required a number of studies to determine how federal funds were being spent.

Just as the Education Amendments of 1972 proved to be a landmark in federal higher education policy making as time allowed for a more objective perspective, shifts in the higher education policy arena that were not noticed or discussed at the time proved to be highly significant in future years. One of these was the movement of policy initiatives from the President to the Congress. All previous higher education legislation had been initiated by the White House. The Nixon administration had attempted to continue this trend, but it could neither interest other policy actors in its initiatives nor mobilize them to act. The higher education associations expressed no interest in Nixon's proposals and even less trust in his intentions. Congress received the proposals but then ignored them as the House and Senate Subcommittees on Education developed their own legislative packages. After some fourteen years of leadership on higher education, the White House was replaced as the lead policy actors by the congressional subcommittees.

Another shift involved the movement of the higher education associations to the outer fringes of the policy arena. In one sense, this was not a major shift. The higher education associations had been only marginally involved in earlier legislation, but the 1972 reauthorization looked as if it would mark the emergence of the associations as major political actors. Representative Green had involved the associations in the process and their long cherished institutional aid program was the centerpiece of the House bill. Despite early appearances, the end result of the legislative process was quite different. The associations failed to gain institutional aid, earned several enemies in the Senate, and lost their champion in the House when Green resigned her subcommittee chair to take a seat on the Appropriations Committee. The move from center stage to backrow balcony produced a number of self-studies as associations looked for answers to what went wrong after such a grand start.

In retrospect, the associations made a number of key errors, many of which were not clearly visible until well after the fact. One error was their failure to gain access to the White House. Not withstanding Moynihan's strong criticisms of the associations, he did involve them in the policy formation process (see Finn, 1977, for a description of the White House working group on education). For their part, the associations neither worked to gain access nor protested their exclusion.

Another mistake was selecting institutional aid as the chief priority for the reauthorization. This mistake might be better described as an interrelated bundle of errors rather than as a single error. The decision to make institutional aid the primary goal of the reauthorization was seemly made without any awareness of the mood of the participants in the policy arena. The Carnegie Commission and Rivlin reports, which helped shape the policy debate, had focused on direct student aid as the most effective way of helping students. In the Senate, Pell clearly made his preferences known and he favored students over institutions. Nonetheless, the associations stood on the issue of institutional aid as *the* policy piece needed to complete the whole of federal higher education policy.

This might be viewed as hard bargaining. In political negotiations, it is not an uncommon tactic to stakeout an extreme position and then move towards a more reasonable settlement position. In using this tactic, parties to negotiations often gain a more favorable settlement than they might otherwise have reached. The associations, however, were not engaged in hard bargaining. Institutional aid was their only position, thus they had no fallback position. Once institutional aid was lost, the associations had no alternative to move to in hopes of reaching a settlement that still favored their terms.

The selection of Representative Green as their champion was also an error, but again it was a compound error rather than a simple mistake. Green certainly appeared to be a perfect choice at the time given her past legislative successes and her support for institutional aid. Yet, in selecting Green, the associations limited their ability to work with other members of Congress because she demanded and got a "zealous commitment" (Gladieux & Wolanin, 1976, p. 131) as a condition for her support of institutional aid. Green's style and demands were summarized by a colleague who stated that "with Edith its kind of like marriage. You can't play the field" (quoted in Gladieux & Wolanin, 1976, p. 131).

It was not just the demand for loyalty that characterized the relationship, but also the requirement, or at least the expectation, that the associations not lobby other members (Gladieux & Wolanin, 1976). The net result was that the associations had no one to turn to when the Brademas group rebelled. In fact, they had no contacts that could inform them of the increasing friction between Green and the other members of the House subcommittee. The selection of Green as their champion meant that the associations had severed their ties with the other major participants in the legislative process. Just as they had no fallback position on institutional aid, the associations had no champions to call on when Green was out maneuvered in conference.

The role of the associations in the reauthorization process and their failure to achieve their policy objectives was summarized shortly after the passage of the 1972 amendments by John C. Honey in a strongly worded *Science* editorial. Honey (1972) charged that "the failure of the Washington-based spokesmen for higher education to contribute significantly to the shaping of those amendments verges on the scandalous" (p. 1234). Their congressional testimony, claimed Honey (1972), was marked by "a paucity of solid data and an over-abundance of wishfulness" (p. 1234). He hoped that the passage of the

1972 amendments would "impress on academia the urgency for quite different approaches" (Honey, 1972, p. 1234). For their part, the associations vowed to learn from the past and to improve in the future.

The last shift that needs to be noted is the change in the size and nature of the policy arena. Before the 1972 amendments, the policy arena was a higher education policy arena. The participants included the White House or executive branch, the subcommittee members and their staffs, the committee members and their staffs, the higher education associations, and some individual institutions and state systems. Lenders under the guaranteed student loan program could also be included, but they were minor participants. With the 1972 amendments, the policy arena was redefined as a postsecondary education policy arena and expanded to include accredited vocational-technical and proprietary schools. In addition to the inclusion of the nontraditional schools, the arena changed over the next few years as the number of lenders and guarantee agencies increased with the growth of the student loan program.

After producing a piece of legislation of the size and scope of the Higher Education Amendments of 1972, it is not unusual for Congress to retire from that policy arena and direct its attention to other policy arenas. This was not the case in 1973. Instead, Congress continued with what was becoming a pattern of almost continual review of the HEA. James G. O'Hara, who had replaced Edith Green as chair of the House Subcommittee on Education, opened a series of hearings on federal student aid issues (Gladieux & Wolanin, 1978). Chief among these was the continuing claim by private schools that they would cease to exist, at least in their present form, if Congress failed to address the special problems of the private higher education sector.

Following the defeat of institutional aid in 1972, private institutions quickly adjusted to the changed political climate in Washington. Instead of asking for aid to institutions, the private institutions framed the issue in terms of the need to preserve a diverse higher education system that would give students a range of choices and multiple points of access. The "tuition gap" became the symbol of the threat to higher education (Herzlinger & Jones, 1990). In fact, the cost of attending a private college was more than four times the cost of attending a public college.

Public institutions rejected the privates' arguments by noting that the public higher education sector already offered what the privates promised (Gladieux & Wolanin, 1978). Public institutions offered access, choice, and diversity at a range of tuition levels affordable to all Americans. As O'Hara listened to the witnesses testifying at the House subcommittee hearings in 1973–74, he became "a partisan of low-tuition public higher education" (Gladieux & Wolanin, 1978, p. 206).

What had started as an inquiry into the plight of private institutions threatened to divide the higher education community into warring camps battling over tuition. The ACE attempted to bring the sectors together behind a program of "tuition offsets" (Finn, 1978). Simply stated, a tuition offset program would allow each sector to continue its tuition policy by offsetting the cost of private higher education through special grants to students in the private sector. While there was interest in the concept, no broad coalition united around the idea.

Rather than uniting as it had in 1972, the higher education community continued to fracture in 1974 and 1975 as Congress prepared for reauthorization. Along with other groups, several public college associations formed the National Coalition for Lower Tuition (Finn, 1978). The coalition's name clearly stated its position on the question of tuition. The American Association of State Colleges and Universities (AASCU) stated its policy position on tuition and student aid when it held that: "No federal or state aid program to the private . . . sector should be at the expense of public college students, either in terms of reduced appropriations for the public sector or increased tuition and student charges at public colleges" (quoted in Finn, 1978, p. 133).

Perhaps sensing that no consensus was forthcoming, Representative O'Hara introduced legislation in February 1975 that reflected his own policy positions (Gladieux & Wolanin, 1978). H.R. 3470, the first of two bills, basically renewed all existing HEA programs. H.R. 3471 suggested radical changes to what had become accepted as the federal student aid policy norm. Among other changes, it removed the BEOG half-cost rule, removed the Supplemental Educational Opportunity Grant (SEOG) program from the campuses and gave it to the Office of Education, removed institutions as lenders under the guaranteed student loan program, and eliminated need as a criterion for college work-study (Gladieux & Wolanin, 1978). Private institutions saw H.R. 3471 as a direct attack on private higher education and as a violation of the long-standing principle of nondiscrimination between public and private higher education.

O'Hara's bills were introduced without cosponsors and did not enjoy support among his colleagues on the subcommittee on education (Gladieux & Wolanin, 1978). But unlike Green, O'Hara was popular with his colleagues, and none of the subcommittee members wanted to oppose him. In addition, O'Hara was planning to run for the Senate, and none of the Democrats on the subcommittee wanted to damage his chances for victory. In short, no one seemed to want H.R. 3471, except for O'Hara, but no one seemed to know how to get rid of the bill without causing at least some political damage.

At the hearings on H.R. 3471, the Consortium on Financing of Higher Education (COFHE) attempted to offer an alternative that could be accepted without embarrassing O'Hara (Bloland, 1985). Formed in 1974, COFHE membership included some thirty institutions that could be "characterized as private, elite, and prestigious" (Bloland, 1985, p. 66). In 1975, it published a widely discussed report on federal student aid. At the hearings, COFHE put forward proposals aimed at addressing O'Hara's concerns while helping private institutions cope with the tuition gap.

Specifically, COFHE recommended repealing the half-cost rule on BEOGs and making SEOGs more tuition sensitive (Gladieux & Wolanin, 1978). The half-cost rule limited BEOGs to no more than half the cost of the tuition regardless of a student's eligibility for a larger grant. The intent of the rule was to prevent students from getting a "free-ride" through college, but many privates had come to interpret the rule as a mechanism for balancing the competition between low and high tuition institutions. The justification for eliminating the rule was to allow students greater access to higher education. Making SEOGs more tuition sensitive would work to insure student choice especially among lower-income students.

The small private schools attacked the COFHE proposals almost immediately. The Association of American Colleges (AAC) and the Association of Jesuit Colleges and Universities (AJCU) led the campaign against the elimination of the half-cost rule, claiming that it would not contribute to choice, would harm small schools, and aid the elite private schools (Gladieux & Wolanin, 1978) Unable to produce a consensus within the private sector, COFHE had little chance of getting its proposal adopted by the subcommittee.

The entire process in the House lacked both a champion and a burning issue to galvanize individuals and groups. The process suffered from the absence of focus and clarity. In an effort to affect closure, Representatives O'Hara, Brademas, and Quie met to hammer out an agreement, but "the result was a firm if amiable stalemate" (Gladieux & Wolanin, 1978, p. 213). In the end, it was agreed to reauthorize the existing programs and save the difficult issues for the next reauthorization.

The outcome in the House matched Pell's expectations in the Senate (Gladieux & Wolanin, 1978). Pell wanted to revise the student loan program and reauthorize HEA for seven years. When the two bills reached conference, there were no major differences to be resolved.

The only compromise of note was one limiting reauthorization to four years rather than the seven that Pell had wanted.

In contrast to previous reauthorizations, the White House played almost no role in 1976. In 1965 and 1968, the Johnson administration had led the policy formation process and Congress had largely followed. In 1972, the process was marked by conflict and a shifting of leadership to the Congress with the rejection of the Nixon administration proposals. Nixon had attempted to play the lead role, but the other members of the policy arena refused to cooperate. In 1976, President Gerald R. Ford essentially vacated the policy arena and conceded leadership to the Congress.

While the Higher Education Amendments of 1976 postponed the more controversial issues until 1980, the legislation did reaffirm federal higher education policy and make some changes in the HEA (McGuiness, 1981). Equal educational opportunity, access, and choice in higher education were restated as the basic goals of federal policy. The maximum BEOG grant award was increased, states were given incentives to establish loan programs, and a new program for lifelong learning was added to Title I of the HEA.

Three new policy actors emerged in the debate over the tuition gap and policy alternatives to assist private institutions. One of the three, COFHE, was discussed above. A new student group, the Coalition of Independent University Students (COIUS), representing students from private, elite institutions was formed and lobbied Congress on HEA. The third policy actor, the National Association of Independent Colleges and Universities (NAICU), emerged from AAC in March 1976 (Hunt, 1977). While it emerged too late to have an impact on the 1976 amendments, NAICU's clearly stated mission was to be a voice for private higher education in Washington (Bloland, 1985).

A final note on the 1976 reauthorization concerns the praise the higher education associations received for their role in the policy process. Senator Pell felt that their role had "been more positive" and that they had helped in the effort to amend and expand HEA (quoted in McNamara, 1976, p. 4). Wolanin (1976), one of their harsher critics in 1972, found that the associations had made progress and were becoming "effective voices in the formulation of federal higher education policy" (p. 184). Gladieux (1977) felt that in 1976 the associations were beginning "to anticipate and take the initiative on emerging issues rather than reacting and having to catch up with events" (p. 43). The basis for this new found admiration of the higher education is difficult to explain. With the exception of COFHE, no higher education group put forward any new ideas. One could also cite ACE, but the concept of tuition offsets was neither a new idea, nor an acceptable idea to the majority of the higher education community. In the House, the higher education associations were not invited to participate in the policy formation process and were forced into a position of responding to the O'Hara bill after it was introduced. In the Senate, Pell was committed to fine-tuning the status quo, thus there was little to lobby for or against. It may be that the new found respect came from personal interactions that were shielded from public view or scholarly analysis. In any case, the political climate and changes in the years ahead would test the perception and the reality of the assessment that the higher education associations were important policy actors.

The beginning of 1977 marked a resting point for the Congress. After dealing almost continuously with some aspect of HEA since 1965, neither side of the Congress had anything scheduled as 1977 started. In the House, William D. Ford replaced O'Hara, who had lost both his seat and his Senate race, as chair of the Subcommittee on Postsecondary Education. The pause to rest did not last long as pressure began to build on the members to do something to alleviate the "middle income squeeze." This was a reference to the belief that the student aid programs helped the poor with access to higher education, that the rich did not need help, and that middle-income students were being squeezed out of higher education because they were too rich for student aid but too poor to pay the high cost of college. The problem of the middle class was compounded by the increase in inflation in general and college costs in particular.

The BEOG program and the guaranteed student loan programs had been linked from the earliest formation of the grant and loan programs in the HEA of 1965. William A. Blakey summarized the link when he noted that the grant "program can't survive without guaranteed student loans," they are "the muscle that pulls the train" (quoted in Stanfield, 1982, p. 1264). The guaranteed loan programs served "as a political alternative to income tax credits" (Fischer, 1987, p. 20). As the perception of a middle-income squeeze grew, tuition tax credits surfaced again as a way of helping middle-income students meet the rising cost of higher education. Opponents of tuition tax credits feared that such a program would break the link between grants and loans, thus reducing the student aid programs to poverty programs for the poor as middle-income parents came to rely on tax credits to finance the cost of sending their children to college. Without middle-income support, there was the reasonable fear that student aid programs would decline for lack of a broad political base of support.

While pressure was building for tuition tax credits to alleviate the middle-income squeeze, empirical evidence indicated that the squeeze did not exist (Gladieux, 1983). The Congressional Budget Office (CBO) examined the issue and found no particular financial squeeze on middle-income students or change in college attendance patterns. Other studies duplicated the CBO findings and confirmed that the middle-income squeeze was a matter of perception rather than of reality. Since politics works on perception, not on policy research, perception was enough to build a base of support for tuition tax credits.

To stop this effort, the Carter administration agreed to support the Middle Income Student Assistance Act (MISAA) of 1978 (Gladieux, 1978). MISAA opened the guaranteed student loan program to all students, regardless of family income, who were enrolled at least half-time in a postsecondary institution (Wilson, 1982). It also expanded eligibility for BEOGs to include more middle-income students. Finally, MISAA raised authorized funding levels for most of the student aid programs.

Described as "an undisguised attempt to create loans of convenience for middle class families" (Doyle & Hartle, 1985, p. 9), MISAA produced a number of changes in the scope and direction of the student aid programs. Chief among these was the expansion of student aid beyond the original focus of insuring equal educational opportunity. With the opening of the loan program, federal student aid started to shift from low-income students to middle- and higher-income students (Gladieux, 1983). The opening of the loan program also signaled the beginning of a shift from BEOG grants as a student aid floor to a reliance on loans as the foundation of student aid. Finally, the increasing emphasis on loans as the vehicle for student aid acted to significantly increase the role of lenders in the higher education policy arena.

The MISAA was followed by the Higher Education and Technical Amendments of 1979. The amendments served three purposes. First, HEA was extended for one year past its 1980 expiration date to give Congress time to work on reauthorization. Next, the definition of an independent student was changed to expand participation in the BEOG program. Last, the special allowance paid to lenders in the Guaranteed Student Loan (GSL) program was increased as a way to encourage more lenders to participate.

The special allowance turned the GSL program into a "gold mine" for lenders (Doyle & Hartle, 1985, p. 9). The special allowance is an interest subsidy of 3.5 percent above the ninety-one day Treasury bill rate. The loan is guaranteed by the federal government, thus the lender is in the unique position of being guaranteed a profit and insured that no loss can occur. This may help explain the growth of the GSL program such that by 1985 it included "some 12,100 banks, 8,650 schools, 58 state and private guarantee agencies, 30 secondary markets, 22 loan servicers, 9 collection agencies, and the ubiquitous Student Loan Marketing Association " (Doyle & Hartle, 1985, p. 9).

The changes brought by MISAA and the Amendments expanded not only the size and scope of the student aid programs, but also significantly increased the cost of the programs. The number of GSL program participants grew from about one million before MISAA to more than two and one half million by 1980 (Gladieux, 1980). With this increase in program participants, loan volume increased from $2.6 billion in 1978 to $7 billion in 1981 (Gillespie & Carlson, 1983). The size and scope of the student aid programs became the central point of contention in the debate over the Higher Education Amendments of 1980 as the Carter administration, along with the congressional budget committees, attempted to place some controls on federal spending, while the congressional education committees moved to continue the expansion of student aid programs (Gladieux, 1986).

With Pell leading the way in the Senate and Ford steering the legislation through the House, the outcome was a victory for the education committees. The Higher Education Amendments of 1980 provided for a number of substantive changes including:

1. Reauthorization of student aid programs through 1985 at a cost of $48.4 billion;
2. Increase in the maximum annual GSL to $3,000 for independent students
3. A new guaranteed loan program for parents—Parents Loan for Undergraduate Study (PLUS);
4. Renaming the BEOG in honor of Senator Claiborne Pell and increasing the annual Pell Grant award to $2,600 by 1985;
5. Establishing Sallie Mae as a lender of last resort; and,
6. Creating a National Commission on Student Assistance to study ways to reduce abuse, fraud, and student loan delinquency. ("Education Policy," 1981; "The Higher Education Amendments of 1980," 1980)

The Higher Education Amendments of 1980 seemed to mark the conclusion of a shift from the White House as the center of power in matters of higher education policy to the congressional education committees and subcommittees as the centers of political power. The Carter administration was virtually a nonplayer in the policy process, not presenting its proposals until the last day of the House subcommittee hearings and firing HEW Secretary Joseph A. Califano the day before he was to testify (Hook, 1980). With the White House missing in action, the higher education associations stepped forward and achieved much of their legislative agenda. In the process, they established themselves as powerful policy actors who were willing and able to work in partnership with the congressional education committees and subcommittees.

As the 1980s started, it seemed to be irrelevant who the president was or who the president would be in the future. The student aid programs had evolved into a vast, highly complex system that could not be radically changed by one person even if that person happened to be the president of the United States. The sense of contentment and complacency among the higher education policy actors is reflected in Breneman and Nelson's (1980) claim that

> [t]he outlook for higher education policy in the nation's capital, then, is essentially "business as usual" during the next decade. No striking new initiatives are apparent, nor are existing programs or purposes likely to change much. The support the federal government provides to students and, indirectly, to institutions will remain vital to the financial well-being of colleges and universities, but the most important decisions about the future of higher education will be made at the state, institutional, and private levels. (p. 245)

The election of Ronald Reagan as president, along with a more conservative Congress, proved such claims to be erroneous. The White House planned to play a major role in higher education policy formation and to make major changes in the HEA programs. In March 1981, the Reagan administration submitted to the Congress a proposal for "Certain Amendments to the Higher Education Act of 1965." If accepted, the proposal would:

- Provide that a student's Pell Grant could not exceed the difference between the student's cost of attendance and the sum of the student's expected family contribution and the amount of self-help, as determined by the Secretary. The self-help requirement could be waived if the aid administrator determined that the limitation could cause severe financial hardship;
- Apply the self-help requirement to the Supplemental Educational Opportunity Grants as well as the traditional family

contribution, assessed on the basis of its resources. The self-help requirement could be waived if the aid administrator determined that the limitation could cause severe financial hardship;

- Limit the amount of any Guaranteed Student Loans made after June 30, 1981 to a student's remaining need—educational costs minus all other aid, the expected family contributions, and self-help;
- Eliminate the provision in legislation which allows the GSL to replace expected family contributions;
- Require need determination for GSL to be calculated under the Federal Need Analysis System;
- Under the Parent Loan Program, allow GSL to be counted as part of the student's expected family contribution in the determination of need, but, no loan may be made to any parent or student which would cause their combined loans for any academic year to exceed the student's estimated cost of attendance minus the student's estimated financial assistance;
- Eliminate the in-school interest subsidy and post-school repayment grace period for GSLs borrowed after July 1, 1981;
- Eliminate administrative cost allowances currently allowed institutions under existing programs. (Wilson, 1982, pp. 16–17)

Doyle and Hartle (1985) summarized the administration's proposals as being "neither well designed nor well conceived" (p. 8), but the effort could not be termed ineffective. Working with a more conservative House and a Republican Senate, the administration was unable to implement many of its proposed program changes, but it was able to achieve much of its higher education agenda through budget cuts. The 97th Congress cut need-based student aid by $200 million from fiscal year 1980 levels, Pell Grants by $200 million, and National Direct Student Loans by $100 million. In addition, eligibility requirements for the GSL were returned to pre-MISAA standards (Stanfield, 1982). The administration was able, through the budget, to negate most of the changes provided for under the Higher Education Amendments of 1980.

In fiscal year 1982, the administration won a twelve percent reduction in student aid funding. In an unusual display of political masochism, the higher education associations delivered congressional testimony accepting the continuing cuts as higher education's "fair share" of a national effort to reduce government spending (Yarrington, 1983). It is not clear that students who saw their aid packages eliminated or reduced felt the same way about the budget cuts as did the leaders of the higher education associations in Washington, D.C.

For fiscal year 1983, the administration proposed budget cuts that would have eliminated more than 2.4 million student aid awards. Anne Graham, assistant secretary of education for legislation and public affairs claimed that the budget reflected the president's belief "that education is predominantly a state and local matter, and that the post-secondary student should be responsible for financing education to the maximum extent possible" (quoted in Stanfield, 1982, p. 1261). ACE Vice President for Government Relations Charles Saunders felt that the proposed $4.3 billion in budget cuts was the administration's way of "sending subliminal signals that it wants to eliminate the federal role" in higher education (quoted in Stanfield, 1982, p. 1264).

Higher education's friends in Congress and the higher education associations "spent most of 1981 learning the rules of the new game, and never seriously played in it" (Wolanin, 1990, p. 228). The proposed budget cuts for fiscal year 1983 finally sparked some resistance from the passive associations. After seeing an early draft of the proposed budget, some twenty higher education associations formed the Action Committee for Higher Education (ACHE) at a meeting in December 1981 (Bloland, 1985). The ACHE undertook a nation-wide campaign, including a grassroots campaign aimed at parents and students, to focus public attention on the threat to student aid. The effort gained valuable support when conservative Republicans Jack Kemp and Orrin Hatch expressed public support for maintaining student-aid funding levels. In the end, the lobbying effort helped produce a one percent increase in student aid funding for fiscal year 1983 over fiscal year 1982. Given the political climate, this was no small victory.

The budget battles of the early 1980s established a pattern of political call and response that continued throughout the remainder of the decade. First, the administration would propose deep budget cuts in student aid programs, then the higher education lobby would react furiously, and finally Congress would substitute its own more moderate proposals. The battle also produced an interesting reversal of roles between the Democrats and Republicans. The administration became the champions of the "truly needy," while the Democrats became the champions of student aid for the middle class. The Democrats favored expanding aid to the middle class, in part, because they believed that the student aid programs would be vulnerable to attack as welfare programs if only the "truly needy" were served. To maintain a political base of support for the programs, the Democrats wanted to preserve aid for middle-class students.

As Congress prepared for the 1986 HEA reauthorization, the political climate for higher education policy making was hostile by any observer's estimate. For the first time in recent history, the president questioned the federal role in assisting students with the cost of higher education. More than just questioning the federal role, Reagan was elected on a platform that promised to abolish the Education Department that was responsible for administering the aid programs. The Secretary of Education, William Bennett, had gained a reputation for inflammatory attacks on higher education along with a willingness to slash his own budget. Coupled with a conservative Congress, the climate was such that any hopes for program expansion, innovation, or reform were dim at best.

These were not the only obstacles to reform as Congress started the reauthorization process. From 1980 to 1986, federal student aid declined by 10 percent in real dollars (Gladieux, 1986). Congress would have to decide whether or not it could afford to bring the programs up to current need levels. The mix of students receiving financial aid had changed as an increasing number of proprietary school students entered the aid programs during the first half of the 1980s. The proportion of proprietary school students receiving Pell Grants grew from 11.5 percent in 1980–81 to 22.1 percent in 1985–86 (Lee & Merisotis, 1990). An increasing number of GSL loans also went to proprietary school students who began to receive the blame for the increasing cost of student loan defaults. While the percentage of students defaulting remained somewhat constant, the volume of loans in default exploded. The total dollars defaulted in 1980 was $2.4 million, but by 1986 the total had reached $1.4 billion (Lee & Merisotis, 1990). The growth in loan volume was also an indicator that the Pell Grant was no longer the primary base for the student aid package. In 1985–86, loans accounted for 50 percent of all student aid (Gladieux, 1986). If Congress wanted to reform the HEA, then it would have to deal with these and other issues.

In some ways, the 1986 reauthorization was a return to earlier reauthorizations in terms of the roles played by the major policy actors. The White House played a largely negative role that acted to define the parameters of reauthorization without presenting any positive proposals. Commenting on the White House role, Doyle and Hartle (1986) noted that "a year after Secretary Bennett's inflammatory remarks, the executive branch is nowhere to be seen. The Department of Education has delayed . . . unveiling whatever ideas it has. . . . [T]he Administration's harsh rhetoric has simply polarized the debate" (p. 34).

As the process unfolded, the White House "made no formal recommendations at all to the House . . . and took what can be described as delayed and desultory action with regard to the Senate" (Keppel, 1987, p. 65).

The 1986 reauthorization was the product of a partnership between the Congress and the higher education associations. In stating this, it is important not to think of the Congress as a monolith. During reauthorization, the Republican Senate was committed to maintaining the status quo. In the House, a bipartisan group lead by Mario Biaggi (D–New York), William Ford (D–Michigan), Steve Gunderson (R–Wisconsin), John McKernan (R–Maine), and Pat Williams (D–Montana) was able to press for some improvements in the legislation. "Caught between the threat of a presidential veto, Senate opposition, and criticism that they were unrealistic about potential funding" (Ozer, 1986, p. 25), the House members were able to maintain some of the reforms, innovations, and funding increases in the bill that came out of conference committee and eventually passed Congress.

Some of the major changes in the Higher Education Amendments of 1986 were:

- Phase-in of Pell Grant eligibility for less-than-half-time students pursuing a degree.
- A $200 increase in the Pell Grant maximum each year beginning with a $2300 maximum for FY 1987 (contingent upon the appropriation process).
- An increase in Guaranteed Student Loan (GSL) limits, to $2625 per year for students in their first and second years and $4000 per year in the third and fourth years. The undergraduate limit is $17,250; the limit for both undergraduate and graduate school is $54,750.
- A three-year GSL deferment for students going into teaching, in areas of need designated by the secretary of education.
- An extension of the grace period for the National Direct Students Loans (NDSL) from six to nine months.
- A stipulation that student aid is not to be counted as income in the evaluation of other federal assistance.
- A $10 million authorization for new Title I programs to provide postsecondary programs for nontraditional students.
- Authorization for new Title IX graduate programs, including grants to institutions to encourage minority participation in graduate education. (Ozer, 1986, p. 25)

Reagan signed the Higher Education Amendments in the fall of 1986. In the signing ceremony, the president made clear his feelings about the legislation:

> This Administration has always supported, and will continue to support, programs properly designed to help our neediest young people acquire higher education. . . .
>
> I do have serious concerns about S. 1965 (Pub. L. No. 99-498), however. The bill does little to meet the Administration's major objectives for higher education:
>
> - Restoring more appropriate and equitable student funding roles to states, schools, students, and their families;
> - Targeting assistance on truly needy students; and
> - Eliminating excessive subsidies to intermediary institutions such as banks, schools, and loan-guarantee agencies.
>
> I am signing this bill because the basic Higher Education Act authorities provide aid to deserving students and support important programs. However, the administration remains committed to improving the higher education programs and to reducing their costs to the American taxpayer. We will continue to propose necessary changes and cost savings. (quoted in Keppel, 1987, p. 51)

With the signing of the Higher Education Amendments of 1986, the HEA was reauthorized into the 1990s. At that time there would be a new president, possibly a different congressional makeup, and perhaps a better economy. The next reauthorization would also be an opportunity to deal with some of the issues that were avoided in 1986. Issues such as the loan-grant imbalance, the size of Pell Grant awards, participation of proprietary schools in the HEA programs, aid delivery systems, and loan defaults would still be viable policy issues during the next reauthorization. A host of new issues would no doubt arise to join the deferred problems.

CONCLUSIONS

The historical events that mark the development of the federal interest in higher education can be interpreted in at least three ways. One is as a series of discrete historical events that act as landmarks in the evolution of the federal role in higher education. As such, the events do little to explain the federal role or the role of the policy actors involved in the formation of federal higher education policy. Instead, the events are merely historical records that tell us what happened on certain days in the past.

A second interpretation is one in which current events are interrelated with past events becoming the building blocks and shapers of future events. This is not to suggest some seamless flow of history, with future events being predetermined by past actions. Instead, a rather messy process of linking policy decisions together in an odd patchwork quilt that forms the whole of federal policy towards higher education is the view that results from this interpretation. Principles and ideology may inform policy decisions, but it is just as likely that guiding principles and ideology are discovered after policy decisions are made.

Continuing with this interpretation, one can see the evolution of the federal role in higher education as the evolution of a national education policy system. This is a third interpretation that builds upon the elements presented in the second interpretation, that is, events and policy actors become interrelated and mutually shape one another. A policy system "can be viewed as an interrelated system which operates to transform inputs from the social system into outputs or policies" (Bresnick, 1979, pp. 189–90). Within the national education policy system, political subsystems form to deal with more discrete and defined policy areas (Bresnick, 1979). The higher education policy arena can be seen as the subsystem that has evolved around federal higher education policy making. It is this interpretation that will help guide this study.

The concept of a higher education policy arena, introduced in this chapter, is discussed in greater detail in chapter 3 along with a discussion of the policy actors who operate in the arena. What is important here is to note that a policy arena tends to form "a closed domain with its own coherence and logic" and to develop "basic concepts, systems of interpretation and reasoning which are given the force of certainties and thus totally escape suspicion" (Callon, 1980, p. 206). These basic concepts emerge from the resolution of tensions and conflicts within the policy arena. Tensions in the higher education policy arena have included conflict and debate over the instrumental versus inherent value of education, student versus institutional aid, loans versus grants, and general student aid versus aid to needy students. The resolution of these and other tensions have produced a series of contested principles or beliefs that guide the higher education policy arena. While these principles are open to contest, many of the principles have gained the force of certainty and are not open to question. The primary principles that guide the higher education policy arena are:

1. Federal grants to states for support of higher education;
2. Federal use of the higher education system to meet national needs for specially educated and trained human resources while recognizing the independence of individual institutions;
3. Federal use of the higher education system as an instrument for social reform;
4. Treatment of higher education as both a public and private good whose cost should be shared between the federal government, state government, the student, and the family;
5. Nondiscrimination between private and public institutions in the awarding of federal grants and loans;
6. Nondiscrimination between nonprofit and proprietary schools in the availability of student aid; and
7. Preference for the use of private agencies in the delivery of student aid.

Higher education associations have evolved as an important part of the higher education policy arena. At times, associations have formed as a direct response to federal policy, but other associations have developed independent of federal action, and some have even resisted involvement with the federal government. In recent years, even resistant associations have reached the inescapable conclusion that some level of involvement is required given the size and scope of the federal interest in higher education. The relationship between mainstream associations and the federal government has evolved to the point where some observers refer to the relationship as a "higher education partnership."

Inherent in any partnership, or other relationship, is the question of power. Looking at the period of policy making from the NDEA forward, power seems to swing back and forth between the White House and the Congress. When the issue is a major policy initiative or change, then the White House is usually the more powerful policy actor. If the issue is one of revision or modification, then the congressional committees and subcommittees on education tend to be more powerful in terms of shaping and determining policy outcomes. Since the early 1980s, the Washington based higher education associations have gained a reputation as powerful policy actors. During the 1980s, the Reagan administration attempted to reduce funding for HEA programs and to eliminate a number of the programs. Despite the efforts of a popular president and an active secretary of education, the higher education lobby was not only able to resist these attempts, but by the end of the decade had actually won increases in student aid funding. Altogether, federal student aid, in real dollars, increased by 33 percent over the course of the 1980s (Hartle, 1990).

While this history describes policy outcomes, it does not explain the role of power in the policy making process. Questions of power— Who has power? What is the source of a policy actor's power? What does power mean in the higher education policy arena? How is power used?—are not addressed in the currently available histories of the HEA. Instead, power is treated in one of two ways. In one, power is assumed or attributed without defining what power means or testing the validity of such claims. In the other, the role of power in policy making is either ignored, omitted, or denied. To begin to address the question of power, the arena in which power is exercised must be more clearly defined.

3

The Higher Education Policy Arena

Political scientists, sociologists, and other students of power have traditionally sought to make explicit the implicit aspects of policy arenas to give the arenas some tangible form or shape with clearly defined boundaries forming the parameters for research. It is this approach that introduced the use of geometric shapes to describe and define policy arenas with the "iron triangle" being perhaps the most famous. While this is a popular approach, the results are less than satisfying. The geometric shapes used to define policy arenas are abstract, static forms that lose meaning as policy arena characteristics shift and change. The authentic, contingent relationships that exist between policy actors are lost when the rich, contextual nature of policy making is compressed into a flat, objective shape.

Some higher education policy analysts have sought to escape the problems associated with the use of geometric shapes by taking an approach that can be described as mapping. Mapping consists of identifying the main policy actors, their views, and their relationship to one another with the final result being a map or description of the policy arena at a given point in time. This offers some advantage over geometric shapes in that a greater sense of dynamism is captured, but one is still left with a static description that is unresponsive to change. Not only is the description static, but the addition or departure of key policy actors renders it inaccurate as a map of the policy arena. Finally, the approach offers no framework for analysis that can be used to explain changes in the policy arena or to explain policy decisions.

The purpose of this chapter is to construct a new approach to defining and describing the social relations that are policy arenas. The intent is to create an approach that captures the dynamic, contingent nature of the higher education policy arena while maintaining the flexibility to adjust to changes in the arena. In addition, the approach will serve as a framework for analysis and explanation. The approach is a definition that relies not on geometric shapes or static maps but on the use of subgovernment characteristics and the concept of community. The concept of community, first introduced in chapter 1, will be developed here and supported by the next two chapters.

The focus of this chapter is the higher education policy arena that has formed around HEA. There are other important higher education policy arenas (e.g., see), but none of the other arenas involve such a large number and diversity of policy actors, nor do other arenas compare in size, range of purpose, or economic and social impact. HEA authorized student aid programs "reached six million students (almost half of all postsecondary students), virtually every postsecondary institution in the country, agencies of every state, and thousands of lenders" (White, 1993, p. 73). Altogether, HEA contains twelve titles authorizing more than seventy programs (Wolanin, 1993). One program, the GSL, has created a multibillion dollar industry where none had existed. The "approximately $21.5 billion in loans, grants, and work opportunities to students" (Wolanin, 1993, p. 90) provided by HEA make this policy arena the most important higher education policy arena and a significant federal domestic policy arena.

The first part of the chapter reviews some early definitions of the higher education policy arena. These are important because of their continuing influence on contemporary scholars and as a background to the approach offered in this chapter. The next section draws on concepts from the subgovernment literature to describe the higher education policy arena in terms of criterion characteristics. While any description is open to criticism for being static, the claim made for this description is that it can be easily adjusted without abandoning or destroying the descriptive framework. The framework is not only responsive to change but can be used to explain change. The last section calls on the concept of community to define the social relations of the higher education policy arena. This may cause some problem for those who like their policy arenas defined with greater mathematical precision but it is community, not geometry, that best defines the social relations that form the higher education policy arena.

EARLY DEFINITIONS

The first attempt to comprehensively define the higher education policy arena might well be Wolanin and Gladieux's (1975) "The Political Culture of a Policy Arena: Higher Education." The authors define the higher education policy arena as being "characterized by substantive coherence, charter legislation, executive, congressional, and lobbying institutions, and a political culture" (p. 179). The substance of the arena is provided by the Higher Education Act (HEA). While the substance is clear, the substantive coherence is not. This may be attributable to the fact that federal programs and decision-making centers are decentralized. HEA is the charter legislation for the policy arena. Finally, the political culture rests on the assumptions of "the primacy of the states, the instrumental view of higher education, the nondiscrimination between public and private higher education, the fragmentation of federal higher education policy, and the relatively low visibility of higher education in federal policy" (Wolanin & Gladieux, 1975, p. 205). For the most part, Wolanin and Gladieux are concerned with defining the higher education policy arena so that it can serve as the background for their larger discussion of political culture. Their definition and description of the political culture covers the contested principles identified in chapter 2 but they present the principles as a unified culture that defines the policy arena. This tends to gloss over the dynamic tensions and conflicts that exist within the arena and that are always available for renewed contest.

While Wolanin and Gladieux may have been the first to offer a description of the higher education policy arena, their work was soon joined by King (1975), Murray (1976), and Finn (1980). The work of these three authors has had a profound effect on subsequent descriptions of the higher education policy arena and continues to influence scholars today. Lauriston R. King's (1975) classification of higher education associations is still used by some scholars as a framework for organizing research on the higher education policy arena. Michael A. Murray's (1976) work builds on King's classification scheme and is cited by some authors as a successful effort to bring the policy arena into sharper focus and detail. Finally, Chester E. Finn's (1980) critique of the education policy arena provides an alternative view that is used even by scholars who disagree with and dislike Finn's analysis.

King (1975) was the first researcher to classify and describe the structure of the Washington higher education associations. He sorted the associations into three categories: major associations, special interest or satellite associations, and a catchall category of individual offices and small associations. The major associations consisted of the Association of American Colleges (AAC), American Association of Community and Junior Colleges (AACJC), American Council on Education (ACE), American Association of State Colleges and Universities (AASCU), Association of American Universities (AAU), and National Association of State and University Land-Grant Colleges (NASULGC). These later came to be called the "Big Six" (Bloland, 1985). The major associations were defined not by size, but by level of activity, namely, that they took "part most regularly and on the widest range of political concerns of all of the Washington-based higher education associations" (King, 1975, p. 19).

The special interest or satellite associations included the Council of Graduate Schools in the United States (CGSUS) and the Council for the Advancement of Small Colleges (CASC). These associations focused not on broad policy issues, but limited their concern to policy issues that effected their highly specialized constituency. According to King (1975) the defining characteristic of the special interest associations is that "except on issues of specific interest to their members, they are generally willing to let the major associations speak for them" (p. 24).

King placed the special interest associations into orbits around the major associations. Orbiting the AAU and NASULGC were associations with research and graduate studies interests such as the Association of American Medical Colleges, CGSUS, and the National Council of University Research Administrators. Orbiting the AAC and were associations that represented "colleges with religious affiliations, and those colleges of marginal status and financial condition" (King, 1975, p. 29) such as the College and University Department of the National Catholic Educational Association and CASC.

The last part of the structure is what King (1975) termed an emerging pattern of "offices representing state systems, small associations of fairly homogeneous institutions, individual colleges and universities, and schools enlisting the services of private entrepreneurs" (p. 31). Some examples of this emerging pattern include the State University of New York (SUNY) office, the Associated Colleges of the Midwest, and Harvard University.

While King's mapping of the higher education policy arena was accurate in 1975, the arena has changed remarkably since his work first appeared. The AAC, one of the two centers, is no longer a major organization having been replaced by National Association of Independent Colleges and Universities (NAICU). The Career College Association (CCA) could probably be added as a major organization, but its representation of proprietary schools certainly differentiates it from the other major associations. The Consumer Bankers Association (CBA), the National Council of Higher Education Loan Programs (NCHELP), Sallie Mae and other groups have also emerged as major policy actors. The dependence of CBA, NCHELP and Sallies Mae on the guaranteed loan program makes it difficult to categorize them and similar associations under King's scheme.

King's classification scheme, while accurate in 1975, has decayed as the higher education associations and the policy arena in which they operated changed. If only the names and number of associations had changed over the years, then it might have been possible to maintain King's classification scheme. What makes it impossible is that changes in the policy arena and the development of contiguous policy arenas have blurred the distinctions between classifications. The fragmentation of policy making has meant that major associations have had to become increasingly specialized to be able to respond to the information needs of Congress and executive agencies. At the same time, special interest associations, especially research and graduate studies, have had to increasingly take part in the policy process because their concerns are impacted by multiple committees, subcommittees and agencies. Because of these changes, the use of King's classification scheme is of limited value in describing the current relationships and roles of higher education associations.

Bloland (1985) and others argue that Murray's (1976) work is an improvement and refinement of King's classification scheme. However, a close examination of Murray's classification system reveals that he changes only the names of the categories first identified by King. Murray replaces King's implied hierarchy of associations with a cluster of associations revolving around core associations. Murray's core groups consists of the same six associations that comprised King's major association group. The satellite lobbies that orbit around Murray's core are unchanged from King's. Finally, King's emerging pattern group is renamed the periphery by Murray.

The use of the core concept might be useful as an analytical device, but Murray (1976) cautions that the "core concept is helpful as a way of describing lobbies but it is somewhat misleading as an analytical device since it masks the deep cleavages which split the lobbies" (p. 82). This warning seems to negate the one advantage gained from dressing King's categories in new conceptual clothing. Aside from the internal weakness noted by Murray, his classification scheme suffers from the same shortcomings as King's and is of limited use in describing the current relationship and roles of the higher education associations.

Unlike King and Murray, Finn (1980) attempts to take a more analytical view of the higher education policy arena using the idea of a "liberal consensus" as his organizing scheme. The idea of a liberal consensus is apparently borrowed from Bailey (1975) who "referred to a 'lib-lab' lobby—a loose association of liberal and labor organizations that shared common values" (p. 23). Finn expands on Bailey's idea in two important ways. First he claims that a liberal consensus not only exists but that it shaped national education policy from 1965 until the election of Ronald Reagan. Second, Finn (1980) expands the definition of the liberal consensus well beyond Bailey's definition of the lib-lab lobby as can be seen in the following answer to his own question:

> What is the "liberal consensus," and how can it be charac-terized? In terms of its major sources and prominent members the consensus has included the Ford and Carnegie Founda-tions and four or five smaller ones; the elite graduate schools of education such as those at Stanford, Harvard, Chicago, and Columbia; the major national organizations of teachers and educational institutions such as the National Education Asso-ciation, the American Association of School Administrators, the National School Boards Association, and the American Council on Education; the various groups represented in the Leadership Conference on Civil Rights; the big labor unions; the political appointees in the education related agencies of the federal executive branch (including, with a few exceptions, those of both Republican and Democratic presidents); half a dozen key Congressmen and perhaps two dozen Congres-sional staff members; a variety of "think tanks," notably including The Brookings Institution and the Aspen Institute; and the writers of education editorials of the major metro-politan newspapers including *The New York Times* and *The Washington Post*. Actively involved at various times during the last decade and a half of the ascendancy of the liberal consen-sus and emblematic of its best ideas and greatest achievements have been such able and distinguished individuals as Clark Kerr, "Doc" Howe, Ernest Boyer, Stephen Bailey, and Samuel Halperin. (p. 25)

According to Finn (1980), the liberal consensus served educational interests well for a time, but then it began "to grow greedy, smug, extreme and, at the same time, defensive" (p. 26). In support of his claim, Finn (1980) cites ten elements that demonstrate a pattern of change away from a broad social interest and toward a narrow self-interest:

> First, the liberal consensus today reveals a preoccupation with questions of educational equity and equality and a pro-nounced lack of interest in the issues of quality. (p. 26)

Second, the liberal consensus today has a generalized abhorrence of tests and other measures of educational achievement. (p. 26)

Third, while the liberal consensus regularly espouses the principle of "accountability," in practice it seems to resent the notion that those who supply resources to educational institutions have a legitimate interest in what is done with those resources. (p. 26)

Fourth, the liberal consensus today is fixated on the concept of "need" and apathetic if not actually hostile to the concept of ability. (p. 27)

Fifth, there is today in the liberal consensus about education a predisposition towards statism and monopoly rather than pluralism and diversity. (p. 27)

Sixth, the liberal consensus in American education is all but helpless in the presence of unreasonableness, which leaves it, the programs it created, and the government that runs them easy prey to victimization. (p. 27)

Seventh, its reliance on government to solve educational problems and regulate educational practices, combined with its proclivity to appease those with extreme or unreasonable demands, means that the liberal consensus finds itself welcoming an ever-larger federal role in education and accepting the associated increase in federal control. (p. 28)

Eighth, the liberal consensus keeps finding itself on the side of formal and informal quota systems and of "reverse discrimination." (p. 29)

Ninth, the liberal consensus today displays a measure of greed, or at least a high degree of tolerance toward others' greed. (p. 29)

Finally, the liberal consensus in education today embodies an unresolved paradox about the role of educators themselves (p. 29).

Finn's work is different from both King and Murray in that he does not seek to describe the higher education policy arena in terms of institutional relationships, but rather seeks to articulate the values and beliefs that define and guide the arena. In his effort to make the case that the liberal consensus that guided education policy for so long and so well has lost its bearings, Finn makes a number of errors that undermine his claims and limit the usefulness of his approach to defining the policy arena. Finn has lumped together policy arenas that are separate both conceptually and in practice. Higher education, vocational education, job training, and elementary and secondary education are separate policy arenas, but Finn combines these and other education policy arenas into one education policy arena without concern for the differences that distinguish the different arenas. As a result, the National Education Association, which is concerned with primary and secondary education, is grouped with the ACE, which is concerned with higher education. At the same time, NASULGC and other major higher education associations are not even mentioned. The "big labor unions" that Finn lists in his definition of the liberal consensus were never that big and have been steadily declining as a political force since the mid-1970s. Labor has not had a significant legislative victory at the federal level in more than two decades. Finally, the claim that higher education would or does welcome an increase in federal control is at odds with the entire history of higher education in the United States. As shown in chapter 2, higher education has been resistant to federal involvement.

None of the above definitions is adequate to the task of defining the current higher education policy arena. Rather than attempting to refurbish one of the above definitions, a new approach is needed that avoids the shortcomings of earlier definitions and accounts for changes that have taken place in the policy arena in the years since those definitions were first presented. The next section moves toward such a definition by defining the higher education policy arena in terms of its characteristics.

CHARACTERISTICS OF THE
HIGHER EDUCATION POLICY ARENA

In contrast to the above definitions of the higher education policy arena, political scientists have developed the concept of a subgovernment to describe and explain policy formation in arenas "insulated from majority influence" (Bond, 1979, p. 651). McCool (1989) defines a subgovernment as a policy arena

> controlled by a closed, three-sided alliance composed of the relevant congressional committees and subcommittees, interest groups, and government agencies. Policy making is usually characterized by autonomy, stability, and low visibility. Conflict is kept to a minimum through bargaining and logrolling and by excluding or coopting potential opponents. . . . These

alliances are most likely to form around distributive policy issues . . . which are characterized by a combination of concentrated benefits and diffused costs. (p. 264)

The concept of subgovernments is introduced here for two reasons. One is that the two terms, policy arena and subgovernment, can be used interchangeably. While the two terms convey the same basic concept and meaning, policy arena tends to denote a more active, contested state of affairs while subgovernment denotes a more mechanical system. The other reason is the existence of an extensive body of literature on subgovernments that extends back over several decades. The knowledge and analytical approaches from this literature are useful in exploring and developing the higher education policy arena.

The term subgovernment probably evokes images of an iron triangle in which Congress, the White House, and interest groups produce policy, isolated from the majority, designed to assist the chosen few at the expense of the masses. This may in fact may describe some subgovernments, but it appears to be more a caricature of the concept than the reality of a subgovernment in operation. A more productive way to think of subgovernments is as a continuum ranging from closed iron triangles at one end to open issue networks at the other end (Hamm, 1986). Criterion characteristics can be used to judge where particular subgovernments fit along the continuum. The characteristics used to describe and define policy arenas are: (1) internal complexity, (2) functional autonomy, (3) unity within type of participant, and, (4) cooperation or conflict among different participants (Hamm, 1983). While these characteristics are used in an effort to give definition and focus to the higher education policy arena, the arena will not be treated as part of the traditional continuum. As discussed above, the case will be made that the higher education policy arena is better described as a community.

Internal Complexity

Internal complexity is used to refer "to the number and variety of participants in the subsystem" (Hamm, 1983, p. 381). By this definition, the higher education policy arena is a low to moderately complex policy arena. The number of key participants is small enough that most, if not all, of the participants know one another personally. Also, the variety of participants, as will be shown, is of a limited range. Finally, the number of committees involved in reauthorization consists of one in the House and one in the Senate.

Congressional Committees

The congressional committees and subcommittees are the central participants in the policy arena and the focus of attention for most of the other participants. They must reauthorize HEA and can hold oversight hearings on HEA programs or any related higher education concerns. The committees, and more importantly the subcommittees, are obligatory passage points for all major policy decisions within the arena. In the House, the key committee is the Education and Labor Committee while in the Senate it is the Labor and Human Resources Committee. The respective subcommittees are Postsecondary Education and Education, Arts and Humanities. The subcommittee members for the 102nd Congress are shown in tables 1 and 2.

While all of the committee and subcommittee members are well positioned to influence the reauthorization process, three members and their staffs were generally regarded as the key policy actors for the 1992 reauthorization. The key policy actor on the House subcommittee is William D. Ford. In part, this is due to his dual role as chair of the full committee and the subcommittee, but it also comes from his more than twenty-five years of involvement and experience with education issues in the House. As noted in the last chapter, Ford was a sponsor

TABLE 1
House Subcommittee on Postsecondary Education, 102nd Congress

Democrats	Republicans
William D. Ford (Mich.) *Chairman*	E. Thomas Coleman (Mo.) *Ranking Member*
Pat Williams (Mont.)	William F. Goodling (Pa.)
Charles A. Hayes (Ill.)	Marge Roukema (N.J.)
Joseph M. Gaydos (Pa.)	Steve Gunderson (Wis.)
George Miller (Calif.)	Paul B. Henry (Mich.)
Nita M. Lowey (N.Y.)	Susan Molinari (N.Y.)
Thomas C. Sawyer (Ohio)	Scott Klug (Wis.)
Donald M. Payne (N.J.)	Thomas E. Petrie (Wis.)
Jolene Unsoeld (Wash.)	Richard Armey (Tex.)
Craig Washington (Tex.)	Bill Barret (Neb.)
Jose Serrano (N.Y.)	
Patsy Mink (Hawaii)	
Robert E. Andrews (N.J.)	
William Jefferson (La.)	
John F. Reed (R.I.)	
Tim Roemer (Ind.)	
Dale E. Kildee (Mich.)	

TABLE 2
Senate Subcommittee on Education, Arts and Humanities, 102nd Congress

Democrats	Republicans
Claiborne Pell (R.I.)	Nancy Kassebaum (Kan.)
Chairman	*Ranking Member*
Howard Metzenbaum (Ohio)	Orrin Hatch (Utah)
Christopher Dodd (Conn.)	Thad Cochran (Miss.)
Paul Simon (Ill.)	James Jeffords (Vt.)
Barbara Mikulski (Md.)	Strom Thurmond (S.C.)
Jeff Bingaman (N.Mex.)	Dan Coats (Ind.)
Paul Wellstone (Minn.)	David Durenberger (Minn.)
Edward Kennedy (Mass.)	
Brock Adams (Wash.)	

of MISAA and has long favored expanding student aid to more middle-income families. During the 1980s, he was one of the Democrats who successfully lead the fight against Reagan administration proposals for deep cuts in student aid programs. For the 1992 reauthorization, Ford called for a major redesign of the HEA loan and grant programs (Cooper, 1992). Among the ideas put forward by Ford were front-loading Pell Grants, eliminating Perkins loans, increasing the size of SEOG awards, increasing aid to middle-income students, and support for direct lending.

The staff director for the subcommittee is Thomas R. Wolanin, who also held the position from 1985 to 1987. Wolanin is known in Congress for his detailed knowledge of HEA and is known in academia for his writing on higher education policy issues. The recipient of a doctorate in government from Harvard University, Wolanin was at one time a professor at the University of Wisconsin but left the academy so that he could make policy rather than merely study policy. Wolanin's introduction to HEA came when he was on leave from Wisconsin working for Congressman Frank Thompson Jr. during the 1972 reauthorization.

Without question, the key policy actor on the Senate subcommittee is the chair, Claiborne Pell. As either the chair or ranking member, Pell has helped shape every HEA reauthorization since 1972. A fixture in the Senate since 1960, Pell has consistently championed equal educational opportunity, nondiscrimination between different types of postsecondary education, and aid to students rather than institutions. Coming into the 1992 reauthorization Pell continued to address his traditional concerns as well as expressing an interest in stricter licensing and accreditation standards for postsecondary institutions as a means of quality control for federal student aid expenditures, expanding aid to middle-class students, and early intervention.

The staff director of the subcommittee is David V. Evans, who has worked for Pell since 1978. During the 1986 reauthorization, Evans was the minority staff director. When the Democrats regained control of the Senate in 1987, he became the subcommittee staff director. Given the broad jurisdiction of Senate committees, Evans has shared the workload on higher education with Sarah A. Flanagan who has been with the subcommittee since 1987. Flanagan is responsible for most of the contacts and interactions with higher education lobbyists.

The third key policy actor is Senator Edward M. Kennedy a member of the subcommittee and Chair of the Committee on Labor and Human Resources. A longtime advocate of education, Kennedy's involvement with HEA dates from its creation in 1965. Kennedy outlined much of his agenda in a *Roll Call* article in early 1991. The issues that Kennedy (1991) saw as important challenges for reauthorization were "the loan-grant imbalance, the integrity of the student loan program, and the excessive complexity of the student aid process" (p. 13). In addition, he expressed an interest in early intervention programs and Pell Grant entitlement.

Terry W. Hartle is the education staff director for the Committee on Labor and Human Resources and a key aide to Senator Kennedy on higher education issues. Hartle, a former policy analyst with the American Enterprise Institute, has also written on federal student aid programs. In some of his published work, Hartle has been critical of the complexity of the system, the role and growth of the guaranteed student loan (GSL) program, and the efforts of higher education associations to promote reform of the system (e.g., Doyle & Hartle, 1985).

While these are the key policy actors, other members of the subcommittees had policy concerns that they communicated and publicized within the higher education policy arena. A number of these issues were reported to the higher education associations through *Educational Record*. In the summer of 1990, Andra Armstrong (1990) reported the views of various House and Senate members in "How the Hill sees Higher Education." Members also used *Roll Call*, public interviews, press releases, and speeches to communicate their reauthorization agendas.

The Executive

While the key policy actors in the executive branch should be as easy to identify as those in the Congress, the Bush administration's policies and personnel were marked by flux and turmoil. In the fall of 1990, Education Secretary Lauro F. Cavazos ruled out separate student aid programs for colleges and trade schools while announcing plans to link aid to academic achievement and student retention rates (DeLoughry, 1990, October 3). In December, Cavazos resigned as education secretary reportedly because White House Chief of Staff John H. Sununu told him it was time to leave (DeLoughry, 1990, December 19).

In January 1991, Bush nominated Lamar Alexander to become the next education secretary. Alexander had served as governor of Tennessee from 1979 through 1987 and had been president of the University of Tennessee system since 1988 (DeLoughry, 1991, January 9). Alexander brought a proven track record on education to an administration that was desperate to make good on Bush's claim of being the Education President, but the conventional wisdom was that he was not appointed on the basis of his education record and experience. One of the reasons some believed he was appointed was his close friendship with Sununu. Another was his reputation as a determined, savvy, political operative who could guide legislation through the Congress. Regardless of the exact reason for his appointment, Alexander had built a solid record as an educational reformer during his years as governor and his appointment was greeted with approval by the education community.

To give Alexander the opportunity to select his own leadership team, the White House asked for the resignations of most of the top Education Department officials (DeLoughry, 1991, April 3). Among those asked to resign was Leonard L. Haynes III, assistant secretary for postsecondary education. While Haynes left immediately, his position was not immediately filled. Instead, Michael J. Farrell, whom Alexander had selected to be assistant secretary for student financial assistance, was asked to fill the postsecondary education slot on an interim basis (DeLoughry, 1991, December 4). In November, Farrell resigned from both positions, but gave no public reason for his departure (DeLoughry, 1991, December 11).

In September, Bush announced the nomination of Carolynn Reid-Wallace to fill the position of assistant secretary of postsecondary education (DeLoughry, 1991, September 18). The announcement of her nomination to the post was favorably received by the higher education community. Reid-Wallace brought a broad range of experiences to the position including a tenure as vice chancellor for academic affairs for the City University of New York System, as assistant director of education for the National Endowment for the Humanities, as dean at Bowie State University, and as an administrator with the National Association for Equal Opportunity in Higher Education. Farrell's resignation announcement came on the same day the Senate confirmed Reid-Wallace's nomination.

The Education Department's instability was symptomatic of the Bush administration's inability to find its footing on education issues and policy. The administration not only had trouble fashioning its leadership team for education but also never seemed to be in sync with other members of the education community. For example, in an effort to give substance and clarity to his claim of being the Education President, Bush announced "America 2000" in a speech at the White House on April 18, 1991. The "America 2000" speech presented the President's strategy to "restructure and revitalize America's education system by the year 2000" ("America 2000," 1991, p. 1). The president did not seem to realize that the congressional subcommittees that would have to deal with the legislative proposals on "America 2000" were already busy holding hearings on HEA. Without considering the merits of the proposals, the message was off-cycle and unresponsive to the needs of the subcommittees who needed to hear what the administration had to say about higher education. The proposals for K through 12 would have to wait a year before the subcommittees were scheduled to reauthorize the legislation for secondary and elementary schools.

In summary, while the White House is the final passage point for HEA in the reauthorization process, the executive branch was in a state of confusion and flux from the very beginning of the process. No one in Congress, Democrat or Republican, seemed to know what the White House wanted from reauthorization or who was in charge. This may be because no one in the White House knew. The best example of this uncertainty is Bush's position on direct loans and Pell Grant entitlement. After initially supporting both, Bush threatened to veto legislation that contained either. The increased level of uncertainty served to increase the internal complexity of the policy arena.

The Associations

The third group of participants in the policy arena are the higher education associations that attempt to lobby the Congress and the executive branch. While they certainly lobby by any conventional definition of the term, most associations claim not to be lobbyists because of their inordinate fear of violating Section 501 (c) (3) of the Internal Revenue Code, thereby losing their tax-exempt status (Bloland, 1985). The number and diversity of higher education associations gives some credence to the lament that "no other segment of American society has so many organizations and is yet so unorganized as higher education" (Babbidge & Rosenzweig, 1962, p. 92). While there are a large number of associations, only a few are recognized as active policy actors, thus it is relatively easy to identify and discuss this segment of the policy arena.

The major higher education associations are housed in the National Center for Higher Education at One Dupont Circle in Washington, D.C., and the address has become a shorthand way to refer to higher education associations. Of the twenty plus associations that reside at One Dupont, only the American Association of Community and Junior Colleges (AACJC), the American Association of State Colleges and Universities (AASCU), the American Council on Education (ACE), the Association of American Universities (AAU), and the National Association of State Universities and Land-Grant Colleges (NASULGC) have been consistently active policy actors in the higher education policy arena. ACE, an umbrella organization, has often attempts to forge consensus positions on policy issues getting as many associations as possible to speak with one voice on the issue before attempting to influence the Congress or the executive branch. The other five associations, all of which are institutional associations, have then provided the expertise on the issues that most impact their member institutions.

ACE has long claimed to speak for all of higher education, but for many years its voice was seldom heard in Washington and its organizational structure all but prevented decision making when Congress did ask for an opinion (Babbidge & Rosenzweig, 1962). By the time ACE cleared policy positions with its member associations and institutions, Congress had either acted on the policy question or else was no longer interested in ACE's views on the matter. It was only after the burst of education legislation in the 1960s, the defeat of institutional aid in 1972, and sharp public criticism from the White House and members of Congress that ACE began to undertake an internal reevaluation and reorganization aimed at improving its governmental relations function. Much of that work, directed by then President Roger Heyns and Vice President Stephen K. Bailey, took place in the mid-1970s.

One of the changes brought by Heyns and Bailey was hiring Charles B. Saunders as the new director of the Division of Govern-

mental Relations (King, 1975). Saunders, now vice president of governmental relations, brought a wealth of experience to the task having
previously served as a Senate staff member, deputy assistant secretary
of education, and acting assistant secretary of education (Bloland,
1985; Graham, 1984). One of Saunders' initial acts was to organize an
informal weekly meeting between members of the major education
associations at One Dupont Circle, the National Association of University Business Officers (NACUBO), and the National Association of
Independent Colleges and Universities (NAICU) (Bloland, 1985).
Saunders later initiated a second weekly meeting with a larger group
of higher education representatives. These informal meetings served
different purposes. The smaller group represented an opportunity for
the major associations to exchange information, identify positions,
and move toward consensus. The larger group acted as a monitor of
events and an information exchange for the participants. The two
groups continued to meet into the 1990s and served much the same
purpose for the 1992 reauthorization.

Consistent with its self-image as the lead association "to coordinate
the formation of policy on the national issues and problems of higher
education" (Bloland, 1985, p. 17), ACE worked to forge a broad consensus on reauthorization issues through the formation of six task
forces. Established in the spring of 1989, the task forces were organized
around the issues of need analysis and the student aid delivery
system, low-income students, middle-income students, graduate and
professional education, program development, and institutional resources. The task force reports were integrated into a comprehensive
set of recommendations for reauthorization that were submitted to
both the House and Senate subcommittees. Joining ACE in signing
the reauthorization recommendations were the American Association
of Community and Junior Colleges (AACJC), American Association of
State Colleges and Universities (AASCU), Association of American
Universities (AAU), Association of Catholic Colleges and Universities
(ACCU), Association of Urban Universities (AUU), National Associa-
tion for Equal Opportunity in Higher Education (NAFEOHE), National
Association of College and University Business Officers (NACUBO),
National Association of Independent Colleges and Universities
(NAICU), National Association of Schools and Colleges of the United
Methodist Church (NASCUMC), and the National Association of
State Universities and Land-Grant Colleges (NASULGC).

ACE's coordinating role and the shared One Dupont Circle address
means that the associations are often lumped together and treated as
one. The terms ACE and One Dupont Circle are often used by con-

gressional staff, observers, and scholars to refer to all of the associations housed in the National Center for Higher Education without any acknowledgment of the differences that define the individual associations. In practice, each association tends to stress what is most important to its institutional members and, at times, to take positions not covered by the consensus agreements that rule One Dupont Circle. AASCU, founded in 1961, might be the best example of an association that has been willing to step out from the One Dupont Circle group and take positions on issues not covered by consensus agreements. AASCU has a consistent record of speaking out for lower tuition and equal opportunity in higher education. As was noted in the last chapter, AASCU's position on tuition has at times put it at odds with other associations. Edward M. Elmendorf, AASCU's vice president for governmental relations and a former assistant secretary of education for postsecondary education in the Reagan administration, has been a visible and effective spokesman.

NASULGC, like AASCU, has a strong record of supporting low tuition and equal educational opportunity. Because so many of its member institutions have graduate schools, NASULGC also speaks out on graduate education, research, and international studies. Jerold Roschwald, NASULGC director of federal relations–higher education worked closely with AASCU and AAU in preparing for the 1992 reauthorization. In addition, Thomas A. Butts, associate vice president for governmental relations at the University of Michigan, worked with NASULGC to develop and lobby for a direct loan program.

AAU was founded in 1900 by fourteen American universities offering the Ph.D. Today, AAU consists of some fifty-six American and two Canadian universities, but its focus remains research and graduate education. Given that AAU's interests often overlap with NASULG's and with CGSUS, John C. Vaughn, AAU director of federal relations, frequently coordinates with these associations to maximize their potential impact on federal policy issues. Vaughn also led the ACE task force on graduate and professional education.

AACJC was established in 1920 to represent the interests of junior colleges. AACJC claims to have a community or junior college in every congressional district, but the nature of this higher education sector is such that many of its issues are state rather than federal issues. This may explain why Frank Mensel, AACJC vice president of federal relations, can also serve as director of federal relations for the Association of Community College Trustees.

While One Dupont Circle is home to the National Center for Higher Education, important higher education groups are also located elsewhere in Washington, D.C. One of the more important of these is the National Association of Student Financial Aid Administrators (NASFAA). NASFAA is often cited for its technical knowledge and expertise. Founded in the mid-1960s, NASFAA now speaks for some 3,200 campuses and 9,000 financial aid officers nationwide (DeWitt, 1991). Traditionally, NASFAA has been noted not only for its technical expertise but also for being the surrogate voice of college students and their parents. In 1992, under the leadership of Dallas Martin, NASFAA sought to expand its traditional role and become an actor on larger policy issues. As part of this effort, NASFAA organized its own re-authorization task force to prepare a full range of HEA proposals for the authorizing committees. In addition, Martin chaired the ACE task force on needs analysis and student aid delivery, but NASFAA did not sign the ACE consensus recommendations. Instead, it presented a separate set of policy proposals developed by the NASFAA reauthorization task force.

Another key association is the National Council of Educational Opportunity Associations (NCEOA). This ten-year-old association represents Upward Bound, Talent Search, Student Support Services, and other so-called TRIO programs directed toward low-income and minority students. Under the leadership of Arnold Mitchem, NCEOA has consistently convinced Congress to increase TRIO funding.

A third association outside One Dupont Circle that must be mentioned in any list of key higher education policy actors is the National Association of Independent Colleges and Universities (NAICU). Just as ACE acts as an umbrella association for higher education, NAICU acts as the umbrella association for higher education's private sector. In preparing for the 1992 reauthorization, NAICU worked with the ACE consensus group and signed the recommendations that came out of the process. Julianne S. Thrift, then NAICU executive vice president, chaired the ACE task force on middle-income students.

Finally, the Career College Association (CCA) speaks for a segment of the higher education community not represented by One Dupont Circle. CCA is the product of a merger between the National Association of Trade and Technical Schools (NATTS) and the Association of Independent Colleges and Schools (AICS). Tainted by egregious student aid abuse scandals, NATTS hired Stephen J. Blair as president in 1985 and gave him the task of cleaning up the organization. Blair, formerly director of policy and program development in the Education Department's Office of Student Financial Assistance, succeeded to the point that AICS, formerly the lead association for the sector, merged with NATTS, largely as a matter of survival. Today, CCA has six full-time lobbyists and a political action committee that donates to Congressional campaigns.

Bolstering the lobbying staff was designed to overcome the political damage caused by the student aid abuse scandals. When possible, Blair hired former congressional staff members to lobby their old committees (DeParle, 1992). The hiring of Patty Sullivan, who had worked for Representative Pat Williams, is the premier example of this tactic. Blair also hired consultants such as Bob Beckel, a member of the Mondale presidential campaign, and Haley Barbour, a member of the Reagan White House, to help CCA prepare for reauthorization.

In chapter 2, the increasing scope and size of the GSL program was mentioned several times. One result of this growth has been the increasing role of lenders and guarantors as policy actors in the higher education policy arena. While bankers may not be educators, the Consumer Bankers Association (CBA) has stressed the role its members play in helping students pay for a college education that might otherwise be denied them due to the unavailability of funds. The CBA plays down the more than $1 billion in profits that commercial banks generate from their student loan portfolios each year, a profit that is virtually 100 percent guaranteed by the federal government (Bluestone & Comcowich, 1992). Instead, it stresses the efficiency with which it delivers loans to students compared to alternatives such as direct loan programs. While CBA speaks for bankers involved in the guaranteed student loan program, the law firm of Colhan and Dean speaks for the CBA. Several members of Colhan and Dean are former congressional staff members with connections to the education committees. John E. Dean, for example, was formerly minority counsel for the House Postsecondary Education Subcommittee (Lee, 1983).

The National Council of Higher Education Loan Programs (NCHELP) is a creation of the GSL program's growth and expansion. NCHELP is a nonprofit association of guarantors, lenders, secondary markets, servicing organizations, private collection companies, and other organizations involved in the GSL program. Jean S. Frohlicker, NCHELP executive director, was involved with the original HEA in 1965 and with every reauthorization since. Like CBA, NCHELP stresses the role it plays in helping students who might otherwise have found college beyond their means. Also like CBA, NCHELP emphasizes it efficiency and the fact that for every federal dollar spent through the GSL program, private markets leverage three to four dollars more for student loans, thus giving the government a bargain while giving students a chance for higher education that might otherwise have been denied.

Sallie Mae, the Student Loan Marketing Association, was created by Congress as part of the 1972 reauthorization. The reason for Sallie Mae's creation was to improve the GSL program by creating a clearinghouse for student loans. Sallie Mae does this by buying student loans from lenders and providing services to lenders and educational institutions involved with the GSL program. By the end of 1990, Sallie Mae owned nearly 30 percent of all outstanding guaranteed student loans (Hyatt, 1991).

Sallie Mae, like CBA and NCHELP, emphasizes the service it provides to students rather than the profits it makes from the service. Lawrence A. Hough, Sallie Mae's president and chief executive officer, likes to emphasize not only the service and efficiency of his organization, but also the way in which it acts to assist middle income students. While Hough speaks publicly for Sallie Mae, much of its day-to-day interaction with the Congress is handled by the Washington law firm of Williams and Jensen.

While other associations and organizations are active, the above are the most active higher education associations in the policy arena. The addition of other, less active organizations would not significantly alter the level of internal complexity of the higher education policy arena. At the beginning of this section, the arena was described as being of low to moderate complexity. Visually, the complexity of relationships and number of participants can be viewed in Table 3.

TABLE 3
Participants in the Higher Education Policy Arena

Executive
President
Education Secretary
Senior Ed Officials
OMB

Associations	Congress
One Dupont Circle Associations	House Education and Labor Committee
CCA	Subcommittee on Postsecondary
NAICU	Education
NASFAA	Senate Labor and Human Resources
NCEOA	Committee
Lender Associations	Subcommittee on Education, Arts, and
	Humanities

Functional Autonomy

Functional autonomy is "the extent to which policies are formulated and implemented within the subsystem" (Hamm, 1983, p. 381). By this definition, the higher education policy arena enjoys a high level of functional autonomy. This is not to suggest that the arena has been immune from attacks on its functional autonomy. The 1968 student conduct debates and the 1972 busing debates are primary examples of other policy arenas seeking to infringe upon the autonomy of the higher education policy arena. Another example is the Reagan administration's use of the budget to implement policy changes that it could not gain through the higher education policy arena. In each of these examples, the higher education policy arena was able to resist and to maintain its autonomy.

A threat to the arena's functional autonomy arose at the beginning of the 1992 reauthorization in the form of an investigation of the federal student loan program by the Senate Permanent Subcommittee on Investigations. Chaired by Senator Sam Nunn, a Georgia Democrat, the subcommittee held a series of hearings as part of an investigation that resulted in the report *Abuses in Federal Student Aid Programs* (1991). The findings were embraced by members of the education committees and subcommittees, who translated the findings into their own policy proposals. The net result was to diffuse the threat to the arena's autonomy without coming into conflict with other legislative policy arenas.

Finally, while there are no instruments for measuring functional autonomy, Hall and Evans (1990) do address the issue of functional autonomy indirectly in their study of the power of congressional subcommittees. Looking at three committees in the Ninety-seventh Congress, one of which was the House Committee on Education and Labor, the authors found that the education and labor subcommittees drafted 88 percent of the committee legislation, dominated the amending of legislation at the committee level, and that the reporting subcommittee lost not a single roll-call vote during the entire Congress. While this is but one study, it provides additional support for the claim that the higher education policy arena enjoys a high level of functional autonomy.

Unity within Type of Participant

Unity within type of participant is simply a way of referring to "the unity among individuals in each sector—agencies, interest groups, and committees" (Hamm, 1983, p. 382). This brief definition of unity conceals the complexity of the meaning of unity when used in discussions of subgovernments. Unity refers to unity between individuals as well as between organizations. An example would be the level of unity between associations on a key policy question. Unity also refers to agreement across sectors. For example, unity on the role of Pell Grants would be rather high across sectors. While it is widely used in describing policy arenas, the concept of unity is not well defined in the literature. Instead of working from an operational definition, researchers use examples from the subgovernment system being studied to support claims of unity or disunity in the system.

The level of unity within the higher education policy arena is rather high. One way in which this can be seen is in the language used by the policy actors. The language used to describe policy issues carries with it an acceptance and understanding of the values that guide the higher education policy arena. For example, "needs analysis" means that students need help attending college, it is the federal government's role to provide that help, and it is necessary to determine how much, if any, help should be forthcoming in a fair and consistent manner. "Equal educational opportunity" means that the federal government should play an active role in removing race, religion, sex, poverty, and other barriers that might prevent children of ability from attending college. "Access" means giving aid to students who are blocked from higher education by financial barriers. The common language and understood values help provide a coherence, unity, and logic to the policy arena.

Since almost no one in the higher education policy arena questions the basic philosophical underpinning of problems and issues, conflicts tend to arise over specific solutions. For example, the issue of whether loans should be given via direct lending or through loan vendors is not an issue of loans, but one of how to deliver loans. The same is true of the loan-grant imbalance. The issue is not student loans, but the proper balance between loans and forms of grant aid. The guiding assumptions and beliefs remain unchallenged with only the solutions open to question and conflict.

Last, unity, particularly between Congress and the associations, has evolved from a long history of cooperative activities aimed at producing workable and popular legislation. The extensive quotations from policy actors in chapter 2 demonstrates that the history has also involved angry disputes, but the policy actors have always overcome these differences to focus on the common goal of aiding students. The resolution of these disputes and the long, shared history of the policy actors has fostered emotional and intellectual bonds that unite the participants.

Cooperation or Conflict

The characteristic of cooperation or conflict among different participants is a function of the communality of interests enjoyed in the policy arena (Hamm, 1983). Communality of interests rests on a number of factors, but interest overrepresentation and circulation of personnel are key concerns in gauging the level of cooperation or conflict within a policy arena. Overrepresentation refers to a greater concentration of interested legislators on a committee or subcommittee than could be accounted for by the normal distribution of legislators. For example, the claim was often made that the oil depletion allowance in the U.S. tax code was a result of oil state overrepresentation on the tax committees (Bonds, 1979). Circulation of personnel is the extent to which "interest groups, agency positions, committee staffs, and personal staffs" (Hamm, 1983, p. 386) move between jobs and sectors within the policy arena.

What one sees in looking at the two education subcommittees is that higher education is well represented by members who have higher education as a major economic interest in their district or state and by members who have a long history of commitment to higher education policy issues. For example, House subcommittee chair Ford has a number of institutions in his district and has a long history of interest and involvement in education issues. Higher education is not a major economic interest in Montana, but Pat Williams has long held an interest in education issues. Tim Roemer is from a district in Indiana that includes an Indiana University campus, the University of Notre Dame, a Purdue University campus, and several small colleges; thus he must be concerned with higher education issues in order to represent his district. Senate subcommittee chair Pell has made his political name with education issues. Edward M. Kennedy has a well-known interest in education and higher education is a major economic interest in Massachusetts. James Jeffords is similar to Kennedy in that he holds a personal interest in higher education and it is a major economic factor in Vermont. While this brief summary does not offer the numerical output of a multiple regression analysis, it is more than enough to establish that higher education interests are well represented and probably overrepresented on the subcommittees.

The circulation of personnel within the policy arena was addressed in the discussion of internal complexity, but additional examples are provided here to reinforce the understanding of the extensive flow of personnel within the policy arena. One example is Beth B. Buehlmann, who was an education policy fellow at the National Institute of Education before she joined the minority staff of the House Committee on Education in 1979, where she remained for some twelve years before becoming the Washington representative for the California state colleges. Another is Lawrence S. Zaglaniczny, currently assistant to the president of NASFAA, who formerly worked for ACE, as a lobbyist for a student higher education group, and as a congressional staffer. Last, William A. Blakey worked in the Education Department during the Carter administration, was later the staff director of the House Subcommittee on Postsecondary Education, and now represents the United Negro College Fund as a member of the law firm of Colhan and Dean. One higher education representative summarized the circulation of personnel by noting that "we are an incestuous lot."

Finally, unity and cooperation or conflict tend to overlap. The common language, shared values, and shared history help create unity and reduce conflict within the policy arena. The exchanges, in articles, papers, and speeches, between the policy actors helps identify and work out disputes as well as helping develop the language of the arena. The circulation of personnel is a major factor in promoting cooperation and encouraging unity by giving participants shared multiple perspectives of the policy arena.

DEFINING THE ARENA

As discussed at the beginning of this chapter, the concept of community is being used to describe and define the higher education policy arena because the concept captures the dynamic, contingent social relations of the policy arena in a way that is not possible with more static approaches such as shapes and mapping. Community is also the metaphor that higher education policy arena participants use "to define and associate the different elements by which they build and explain their world" (Callon, 1986, p. 201). Many policy actors define the community in terms of a constructive partnership that benefits all members of the community.

Higher education partnership is also used by policy actors to describe the social relations in the policy arena. The exact nature of the partnership varies depending on which policy actor defines the meaning of higher education partnership. For example, one higher education association representative viewed the relationship as a partnership because of the low level of conflict the arena exhibited compared to other policy arenas she had worked in prior to entering the higher education policy arena. In addition, the opportunity for discussion, input, and participation seemed to distinguish the arena as a partnership.

A higher education lobbyist also viewed the social relationship between participants in the policy arena as a partnership, but one that had deteriorated due to neglect by the Reagan and Bush administrations. The condition of the partnership today is one in which "there's a strong relationship between Congress and the lobby," but the executive has "been pretty ineffective" (Personal interview, February 27, 1992). NASULGC's Jerold Roschwalb echoed this view of the higher education partnership suggesting that perhaps "it characterizes it too neatly in some respects. . . . [T]here's a more solid relationship . . . between the associations and the Hill . . . [T]he Department . . . just hasn't been there for awhile" (Personal interview, February 27, 1992). Thomas Wolanin summarized it more succinctly stating "a higher education partnership does exist, but the White House role is that of veto agent" (Personal interview, May 7, 1992).

The policy actors' self-definition of the policy arena as a community or partnership matches well with definitions and descriptions of community in the literature. For example, Bellah and colleagues (1985) define a community as:

a group of people who are socially interdependent, who participate together in discussion and decision making, and who share certain *practices* (which see) that both define the community and are nurtured by it. Such a community is not quickly formed. It almost always has a history and so is also a *community of memory*, defined in part by its past and its memory of its past. (p. 333)

Suggesting that higher education policy actors are socially interdependent would be stretching the reality of the arena to fit the definition, but other elements of Bellah's definition fit quite comfortably. The policy actors do participate together in discussion and decision making. The community does not operate by consensus but participants are allowed extensive input into the bill writing process. The community also shares common practices that define and maintain the community. The subcommittee hearings, position papers, and bidirectional lobbying are examples of practices that define and maintain the community. Finally, a community memory is maintained by long-term members of the arena such as Representative Ford and Senators Pell and Kennedy and is renewed with each new reauthorization as the old members of the community educate the new members about HEA, its past, its purpose, and its future.

David A. Hollinger (1985), in an essay on intellectual history, offers a definition of community that is centered on participation in a discourse. In some ways this is a loose definition of community because it means that anyone who joins the discourse is part of the community. In other ways it is a strong definition because

> participants in any given discourse are bound to share certain values, beliefs, perceptions, and concepts—"ideas," as these potentially distinctive mental elements are called for short— but the most concrete and functional elements shared, surely, are *questions*. . . . Questions are the points of contact between minds, where agreements are consolidated and where differences are acknowledged and dealt with; questions are the dynamisms whereby membership in a community of discourse is established, renewed, and sometimes terminated. (Hollinger, 1985, p. 132)

The higher education policy arena reflects many of the characteristics of Hollinger's community of discourse. The contested principles in chapter 2 demonstrate a community concerned with questions from the earliest stages of its development through to the present. Equal educational opportunity was the value and belief that guided the Johnson administration's original vision of HEA and continues to play a key role in decision making today. Access, equal educational opportunity, and needs analysis are part of the common language and shared values that help guide discourse and provide coherence, unity, and logic.

Describing the higher education policy arena as a community and matching its characteristics with definitions of community from the literature gives some focus to the concept of community but begs the question of what type of community is being discussed. It is important to establish the exact type of community because this will become the context for the discussion of the meaning of power in chapter 5. The basis for defining the nature of the community that is the higher education policy arena are the criterion characteristics from the subgovernment literature. From the description generated by the application of this descriptive framework, the exact nature of the higher education policy community can be interpreted.

The interpretation that follows has its roots in John Dewey's (1927/ 1988) communication community concept. Dewey's communication community is used because the history of the policy arena suggests a community bonded by communication. The communication community forms the basis of collective action in the higher education policy arena. Through the experience of collective action policy actors have developed a common language as well as widely understood signs and symbols that convey shared meanings in the arena. From the experience of collective action, emotional, intellectual, and moral bonds have evolved to link and bind the members of the policy arena. These different aspects of a communication community are developed below in greater detail.

Before discussing these aspects, it is necessary to develop Dewey's concept of a communication community in greater detail. A more complete development is required because Dewey himself did not fully develop the concept after suggesting it in *The Public and Its Problems* (1927/1988). Dewey's theory of a communication community starts with, rather than ends in, the process of collective action. The product of collective action, regardless of how well it is conceived and planned, produces unintended or unanticipated consequences for the public. As these problems become apparent, the institutions responsible for implementing the public will and the public interact to produce a new decision. Of paramount importance in this process is communication between individuals and institutions who are either affected by a decision or are concerned with the consequences of any new decision. Communication is what bonds the community together. The public, a true democratic public, emerges from the communication required by group problem solving. The same is true of democratic governments that exist as a function of the collective action process. Communication for problem solving, not force of arms, becomes the mechanism for social order in the communication community.

As sketched by Dewey, the communication community is a lively, free-wheeling society, but one that also places a heavy moral and political responsibility on its citizens. Individuals must be aware of community issues, the consequences of collective actions, the needs of society, and must make decisions based on the needs of the community without the possibility of passing the burden for decision making on to some higher authority or outside agent. In the communication community, power as domination is replaced by power as problem solving, thus the public must take responsibility for solving its problems. If the public fails to take responsibility, there is no external system of social control, and the internal system of social order begins to unravel.

Dewey (1927/1988) claimed that the communication community would "have its consummation when free social inquiry is indissolubly wedded to the art of full and moving communication" (p. 184), but recognized that certain prerequisites were necessary before this consummation could be achieved. One of the prerequisites was a common language that could be used and understood by all of the community. Language by itself was not enough to foster fully understood communications. The public also needed widely understood signs and symbols to convey shared meanings. In addition, groups needed to interact in cooperative activities because "the pulls and responses of different groups reenforce one another and their values accord" (Dewey, 1988, p. 148). The shared activities also produce emotional, intellectual, and moral bonds that help bind the community. As these prerequisites are met, then a community evolves that is capable of transforming the power of domination into the power of problem solving.

Returning to the history of the higher education policy arena, one discovers a community born from collective action. Its early roots can be traced to the debates over the Northwest Ordinance of 1787, the national university, and the Morrill-Land Grant Act of 1862. The Association of American Agricultural Colleges in 1887 and the National Association of State Universities in 1895 were formed in response to the federal role in higher education and in an effort to better communicate the problems and needs of higher education to the federal government. While these are the early roots of the community, its growth was slow because there was limited federal action, little need for collective action, and almost no reason for communication.

The community did not begin to take its present form until well into the 1960s. Some associations formed in direct response to federal policy decisions, while others formed to fill the needs of their members for communication between similar institutions. Whatever the reason for their original formation, the associations reached the inescapable conclusion that some level of involvement with the federal government was required given the increasing size and scope of the federal interest in higher education. Federal decisions were impacting colleges and universities more directly than ever before as government programs ranging from national defense to social equality were created with institutions of higher education serving as the instrument of implementation. While institutions might have followed a path of resistance, the only effective way to influence federal action was to enter into a dialogue with federal policymakers. In particular, with the congressional leaders responsible for federal higher education policy formation and the executive agencies charged with implementing policy.

The federal government experienced a similar need to enter into a dialogue with the associations representing colleges and universities in order to implement its own policy agenda. The first HEA focused on providing equal educational opportunity for low income and lower-middle-income students with aid programs administered primarily though campus officials. Subsequent reauthorizations expanded this focus to include more middle-income students and created various loans under the GSL program to facilitate the delivery of aid to these students. In addition, Congress expanded the definition of higher education to include a broader range of postsecondary education, thus expanding the number and type of potential aid recipients. To accomplish their policy goals, federal higher education policymakers had to enter into a dialogue with the associations. Policy actors in the federal government could not have successfully imposed programs on colleges and universities just as those institutions could not have successfully resisted the implementation of federal programs. The parties had a mutual need to communication and cooperate.

Communication did develop, but not quickly or easily. When higher education policy emerged as a distinct part of federal policy making with the passage of the 1965 HEA, the Johnson administration did not include associations in the development of the legislation and limited congressional involvement. The associations were more involved in 1972, but not as active participants in a discussion over how to refine and expand the federal student aid program. The associations, dependent on Representative Green, lacked the ability, knowledge, and skills to participate in the debate. It was after this failure that the associations began to reorganize, and in some cases to organize for the first time, for participation in the discussions that formed and shaped federal higher education policy.

At least three factors contributed to the development and maturation of the communication community. One, already suggested, was the need of the various policy actors to discuss programs to insure that student aid programs were well conceived, planned, and implemented. Once implemented, programs usually hit snags, produce unintended or unanticipated consequences, and otherwise encounter problems that create the need for new communication, consultation, or planning. This process of interacting to resolve unanticipated problems produced a pattern of communication for problem solving that became the norm for the community. This is not to suggest that all efforts to influence policy actors through communication was altruistic, because it was not and is not. Instead, what is suggested is that ideas, discussions, suggestions, and recommendations were held to the test of helping students achieve equal educational opportunity.

A second factor is the longevity of key policy actors and the history of shared activities that comes from that longevity. Representative Ford and Senators Kennedy and Pell were part of the first HEA and remained as key policy actors in 1992. Others, such as Representative Green and Senator Stafford played key roles for a long number of years before retiring from the community. Some House and Senate staffers such as Thomas R. Wolanin have remained active in the community for a significant number of years helping develop an institutional memory that anchors the community and helps carry it into the future. Wolanin and Lawrence E. Gladieux (1976) helped define the higher education policy arena as a community with their book *Congress and the Colleges*. Finally, some policy actors have remained active for an extended duration, but have moved within the community. Beth B. Buehlmann, William A. Blakey, John Dean, Jean S. Frohlicker, and Lawrence S. Zaglaniczny were cited above as examples of the extensive circulation and flow of personnel within the policy arena. This movement has contributed to the maturation of the communication community as policy actors have shared experiences as well as gaining multiple perspectives.

The third factor is the need and demand for communication between policy actors. The 1972 reauthorization strongly underscored the need for higher education associations to participate in a dialogue with federal policymakers. Honey (1972) strongly emphasized this point when he charged that "the failure of the Washington-based spokesmen for higher education to contribute significantly to the shaping of those amendments verges on the scandalous" (p. 1234). The need to participate in a conversation over higher education policy was a mutually expressed need that was expressed and even demanded by federal policymakers. In 1970, Daniel P. Moynihan's sharply worded criticism of the federal higher education associations revolved around their failure to engage in a debate over President Nixon's higher education proposals. Senator Pell was equally critical of the higher education associations in 1972 for their failure to take "the trouble to reflect on and study our ideas which we think can help solve the problem" (quoted in Gladieux & Wolanin, 1976, p. 95).

Following the 1972 reauthorization, the higher education associations moved to increase their ability to communicate with their members, with each other, and with federal higher education policy makers. In some cases, this meant hiring new personnel and creating new offices to handle government relations. The structures for communication ranged from closed, elitists groups to open, egalitarian gatherings. One of the older, more elite, structures for communications is the Secretariat, which was formed in 1962 by the Big Six and five other associations. While the Secretariat was viewed as a powerful, exclusive group, growth in its membership limited the organization's ability to function as a decision-making body. While it continues, the heads of the Big Six formed the Brethren to exchange information and coordinate action. The government relations officers of the Big Six dubbed themselves the Sons of the Brethren and also met to exchange information, ideas, and intelligence. Finally, the Monday and Friday groups, discussed above, brought together higher education representatives to exchange information.

To a considerable degree, communication is the reason for the community's existence. As noted above, the community evolved from the need to respond to the growing federal role in higher education, to communicate the needs of higher education to the federal government, and to communicate between institutions. The reauthorization process reinforces the need for communication. Programs created or continued under previous reauthorizations have to be reviewed and considered before any new decisions can be made. Before new programs can be considered, information to support the need for a new action has to be collected and disseminated. In order to meet the needs of students and institutions, federal policymakers have to hear those needs. Always short on time and information, policymakers look to program constituent to provide information, collect additional information, and build support for programs and program ideas.

The structure of the reauthorization process demands communication. The Education Department and the education subcommittees all request written submissions from interested parties as part of their preparation for reauthorization. Federal policymakers and policy actors constantly lobby one another as written submissions in the form of position papers and recommendations are prepared. Bidirectional lobbying keeps policy proposals within the realm of the possible and keeps policy actors and policymakers in touch with one another. The mutually shaped and tested position papers and policy recommendations are the most practical example of the communication community.

The subcommittee hearings are the most visible example of communication created and demanded by the reauthorization process.

The information gained through the hearings could easily and more efficiently be communicated through written submissions. The hearings are a public ritual symbolizing the communication community and its commitment to problem solving. Subcommittee members listen as problems and solutions are identified and discussed. The witnesses pledge their support to solving problems and removing barriers to participation in higher education. The members respond in kind, pledging their support to solving the identified problems and implementing the suggested solutions.

Finally, in making the case that the higher education policy arena is a communication community, no claims are being made about the meaning of power. Dewey claimed that power in a communication community would be replaced by problem solving, but to accept that definition of power at this point would mean forcing the communication community definition of power on the data instead of letting the meaning of power emerge from the data. Before the meaning of power can emerge, the current social context of policy making must be examined. In doing this, the definition of the community based on its historical context may shift and change suggesting a different type of community.

CONCLUSIONS

One of the difficulties in approaching the higher education policy arena as an area of study has been the absence of a definition and description that captures the arena's dynamic social interactions and relationships. Among the first to offer a definition of the arena were Wolanin and Gladieux (1975), but they were primarily concerned with providing a background for their larger discussion of political culture. Today, that definition is skeletal, dated, and of limited value in defining a policy arena that has changed substantially in the more than two decades since the definition was first offered.

King (1975), Murray (1976), and Finn (1980) have also offered definitions of the higher education policy arena. King's is perhaps the best of the three, but it has decayed over time. This is because King was presenting a description and definition of the policy arena as it was rather than a framework that could be used to study the arena as it evolved. Murray basically repeated King's earlier work, but dressed it in new conceptual clothing. Finn's effort is seriously flawed and probably continues to enjoy some mention on the basis of his reputation rather than on the merits of his work.

While any definition of the arena will be time- and context-bound, it is possible to use the subgovernment literature to create a framework for describing and defining the higher education policy arena in a way that allows for some adjustment and flexibility to account for changes in the characteristics of the policy arena. The criterion characteristics of internal complexity, functional autonomy, unity within type of participant, and cooperation or conflict are helpful in bringing the policy arena into focus and for adjusting that focus as the policy arena changes. Using these characteristics as a descriptive framework, researchers can discuss shifts and changes in the arena without discarding the framework. Also, changes in the arena can be explained by relating them to the criterion characteristics. The flexibility of this approach represents a significant improvement over earlier descriptions of the policy arena.

The description that comes from the application of this descriptive framework suggests a communication community. Dewey's concept of a communication community starts with the process of collective action. Through the experience of collective action policy actors have developed a common language as well as widely understood signs and symbols that convey shared meanings in the arena. From the experience of collective action, emotional, intellectual, and moral bonds evolve to link and bind members of the policy arena. At the core of this community is a continuing, mutual need to communicate and cooperate.

While Dewey's communication community concept helps define the type of community, it is too soon to extend the concept to include Dewey's definition of power. The meaning of power must emerge from the historical and social context of the community. The next chapter addresses the social context of policy making and continues to test the concept of community. The question of the meaning of power is reserved until chapter 5.

4

The Social Context of Policy Making

As discussed above, the meaning of power is not universal but must be interpreted within the social context that holds power roles and relationships. The broad outlines of the social context of the higher education policy arena were presented in chapter 3. The purpose of this chapter is to complete that outline by filling in the details that collectively form the social setting for policy making. Like a pointillist, the task is to create a whole picture from a collection of dots. Ideally, the researcher would enter the policy arena in its formative stages and observe how problem definitions and solutions arise from the arena's primordial beginnings and then trace those problem definitions/ solutions through to the present. Of course, this is impossible in the case of the higher education policy arena and probably impossible in any policy arena.

Instead, one is faced with the problem of stepping into a developed policy arena that is awash with problem definitions/solutions. The history of the higher education policy arena reveals that problem definitions/solutions form, appear, disappear, reform, and reappear as actors constantly seek to translate their definitions/solutions into policy decisions. An apt description of a policy arena at work might well be found in Michael D. Cohen and James G. March's (1974) "garbage can" theory of decision making. In this theory, decision making depends on the mix of "problems and solutions . . . , on the labels attached to alternative cans, . . . on what garbage is being produced at the moment, and on the mix of cans available, and on the speed with which garbage is collected and removed from the scene" (Cohen & March, 1974, p. 85). The decision that comes out of the garbage can is a function of the interaction of problems, solutions, participants, and choice opportunities.

Cohen and March's garbage can reflects much that happens in the sociology of translation. Nothing is neat and clean, new contents are frequently added to the mix, and policy actors are constantly seeking to provide their definitions and/or solutions as *the* definition or solution. This makes it impossible to create an objective shape or map that defines the social context of the arena. It is, however, possible to create a description of the social context of the policy arena that then can be used to interpret power. The starting point for this description are the events that foreshadowed the reauthorization process and helped define issues that would become central to the process. These events meant that issues such as the loan-grant imbalance, program integrity, needs analysis, simplification, and student loan default rates would be waiting when the reauthorization process started. Once the process officially started, a new set of issues was added as members of Congress, the higher education associations, the White House, and other policy participants moved to build support for their reauthorization issues. These issues were articulated and presented to the community through position papers and recommendations. Subcommittee hearings were then used as a platform to restate and reemphasize policy positions and recommendations. Finally, in considering how demands, interests, problems, and solutions were translated into the policy decisions that became the Higher Education Act of 1992, particular attention is given to the issues of direct loans and Pell Grant entitlements.

FORESHADOWING

Explicit in the sociology of translation is the view that policy decisions do not resolve policy issues but merely place those issues in black boxes that are invariably reopened. Any number of factors can lead to the reopening of these black boxes, but the primary factor is a growing awareness that problems continue to exist despite the apparent closure of policy issues. A review of chapters 2 and 3 shows that after each legislative decision on higher education policy a number of new problems/solutions began to bubble up and set the stage for a new cycle of policy decisions. While various events foreshadowed the Higher Education Act of 1992, the Higher Education Assistance Foundation (HEAF) crisis, the Nunn report, and the 1990 budget agreement were most important.

HEAF

HEAF was one of some fifty-five agencies that function as a form of middle management in the federal GSL programs. While all of the guarantor agencies performed similar functions, HEAF was distinguished from the other agencies because of its size its loan portfolio was more $9.6 billion in 1990 and by the fact that it was a national agency guaranteeing loans in several different states. Despite its size and range, HEAF lost $44 million in fiscal year 1989 and another $40 million through the first ten months of fiscal year 1990 (DeLoughry, 1990, August 1). When HEAF's problems became public in the summer of 1990, the higher education policy arena was shocked and feared that the HEAF crisis might undermine public support for a GSL program that had suffered a steady stream of criticism in the 1980s.

As the story gained attention, analysts blamed the HEAF crisis on poor management and on conflicting federal student aid policy goals. Many of HEAF's problems could be traced to its decision in the early 1980s to aggressively pursue loans made to proprietary school students. These loans, considered high risk because of the likelihood of student default, soon made up half of HEAF's portfolio (Pitsch, 1990). As the possibility of student defaults became reality, HEAF's loan default rate exceeded 5 percent, triggering federal rules that reduced the reimbursement rate to less than 100 percent of loan value. For some loans, HEAF was being reimbursed at just eighty cents on the dollar, thus creating a serious cash flow problem for the agency.

HEAF had managed to avoid problems created by its cash flow difficulties in previous years thanks to the rules of the student loan program and to loans from the Student Loan Marketing Association (Sallie Mae). Under the rules of the GSL programs, the federal government reimbursed HEAF at 100 percent of the value of its defaulted student loans when HEAF's default rate was less than 5 percent of its total volume of loans. At the beginning of each new academic year, when HEAF added to its total loan volume with new student loans, its overall default rate was reduced so that in October, the beginning of the federal fiscal year, the federal government would again reimburse the agency at 100 percent of the value of defaulted loans. In addition, HEAF had borrowed more than $800 million from Sallie Mae to help cover its cash flow problems. In August 1990, HEAF borrowed another $200 million, hoping to make it safely through the beginning of the academic year and on to the beginning of the new fiscal year (DeLoughry, 1990, August 8).

While its managers were certainly guilty of poor management, conflicting federal student aid policies added to HEAF's woes. Starting in the early 1980s, Congress attempted to reduce the public cost of federal student aid by emphasizing loans over grants. Many students, especially high-risk students, accepted loans as the only means available to pay for higher education. High-risk students who fail to graduate tend to default on their loans because they have no income and no skills to sell in the marketplace to earn an income. The default problem was compounded through abuses of the GSL programs by a number of schools in the proprietary sector. At the very time defaults and abuses were on the rise, the Education Department, under the leadership of William J. Bennett, was downsizing its oversight offices as part of the Reagan administration's plan to reduce the size of the Education Department. One proprietary school representative noted that Bennett heaped abuse on the proprietary sector but did nothing to help the sector eliminate the bad schools and actually made it easier for bad schools to exist by reducing the Education Department's ability to monitor and review institutions participating in GSL programs (Personal interview, October 19, 1990).

This view of Bennett was reinforced by a John B. Lee, a higher education consultant, who described the fracturing of what had been a cooperative relationship between the White House, the Congress, and the higher education community prior to Bennett's tenure as education secretary:

> [The] Bennett group didn't particularly care about education in an operational sense or how can they do a better job. . . . You had Bennett lofting bombs into the ACE homes and screaming at Kennedy and it was just amazing. It was kind of warfare. . . . And the bureaucrats in that situation just sort of put their heads down and sort of said, "This guy will leave town some day and I'm not going to say anything or do anything that's going to get me in trouble in the meantime." So . . . the Department of Education disappears, they're having their S&E, staff, and expenses budget being cut. And the OMB guys are saying, "Hey, we thought you guys would come back and argue. . . ." Well, they never did so that it cuts too close and all of a sudden there's no heart to the operation of the program. (Personal interview, February 24, 1992)

As the volume of defaulted loans increased, Congress decided to penalize agencies and institutions with high default rates rather than limit access to the loan program. It is difficult to see the logic of this approach since it did nothing to limit loans to high-risk students or deal with unscrupulous institutions that abused and defrauded the loan programs, but this is what Congress decided to do in the face of a growing volume of defaulted loans. It was this conflicting web of federal student aid policies, coupled with poor management, that put HEAF on the brink of bankruptcy in the summer of 1990.

Despite the loan from Sallie Mae and assurances by Education Secretary Lauro Cavazos that everything would be fine, the Education Department dissolved HEAF in October. Sallie Mae was given responsibility for overseeing the distribution of HEAF's $9.6 billion loan portfolio (DeLoughry, 1990, October 10). Tentative plans called for HEAF's loans and guarantor responsibilities to be divided among some twenty agencies. What had once been the nation's largest student loan guarantor had moved from financial crisis to historical artifact in a mere three months.

The Nunn Committee

Almost simultaneous with the HEAF collapse was the conclusion of the public hearings phase of the Nunn committee investigation of abuses in the federal student aid programs. The Nunn committee was a shorthand way to refer to the Senate Permanent Subcommittee on Investigations, chaired by Georgia Democrat Sam Nunn. While the subcommittee does not have higher education responsibilities, the chair is free to review programs of his choice. In the fall of 1989, Senator Nunn started an investigation of the federal student aid system with particular interest in the GSL program. Following a series of highly publicized hearings, the investigation concluded in the fall of 1990 while the subcommittee retired to write a report of its findings.

Part of Nunn's concern was the ever-increasing volume of loan defaults. While the net default rate had remained around 10 percent, the costs of defaults had risen from $263 million in fiscal year 1980 to $2.4 billion in fiscal year 1990 (Fraas, 1990). Put in different terms, default costs had risen from 16 percent of the cost of the GSL program in 1980 to 45 percent of the cost in 1990 (Fraas, 1990). Some part of the increasing volume of defaults can be attributed to the doubling in loan volume from 1983 to 1990, but during the same period loan defaults increased more than 300 percent, indicating that the default problem was not merely a function of program growth (Permanent Subcommittee, 1991).

Another part of the Nunn's concern about the GSL program was the sense that some schools in the proprietary sector were knowingly and actively engaged in fraud and abuse. This view was also held, and widely publicized, by former Secretary of Education Bennett, who accused trade schools of recruiting unprepared students who could not benefit from the training and who would be unable to repay the loans they had taken to enter school. Whatever the exact cause of the problem, proprietary school borrowers defaulted at a rate of nearly 40 percent compared to about 10 percent at four-year colleges (Fraas, 1990).

To focus attention on his concerns, Nunn organized the hearings around a series of case studies (Permanent Subcommittee, 1991). One case study focused on the American Career Training Corporation (ACT) of Pompano Beach, Florida. ACT combined a program of home study and campus study to prepare students for careers as secretaries and travel agents. The subcommittee found that ACT employed 23 faculty members, 169 commissioned sales representatives, and 70 financial aid staff. Enrollment contests for sales representatives helped generate more than $140 million in GSL program loans between 1985 and 1989. The revenues from rising enrollments were used to intensify recruitment efforts and to boost administrative salaries while instructor salaries and teaching resources remained static. As the availability of student loans grew, the tuition at ACT jumped from $1,295 in 1985 to $2,195 in 1989 with a concomitant increase in profits from an operating loss of $90,926 to a net profit of more than $3.8 million at the end of 1988.

A second case study centered on the Culinary School of Washington, D.C. (CSW). CSW was plagued by problems throughout its history, but maintained its GSL program eligibility. For example, the inspector general found that CSW was guilty of making numerous misrepresentations to students. In another example, a legal services lawyer representing former CSW students who had incurred loans of $8,000 in learning to be chefs reported that their training consisted of working in a water treatment plant cafeteria, without pay. CSW closed in 1990, but was able to accumulate a loan volume of $19 million during its eight years of existence. Despite numerous problems, CSW was still eligible to participate in the GSL program when it closed its doors.

The most publicized of the cases the Nunn committee examined was the collapse of the First Independent Trust Company (FITCO) of Sacramento, California. FITCO entered the student loan market in 1980 after the 1979 Technical Amendments to HEA created provisions encouraging lenders to make loans available to proprietary school students. By removing the ceiling on the special allowance that had been placed on loans to proprietary students, Congress opened a lucrative new market to lenders such as FITCO. In fact, FITCO and other lenders were not only presented with a new market, but with a guarantee that loans would be repaid plus a special allowance payment of 3.25 percent above the 91-day Treasury Bill rate as an incentive to participate in the GSL program.

FITCO entered the new market with gusto. It quickly became the largest GSL lender in California and by the late 1980s was the second largest GSL lender in the country. To increase its business, FITCO would quickly sell its loans, guaranteed by HEAF, to a secondary market, the California Student Loan Finance Corporation (CSLFC), thus clearing its books to generate new student loans. To give business still another boost, FITCO entered into an agreement with United Education and Software (UES). UES owned twenty-six schools in California, as well as a student loan servicing company. The school arm of UES used FITCO to originate loans to its students, while the servicing arm contracted with FITCO to service the same loans. Not satisfied with its level of participation in the GSL program, FITCO effectively lobbied for an amendment during the 1986 HEA reauthorization that waived the requirement that student loans make up no more than 50 percent of a lender's total loan portfolio. By the end of the 1980s, FITCO's lending operation had reached such a frenzied pace that student loans were often originated and then sold to CSLFC before the student's check could be processed and issued.

In 1989, California banking regulators shutdown FITCO. Among other problems, the lender was simply unable to keep up with the $1.5 billion in student loans that it had generated, primarily to proprietary students, over the course of the decade. Despite its collapse, FITCO denied any wrongdoing or any mistakes. Deno Evangelista, FITCO president, called the Nunn committee claims against his company "unbelievable" and blamed "everyone" for the problem except for FITCO, which was blameless (quoted in Myers, 1990, p. A29).

The Nunn committee did not produce new issues for the policy arena to consider, but rather sharpened the focus on existing issues before higher education policy actors could formally present their problem definitions/solutions. Some policy actors attempted to build on this opportunity to define issues before the policy arena could move toward reauthorization. Charles B. Saunders, ACE senior vice president, claimed that Nunn had "certainly zeroed in on the principal problem in the proprietary sector. I think this helps to make a stronger case for differentiating between the collegiate sector and the short-term vocational programs" (quoted in DeLoughry, 1990, October 17, p. A23). Others were more than content to save the issues for problematization within the higher education arena. David V. Evans,

Senator Pell's staff director, claimed that "the [student aid] program over all, works very, very well" and that the Nunn committee had merely publicized "sensational aberrations in the program" (quoted in DeLoughry, 1990, October 17, p. A28).

The Budget Agreement

The last foreshadowing event discussed here is the 1990 budget agreement. The purpose of the agreement was to reduce the federal budget deficit over a period of five years by limiting the movement of funds between budget accounts, restricting the creation of new entitlement programs, placing spending caps on budget accounts, and directing program savings toward deficit reduction (DeLoughry, 1990, November 7). In addition the federal budget was divided into three broad accounts: defense, domestic, and international. Spending walls, popularly known as fire walls, prohibited the transfer of funds between accounts unless the transfer was approved by a three-fifths majority in the Senate and by a two-thirds majority in the House (DeLoughry, 1992, April 25).

The immediate impact of the five-year budget agreement was to limit the flexibility and creativity of the higher education policy arena before the policy actors were able to consider reauthorization issues. The budget agreement also increased the possibility for conflict between the higher education policy arena and other policy arenas falling under the domestic account. Newton O. Cattell, Midwestern Universities Alliance director, summarized the possibility of increased conflict when he ironically stated it "will be fun, won't it, to see our health people fighting our student-aid people" (quoted in DeLoughry, 1990, November 7, p. A27).

In summary, the HEAF crisis, the Nunn committee, and the 1990 budget agreement helped set the stage for the reauthorization process by problematizing a range of issues that would be clearly focused and waiting when the formal reauthorization process started. Given the history of the policy arena, it is almost certain that issues such as accreditation, the loan-grant imbalance, program integrity, program review and oversight, separate student aid systems, and student loan default rates would have been issues during reauthorization, but now the issues were problemized and waiting for the higher education policy arena to act. Foreshadowing events merged with the beginning of reauthorization to give the policy-making process an ongoing or continuing sense rather than being a once every five year event.

Issues, problems, and solutions would not wait for the official start of reauthorization.

REAUTHORIZATION

The official start of the reauthorization process is usually marked by either the Education Department's request for comments on reauthorization or the first congressional hearings on reauthorization. While these might be accurate in a formal sense, a more appropriate beginning point is with the release of trial balloons by members of the higher education policy arena. Trial balloons serve the dual function of problematization and interessement as some policy ideas crash while others spark interest, support, and movement toward a policy idea. Virtually all members of the policy arena participated in launching trial balloons in a prelude to reauthorization that moved almost seamlessly into the formal reauthorization process.

One of the first came from ACE President Robert H. Atwell, who suggested that it was time to consider separate student aid systems for the traditional schools and the proprietary sector. Richard F. Rosser, NAICU president, gave support to Atwell's suggestion noting that "it may be you just have to write different regulations. These are for-profit institutions. The motivation is simply different" (quoted in Vobejda, 1989, p. A19). College and university presidents moved to support the idea for separate systems citing the need to protect students and the student aid system. Robert G. Bottoms (1990), DePauw University president, spoke for many campus leaders when he wrote "sure we need beauticians, but not at the expense of university education" (p. A23).

Viewing the proposal as a serious threat to its continued existence, the proprietary sector quickly organized a campaign to defeat any consideration of a two-track student aid system with separate funds and regulations for proprietary schools. NATTS started a $1 million grassroots media and lobbying campaign some two years before Congress scheduled the first hearings on HEA (Vobejda, 1989). Stephen Blair, NATTS president, defined the issue as one of making "sure that people have the choice to attend the school they want" (quoted in Vobejda, 1989, p. A19). From Blair's perspective, those who supported separate systems were guilty of elitism and a desire to exclude poor and minority students from higher education.

In the summer of 1990, several members of the policy arena used a special issue of *Educational Record* to float policy ideas and proposals.

Representative Pat Williams, then chair of the Subcommittee on Post-secondary Education, discussed the need to expand access to higher education by expanding aid to low and middle income students. Representative William F. Goodling, ranking Republican on the House Education and Labor Committee, identified the need to provide a balance in student aid packages between loans, grants, and other types of aid. Several members of Congress expressed a concern over loan default rates and the need to insure program integrity.

One the more interesting articles in the special issue was a panel discussion between David V. Evans of Senator Pell's staff, Richard T. Jerue of Representative Williams's staff, and D. Bruce Johnstone, chancellor of the State University of New York. Evans called for a fundamental change in the nature and structure of student aid programs under HEA. Jerue echoed Evans's call stating "that this has to be a bold reauthorization—one that looks at the programs much more critically than in the past" (Johnstone, Evans, & Jerue, 1990, p. 32). In response to the calls for bold, visionary changes in HEA, Johnstone defended the status quo. As the higher education representative on the panel, he emphasized that "what we must keep in our minds is that the programs, for all of their inadequate dollars and patchwork appearance, *do* work. The system may look a little funny, at least to the first time observer. But it is *not*, I submit, fundamentally broken. Let us fix it up" (Johnstone, Evans, & Jerue, 1990, p. 33). This difference over the level of change needed to move HEA into the next century established a pattern for reauthorization in which members of Congress and their staffs called for historic changes only to hear a timid response from the higher education associations.

This pattern was repeated at the January 1991 ACE annual meeting in San Francisco. At a session titled "Reauthorization of the Higher Education Act: Issues and Policies," congressional staff members Beth Buehlmann, Sarah Flanagan, Terry Hartle, and Tom Wolanin called on the higher education community to join with the Congress to produce an historic reauthorization that would form the foundation of student aid for the next century. The response from the audience and from higher education representatives on the panel was one of "Let's not be too hasty with change, and let's not change my program." At a session called "Improving Quality on Campus in the 1990s: Who Will Pay?," the message from panel members David Breneman, Art Hauptman, D. Bruce Johnstone, and Shelia Kaplan was equally cautious. Johnstone repeated his message of "Let us fix it up," while the other panel members questioned the need for any major changes in the current aid system. After the session, a University of California administrator said to the author that "if Bruce Johnstone doesn't have any new ideas, then there aren't any new ideas." The statement summarized the higher education community's reticence to enter into a dialogue with the Congress and the White House on rethinking the student aid system.

As Congress moved closer to the beginning of reauthorization, members increasingly floated their ideas for reauthorization to gauge response and interest. Among the most important of these were the ideas presented by William D. Ford, the new chair of both the House Committee on Education and Labor and the Subcommittee on Post-secondary Education. Like other members of Congress, Ford wanted more than a "reauthorization where we dust off the furniture and rearrange it" and called on the higher education community to "do a little bit different kind of thinking than they have been doing" (quoted in Cooper, 1991, p. A9). Ford also presented his own thinking for consideration and discussion within the policy arena. Among the ideas that Ford presented were a front-loading proposal, an end to the Perkins' loan program, consideration of a direct loan program, and expansion of aid to students from middle-income families. Finally, Ford made it absolutely clear that he would not support separate student aid programs. In his own words, "if we say that one kind of student is more worthy than another, then we will have a federal policy of class structure in post-secondary education that I am absolutely never going to support" (quoted in Cooper, 1991, p. A9).

Congress and the higher education associations were not the only participants in the prelude to reauthorization. In the fall of 1990, Education Secretary Cavazos announced that he would propose major changes in the shape and focus of HEA student aid programs (DeLoughry, 1990, October 3). Cavazos indicated a desire to link student aid to student academic achievement and to institutions' retention rates. In addition, Cavazos also expressed an interest in combining the various fellowship programs to form one consolidated program. Finally, he made it clear that the Bush administration would not support separate aid systems.

Two months after outlining his ideas, Cavazos was asked to resign. Reportedly, the reason for the resignation request was that Bush wanted to find a high-profile education secretary who could help him fulfill his promise to be the Education President (DeLoughry, 1990, December 19). Whatever the reason for Cavazos's departure, ideas continued to float out of the White House. In January 1991, an unnamed source told *The New York Times* that the administration was considering a direct loan proposal that would eliminate the role of lenders in the student loan programs (Pear, 1991). In September, President Bush urged colleges to demand a Pell Grant entitlement from Congress and to push for increased aid to low- and middle-income students ("Washington Update," 1991).

With both the Congress and the White House suggesting major changes, an historic reauthorization seemed possible. Commenting on the White House and Congressional roles, Tom DeLoughry, a writer for *The Chronicle of Higher Education*, believed that "we're looking at some bold ideas, and the tradition in education has been that the Congress outdoes anything that the administration wants. . . . [N]ow if the president's going to be an activist . . . and the president is talking about overhauling programs, there's going to be increased pressure on them to do major things rather than tinker" (Personal interview, February 28, 1992). John Dean, who represented the Consumer Bankers Association, was also enthusiastic suggesting that the Bush administration would send up legislation on all HEA titles and would "have dramatically more credibility than Reagan did. You know, Reagan would come in, you'd take a look at Title II, and let's see what we're going to do for libraries and it was X it out. Zero for the libraries" (Personal interview, January 11, 1991). The appointment of Lamar Alexander as education secretary only served to increase the sense that history was in the making.

Considering the ideas floated by the Congress and the White House during the prelude to reauthorization, historic change was not only possible but seemed highly probable as reauthorization approached. For the first time since 1972, plans for major program reform and restructuring, rather than marginal tinkering, appeared on the agendas of the primary policy actors. The only policy actors who appeared to be hesitant to embrace an agenda of change were the higher education associations. Comfortable with what they knew, the associations were reluctant to give up known programs for untested promises.

Position Papers and Recommendations

Trial balloons are part of the communications process within the higher education policy arena. The small size of the arena makes it easy for anyone to participate. To continue the balloon metaphor, one need not prepare for a trans-Atlantic flight because a simple hot-air balloon tethered to the ground is sufficient to float a proposal. Once in the air, proposals serve several purposes. One is to gauge support for policy proposals or ideas. Another is to identify how policy actors will line up around issues based on responses to trial balloons. By watching other actors' trial balloons, an actor can judge what to include in recommendations to the subcommittees. Finally, the information gained from trial balloons feeds into the formulation of position papers and recommendations that are presented to the subcommittees.

NASFAA

While the information gathered during the prelude feeds into the formulation of position papers and recommendations, most associations begin preparing for reauthorization a year or more in advance of the anticipated request for recommendations from the subcommittees. NASFAA's preparation for reauthorization is a good example of how long and complex a task it can be for a higher education association to reach the point of presenting recommendations to the subcommittees. A NASFAA representative explained the process noting that "[we] really began looking at reauthorization over a year ago. And a year ago, not last July [1990], but two years, when Kathleen McCullough, assumed the responsibility of coming in as the Chairman of our Board of Directors, we at that time had sat down and began to talk" (Personal interview, January 10, 1991). From these talks, it was agreed to appoint "a task force, a reauthorization task force, for NASFAA, to be in charge of developing and soliciting information to do our recommendations" (Personal interview, January 10, 1991).

Appointing a task force or working group to prepare recommendations for reauthorization is somewhat the norm for higher education associations, but NASFAA went beyond this to create a process that in many ways replicated what a congressional committee might do in terms of information gathering and oversight. As the representative explained,

> we set up a public hearing process . . . kind of paralleling what Congress does on oversight hearings. And we did that in each of our six [regional] meetings during the course of that year. In addition, we got invited to several state meetings . . . like California for example. California at their state meeting may have 800 to 900 people. . . . [W]e took testimony. . . . And so we got a lot of written statements and people came, and it's kind of a good learning experience too for them about how to testify and got through it. We held it like a hearing and gave certain time to scheduled people and so on and asked questions afterward. (Personal interview, January 10, 1991)

From this process, NASFAA identified three broad themes for reauthorization: simplicity, integrity, and rectifying the grant/loan imbalance. Rather than trust that it understood the recommendations and proposals that followed from these themes, NASFAA's leadership continued to test the themes, proposals, and recommendations with the membership. Prior to its 1990 annual conference, NASFAA published the themes and possible recommendations for the membership to consider then

> put those out just before our annual conference in Boston last year. And then at the annual conference what we did is we had, on one of the mornings we had kind of a panel discussion with some aid administrators, but also three or four other people that we had identified that had really been more in a policy arena looking at student aid matters. Bruce Johnstone . . . had been very involved in student aid. David Longanecker . . . Maureen McLaughlin . . . Martin Kramer . . . people like that . . . to kind of broaden the discussion, get kind of a point of view on some of these things and maybe some people to even challenge some of the assumptions and stuff beyond what we look at in the aid community. We had kind of a roundtable or kind of a panel discussion, open discussion, one morning for about an hour and a half, and kind of went through these key issues that we heard. And then we broke all of these people who were in attendance as conferees up into subgroups and just had for about another hour of just letting them talk about these issues and expressing some of the things and what they thought and their things. And we had kind of just simply did a pairing of numbers as they came in by assigning random numbers to people to do it so that we'd make certain that in any one group that it was going to have some cross-sectional kind of things . . . the task force people all set in to monitor the sessions, or somebody on our staff that was involved in it. And then we took those comments and then the task force took all of that material, compiled it, came up with tentative recommendations. We sent that out to the membership, got feedback one more time . . . put that together, and took the tentative recommendations to the Board of Directors. (Personal interview, January 10, 1991)

The final recommendations from this process were published in NASFAA's *Recommendations for Reauthorization* (May 1991). The recommendations in the NASFAA plan were designed to meet four goals:

1. That the model equitably target funds, especially to those with the lowest incomes;
2. That the process assure access to postsecondary education;
3. That the system be understandable; and
4. That the data required support accuracy.

When NASFAA representatives presented testimony at subcommittee hearings, they repeated the four goals over and over, as well as emphasizing that the goals and specific recommendations had emerged from a process that had maximized member participation.

ACE

Like NASFAA, ACE organized a task force effort designed to determine the problems and needs of the higher education community and to produce policy recommendations to address those issues. In the spring of 1989, ACE formed six task forces to review HEA provisions and identify reauthorization issues. While membership on the task forces was open to all Washington higher education associations who chose to participate, some felt more welcome than others, given ACE's attitude toward the proprietary sector. The six task forces and their chairs were: Needs Analysis and the Student Delivery System, chaired by NASFAA president Dallas Martin; Low-income Students, chaired by Edward Elmendorf, AASUC vice president for governmental relations; Middle-income Students, chaired by Julianne Still Thrift, NAICU executive vice president; Graduate and Professional Education, chaired by John Vaughn, AAU director of federal relations; Program Development, chaired by Clyde C. Aveihle, director of federal relations, California State University System; and Institutional Resources, chaired by Mary Jane Calais, NACUBO director of public policy and management programs.

As the task forces considered issues and recommendations, ACE made it clear that the process was one of gathering ideas and stimulating discussion. When ACE (1989) published its *Background Papers on HEA Reauthorization Issues*, the cover memo left little doubt that the "task force reports are preliminary: *their recommendations do not represent a consensus of the national associations. Rather, they identify issues and concepts for further consideration and debate*" (emphasis in original). While ACE attempted to send a clear message about the exact purpose and intent of the task forces, either the message was not as clear as ACE thought or else the message was not clearly received by all members of the higher education community.

For example, a United States Student Association (USSA) representative on a task force, felt that "ACE wanted to develop a community-wide consensus" through the task forces" (Personal interview, February 24, 1992). Unfortunately, ACE discontinued the task forces before a consensus could be achieved. One possible reason for this was that ACE had obtained all the information that it needed, thus the process no longer served a useful purpose. Whatever the reason, the USSA representative believed that the process had helped "bring the higher education community closer together" (Personal interview, February 24, 1992).

In contrast to the USSA representative, a NASFAA representative felt that the task forces got off to a great start, but was disappointed with the outcome of the process. As experienced by the representative

Charlie Saunders, through ACE and kind of the umbrella group of most of the associations, had kind of organized a series of some task forces to look at some specific areas. . . . [I]f you wanted to be on one of these, let Charlie know and you could join the group. . . . [T]he group that I was with, I think we had about 12 or 13 people. . . . We met several times. I think my group met about 10 or 11 times, and we really looked at those things under our charge. . . .

And . . . fed that back in through ACE to Charlie and so on. He kind of put that into a single piece, circulated it out again, and it went back basically to the presidential associations. The Big Six up there, and kind of shared amongst the Secretariat members to see what they were going to do. And the idea was as they would review it and chew on it, go through some things and at that time, as was laid out the plan, we were all going to . . . come back and then we would proceed now to kind of phase two which would be to get those groups to move on and try to answer those questions. . . . Well the first part of it went pretty well. It took longer than what Charlie had originally designed because the groups had trouble getting together because we're dealing with busy people. But nevertheless . . . we got it done, and it went into kind of a black hole. . . . The presidential groups looked at it, a bunch of people chewed on it, and that was kind of it. And we waited and waited and . . . well, to make a long story of it, not to be critical of anybody, but the bottom line is the groups never really got reconstituted. . . .

[T]here have been discussions amongst the six basic presidential associations. . . . [T]he six of them, both with the respective heads of those associations, and their chief governmental relations people, have met and have gone through a lot of that. And so they had a number of meetings on their own. But that has been a closed-door process to everybody else in the community, with a couple of exceptions. . . . [T]he presidential groups kind of decided that they were going to meet and get together and resolve their differences and stuff so they could have a more united front. They decided they should do that unto themselves.

I'm disappointed in it. Because I was really encouraged by how the process had started. I'm not saying that it's too late yet, and there's still time. . . . I just have to be frank about that because I think . . . what's trying to be done is that the decision with the input that they had is going to be a decision that's going to be decided on high, and then somewhat given back down to everyone else to say here it is, this is what you're supposed to kind of fall in and do. . . . ACE and the presidential associations view themselves as higher ed. (Personal interview, January 10, 1991)

Once the information flowed back into One Dupont Circle, the Big Six negotiated a basic set of policy recommendations that were acceptable to the participating associations. From this basic set of recommendations, ACE, consistent with its self-image as the lead association "to coordinate the formation of policy on the national issues and problems of higher education" (Bloland, 1985, p. 17), worked to forge a broad consensus. The end product of this process was a comprehensive set of recommendations for reauthorization that were submitted to the House and Senate subcommittees. Joining ACE in signing the recommendations to the subcommittees were the American Association of Community and Junior Colleges (AACJC), American Association of State Colleges and Universities (AASCU), Association of American Universities (AAU), Association of Catholic Colleges and Universities (ACCU), Association of Urban Universities (AUU), National Association for Equal Opportunity in Higher Education (NAFEOHE), National Association of College and University Business Officers (NACUBO), National Association of Independent Colleges and Universities (NAICU), National Association of Schools and Colleges of the United Methodist Church (NASCUMC), and the National Association of State Universities and Land-Grant Colleges (NASULGC).

While disappointing to some, the process did produce a set of recommendations acceptable to a broad cross section of higher education associations. Of these recommendations, the agreement on the Pell Grant formula was the most surprising. As discussed in earlier chapters, the formula has always been a difficult and sensitive issue for public and private institutions to resolve with each sector fearing the other might gain some undue advantage. As described by a NCHELP representative, this early agreement was far different from the traditional approach in which the "formulas for Pell are one of the last things studied, and Ford locks everybody in a room" to fight over the formula (Personal interview, February 25, 1992). Once an agreement is reached, you "crawl across the floor and scratch on the door" (Personal interview, February 25, 1992).

The proposed changes in the Pell Grant program balanced the needs of private and public institutions. First, the proposal recommended that the maximum award be increased from $2,400 to $4,000 and that annual increases be linked to the Consumer Price Index (CPI). In addition, the proposal altered the formula for determining individual Pell Grant awards to make the maximum award equal to $2,500 for living expenses plus 25 percent of tuition (not to exceed $1,500), minus the expected family contribution. Next, the proposal addressed middle income concerns by recommending a change in the formula to extend eligibility to families with annual incomes of up to $43,300. Finally, the Education Department would be required to borrow from the upcoming fiscal year whenever current-year Pell Grant funds were insufficient.

This proposal was designed to deal with the difficult problem of program entitlements. Under the budget agreement, new entitlements were extremely difficult to create. At the same time, key members of the subcommittees were pressing for a Pell Grant entitlement and expected support from the higher education associations to support their position. The ACE group was caught between the reality of the budget and pressure from political friends who had been helpful in the past and who would be important in the future. The borrow-ahead proposal was an inventive escape from a difficult position. The net effect of the proposal, if accepted, would be to transform the Pell Grant program into a functional entitlement without violating budget agreement restrictions on creating new entitlements.

UNCF

The United Negro College Fund (UNCF) engaged in a preparation process that was different from NASFAA and ACE, as well as being different from UNCF's traditional role. Part of what made UNCF's preparation different is that it is simply much smaller and more focused than ACE, NASFAA, and other broad based associations. This meant that when UNCF began working on its "reauthorization proposals more than a year ago [1989], both our governmental affairs committee and our 41-member institutional presidents . . . directly participated in the development of our reauthorization proposals" (William Blakey, personal interview, February 26, 1992).

UNCF's recommendations were different from its more traditional approach because

> in an unusual and historical way UNCF made a conscious decision not to stay within the four corners of what had historically been the interests of historically black colleges. That is they went outside Title III and Title IV in particular and made recommendations affecting their institutions and the career and post-graduate, in particular, aspirations of African-Americans and other minority groups. In a sense, that sort of caught the rest of the higher education community by surprise and/or they simply ignored those recommendations. At the staff level and at the presidential level, however, an intensive effort was made to identify issues and individuals in Congress who were interested in those issues to . . . carry UNCF's water in the reauthorization process . . . for example, like Paul Simon, like Eleanor Holmes-Norton, and Congressman Charles Hayes, who were interested in issues and pulling together not just UNCF schools but other schools in our black college family to move things along. (Blakey, personal interview, February 26, 1992)

The planned interaction between UNCF and the subcommittees might have been more sophisticated than was the case with other associations, but every major association engaged in bidirectional lobbying with the subcommittees. Bidirectional lobbying is used to describe communication between the associations and subcommittees in which each attempts to interest and enroll the other in support of its problematization. William Blakey, who represented UNCF during the reauthorization, explained that this is especially important for an association because once a member takes "on the issue as his or hers you're more than halfway home at that juncture because then you have somebody, both staff and member, who is involved in the process who in effect becomes your advocate . . . they advocate for what is not your program any more; it's his program" (Personal interview, February 26, 1992). The members and their staffs also lobby the associations to take certain positions so that they can then claim it is not a member's personal interest, but the public will that is being served by a policy proposal. A NCHELP representative expressed fascination and amazement over the fact "that there are lots of articles and things about lobbies . . . but . . . never an ounce of attention to the way Congress uses lobbies" (Personal interview, February 25, 1992).

Bidirectional lobbying takes many forms and serves a variety of purposes. One purpose is as source of information about what is going on in the field or within the subcommittee. A NCHELP representative described a process in which members and staffs "cross-check us against each other . . . someone comes in with a tale of woe or a tale of luck, you check it out with someone else whose opinion you respect" (Personal interview, February 25, 1992). For the associations, its "a reality check to make sure that we don't go off on a tangent where we think this makes sense and nobody else does . . . it's a dynamic situation, what we hear backs into the position we take" (Roschwalb, personal interview, February 27, 1992).

While association representatives, subcommittee members, and subcommittee staffs are aware of their participation in bidirectional lobbying, it is not thought of as lobbying. Instead, it is described in terms of communicating policy positions, information sharing, or normal conversation. Bidirectional lobbying is thought of as a conversation or an exchange of information rather than as a form of lobbying. This can be seen in the description provided by a NASFAA representative:

> I was at a dinner meeting last Friday with Paul Simon and a small group of people [who] wanted to talk about kind of setting the agenda and talking about some things and what we were thinking of—sharing with us what some of his thoughts were of the upcoming reauthorization. Now he's very optimistic, thinks this is a time for really big initiatives, thinks we've got a chance to really go forward and so on. But you know he was not only asking us what we see as some of the issues and things that concern us and the things we'll

be dealing with, but he shared with us some of the things he wants.

In talking to staff people . . . , they sometimes just share with you some little issues or things that maybe they have picked up from the boss, or they sometimes find out a little additional kind of things that are kind of out there, you know, and if you know somebody that kind of has an interest in this section or that, it's always a good idea, because as we begin to go through this you kind of get an idea then, and okay, well, maybe can I begin to help support this, or how can I get information to do something. . . . Well, it's helpful to us if you know [what] somebody's thinking about . . . on the subcommittee. . . . That's probably something you want to know.

So when you have these kind of discussions sometimes it's good, and in these kind of informal ways . . . you get a chance to talk about this to kind of at least say, Well what about this. . . . And its better to do those kind of conversations and to find out what people are thinking and stuff, if you can, one-on-one. (Personal interview, January 10, 1991)

The extent of bidirectional lobbying within the policy arena means that position papers and recommendations are a product of mutual shaping rather than the product of an individual association. In the ACE, NASFAA, and UNCF examples, the proposals were first shaped by internal negotiations as the associations attempted to fashion positions acceptable to their members. As proposals took form, they were then discussed with subcommittee members and staffs to create a set of policy recommendations with a chance of being translated into legislation. The recommendations the associations submitted to the subcommittees were the mutually shaped and tested product of the larger community of higher education policy actors.

Hearings

Like position papers, subcommittee hearings serve multiple purposes for policy actors. First, the hearings are an opportunity to restate and reemphasize problematizations offered earlier in the process. Second, the hearings are an opportunity to interest and enroll policy actors in support of particular positions. Finally, the hearings serve the goal of mobilization by giving policy actors specific activities and responsibilities to carry out in support of problematizations.

The hearings also serve the needs and interests of subcommittee members. For example, a subcommittee member with a certain program interest or policy goal can schedule a witness to reinforce her/his position. The hearings are also an opportunity for subcommittee members to be featured in their district or state. By bringing a congressional subcommittee hearing home, the member can show the voters how he/she is working to represent their interests and needs in Washington. Finally, by going into the field, the members demonstrate an interest and responsiveness to the voice of the people.

While the hearings are important for all of the above reasons, their value is often discounted because they are scheduled and controlled by the subcommittee staff. Still, as one higher education representative noted, it is impossible to control everything and it is certainly impossible to predict the public impact of a witness. For example, Representative Ford

had the greatest hearing ever done in education out at Oberlin. . . . [A]fter two or three people, the president of the campus spoke, he said that we have to take a few minutes break to set up for the next hearing, which sounded bizarre to start with, and a bunch of heavy, big guys, campus football types, wheeled in a Steinway, right smack in the middle of the hearing room. And then a young man was called up, from the Cleveland ghetto, scared, very unsure of himself, and he was introduced as his testimony, he was going to perform the testimony, the kid sat down and played the Polonaise, Chopin Polonaise, brilliantly. And the usual . . . he spoke for just a couple of minutes, he was asked questions. He has no money, his family has no money, he's there because he's got a Pell grant, he's got his work-study, he's got his loan, he's got the university putting up a lot of money for him, and that was the best piece of testimony about student aid ever. And if you want to see it, the notes are in the book. (Roschwalb, personal interview, January 10, 1991)

While some witnesses do have this type of impact, the primary role of the hearings is to restate, reemphasize, and reinforce positions presented earlier in the reauthorization process. To do this, associations often present witnesses from different levels of the organization and from the field. ACE, NASFAA, NASCLGU, and other groups sent multiple witnesses to the hearings insuring that their views on problems and solutions would be repeated several times for subcommittee members and other members of the policy arena to hear. For example, Robert Atwell, John Brademas, Thomas Ehrlich, Edward M. Elmendorf, José R. Gonzalez, Reginald Wilson, and others presented testimony on issues of interest to One Dupont Circle associations. NASFAA witnesses include Natala K. Hart, Elizabeth Hicks, Dallas Martin, and others. NATTS was represented by Stephen J. Blair but also brought in a number of representatives from the field, including students, to demonstrate, in human terms, the value of proprietary school education to the individual, the community, and the nation. Finally, Jean S. Frohlicker presented testimony for NCHELP, but representatives of loan programs from throughout the nation also testified, perhaps as a reminder to subcommittee members of the economic importance of the GSL program.

While the primary role of the hearings was one of renewed emphasis on established positions, the hearings helped give a real boost to the United States Students Association's (USSA) status as a policy actor. Historically, student groups have not been major policy actors, but this changed when USSA was given responsibility for organizing a hearing at which students would tell subcommittee members what the programs were like from a student perspective. The student group "was given unprecedented freedom" in organizing the joint hearing "because members of the House and Senate subcommittees were so interested in hearing from the students" (DeLoughry, 1991, March 27, p. A23). The only restriction placed on USSA was that one student had to be from Connecticut, the home of Senator Christopher J. Dodd who was to chair the hearing. The association was wise enough to bring representatives from a variety of schools including Rhode Island and Michigan institutions.

The Chronicle of Higher Education reported that the students had provided Congress with "gripping testimony about how inadequate aid had forced them to eat food donated by friends, to sell blood for cash, and to take out large loans" (DeLoughry, 1991, March 27, p. A23). Senator Dodd credited the witnesses with being "about as eloquent as any one of us has heard, regardless of how long we've served" (quoted in DeLoughry, 1991, March 27, p. A24). Representative Ford urged them to continue the good fight noting that "I'm not advocating burning any campuses or shutting them down, but if it's necessary, I'm not telling you shouldn't" (quoted in DeLoughry, 1991, March 27, p. A23). Finally, Sarah Flanagan, a member of Senator Pell's staff, claimed that the students had "set the tone of the priorities of the reauthorization" (quoted in Schonberger, 1991, p. A1).

The hearing helped increase USSA's political capital and to earn it the label of Bill Ford's favorite higher education group. Being tabbed as Ford's favorite lobbying group had a number of pluses and a few minuses for USSA. On the plus side, USSA found that it was much easier to get into congressional offices to present their positions on reauthorization. Acceptance from other higher education associations increased and USSA was invited to participate in ACE's Friday meetings, but still remained outside the communications loop of the Secretariat. On the minus side, USSA ran into the criticism that can come from being too successful in Washington. A CCA representative claimed that USSA only had influence because "Bill Ford loves that little thing that is their lobbyist and thinks that she can do no wrong. If Ford didn't have a relationship with her, then USSA would not be powerful" (Personal interview, February 25, 1992). Despite USSA's success with the hearing, the association was also criticized for not doing much with student testimony and not taking advantage of its base.

If USSA was the surprise star of the hearings, then the Bush administration was the major disappointment. Coming into the hearings, the administration had sent a number of messages indicating its intent to be a major player in the reauthorization process and to propose fundamental changes in the HEA programs. The appointment of Lamar Alexander as education secretary reinforced the notion that the administration would enter into a serious dialogue with Congress and higher education policy actors to fashion major changes in higher education policy. A different message was delivered during the hearings.

On Thursday, April 11, 1991, Lamar Alexander presented the administration's vision of higher education policy for the 1990s to the Senate Subcommittee on Education, Arts and the Humanities. After presenting a brief historical perspective of the federal role in higher education, Alexander identified the themes that should guide the reauthorization process. The three primary themes that would drive the administration's proposals were: "(1) improving access to post-secondary education for all Americans, (2) improving educational quality and rewarding excellence, and (3) ensuring integrity and improving service delivery in all HEA programs" (Alexander, 1991, p. 5). The proposals that flowed from these themes included increasing the size of the Pell Grant awards by reducing the number of eligible participants; a merit based award of up to $500 for high-achieving Pell Grant recipients, to be called the Presidential Achievement Scholarship program; an increase in GSL limits so that students could borrow

33 percent more in the first year and 25 percent more in each subsequent year; sharing the risk of student loan defaults with the states; an early intervention program; and, collapsing all graduate fellowships into one program to be called National Graduate Fellowships. Finally, the administration, which had suggested replacing GSL with a direct loan program, had no proposal on alternatives to GSL, but Alexander promised to keep the subcommittees informed.

For Democrats on the subcommittees, Alexander's testimony was not a vision of the future, but a rerun of the past. Virtually all of the administration's proposals had been presented previously during the Reagan and Bush administrations and had been rejected by the Congress. Tom Wolanin observed that the White House was a player only to the extent that Congress had forced it to be a player by demanding recommendations at the front end of the process (Personal interview, May 7, 1992). Before the hearings ended, administration representatives would testify thirteen times, but this was primarily because the subcommittees had scheduled and demanded testimony. On the Senate side, Robert Shireman, a member of Simon's staff, described the White House role as one of "too little, too late" (Personal interview, May 5, 1992). The administration lacked a clear agenda for reauthorization. If the administration had a clear agenda, then it was known only to them and never communicated to the Senate subcommittee (Shireman, personal interview, May 5, 1992).

The change in the administration's position, or at least in the congressional perceptions of its position, was rather vexing to Republicans on the subcommittees. For many Republicans, HEA was the opportunity to make good on Republican education claims on the eve of an election. The difference between the White House and House Republicans was explained by a Republican staff member, who described the Bush administration as having "very different ideas about education" which often puts them at odds not only with the Democrats, but also with Republicans (Personal interview, May 6, 1992). The staffer noted that "Coleman and Goodling always listen, but seldom act on the administration's agenda because it is not consistent with their view of education" (Personal interview, May 6, 1992). Another Republican staff member was more blunt in describing the president as the "no man" (Personal interview, May 6, 1992). This was very frustrating for Republicans because instead of receiving positive leadership and direction from the White House they could only learn what the administration was against. When asked by Republicans to communicate an agenda, the president became the "I don't know man" who could not explain what the administration stood for in reauthorization. A Senate staffer offered a more charitable Republican view of the administration, suggesting that it merely had "a very limited agenda" (Personal interview, May 4, 1992).

Part of the disappointment with the administration might have come from the unrealistic expectation generated by the appointment of Alexander. Phrases such as "political savvy," "forceful," and "strong and assertive leader" were so often used with Alexander's name that one might have thought that these were his middle names. Whatever attributes he might have brought to the job, Alexander could not live up to the expectations generated by his appointment. A primary reason underlying his inability to meet expectations was that he never became involved in a discourse with the Congress, the higher educa-tion associations, and other higher education policy actors over the future of higher education policy. A higher education policy arena participant suggested that the lack of involvement and interaction with policy arena participants might have been because "the secretary himself didn't, didn't really want this to be his number one priority. I mean, when ever we asked him what his priorities were, he would say America 2000 and the higher ed act. And I think there was a long way between one and two because he was traveling every week to a different America 2000 state and leaving the higher ed stuff to people at home" (Personal interview, February 28, 1992).

Whatever the reasons for the administration's and Alexander's failure to meet expectations, the result was tremendous frustration and disappointment among policy arena participants. William Blakey might well have spoken for the majority of policy arena participants with his observation that

the secretary, or the president, or whomever, I think made critical mistakes. One, they put out their time and effort, . . . into their America 2000 proposal which was off-cycle and unresponsive. I mean it was what they wanted to do. There's no hew and cry out there in the nation about having the federal government tell the states and local jurisdictions what to do about their schools. . . . [S]o America 2000 has ended up being a gigantic public relations exercise and by and large a failure to the extent that they spent their time and energy on that and not on the thing that Congress was working on, they missed the boat.

[Alexander has] made some missteps and I think signif-icant ones. One, he's on the wrong train in terms of America 2000, that's not the train that's due into the station. It's not the one anyone wants to ride on. And then on the issues on which he has been involved in higher education issues, minority scholarships, and the Middle States diversity controversy in particular, he's wrong. . . . It's hard to say because I have a jaded perspective. My perspective is I had very, very, very, very great expectations of him. He was the first secretary of education and the first secretary who has been the chief steward for education since Joe Califano, who had the kind of respect and clout within the administration—who could have done some real good during his tenure. He could have made George Bush a real Education President. And I would say virtually by almost every measure, he has blown it. (Personal interview, February 26, 1992)

The hearings concluded what Ken Holdsman, a member of Andrew's staff, termed the first step in the policy-making process. A step that Holdsman defined as a information gathering "a wide-open process, a two-way street with information going back and forth" (Personal interview, May 4, 1992). The information gathering phase of the policy process included more than sixty Congressional hearings and involved more than 500 witnesses. When the hearings started, an historic reauthorization seemed a real possibility, but the prospect of fundamental change was much more distant after the hearings. The Bush administration had offered a set of proposals that had been rejected once by the Congress while the higher education associations recommended a continuation of existing programs with some incremental changes at the margins. If history was to be made, then it would have to be made by the subcommittees in the drafting of the reauthorization legislation.

FROM MARKUP TO PASSAGE

As the two subcommittees moved from gathering information to writing legislation, the unique traditions of the two sides of Congress and the personalities of the subcommittee members combined to produce quite different approaches to the bill writing process. The House side was open to continuing participation and scrutiny by higher education policy actors. While it was open, Representative Ford and Staff Director Wolanin drove the process in general and the drafting of legislation in particular. A participant at the subcommittee level attributed about 90 percent of the bill to Ford, Wolanin, and the subcommittee staff (Personal interview, May 4, 1992). The process incorporated ideas that were originated by other members as long as a member's proposal was not in conflict with what another member wanted.

The personalities of the House also helped shape the way the bill writing process unfolded. In discussing Wolanin, a policy arena participant suggested "he could sit there writing the bill in the middle of a hurricane if everybody was circling around him yelling at him" (Personal interview, February 28, 1992). As the process of writing the legislation moved forward, "he continued to talk to them, you know, to give some idea of what he wanted" (Personal interview, February 28, 1992). AASCU's Barmak Nassirian cautioned that differences in appearances are not the same as differences in practice noting that in the end "Wolanin is not necessarily any less flexible once he makes up his mind than than Dave Evans, nor is Mr. Ford any less autocratic than Mr. Pell " (Personal interview, February 28, 1992).

In contrast to the more open, free-wheeling style of the House, the Senate subcommittee took a closed door approach to writing the reauthorization bill. The subcommittee divided the work process into tiers (Personal interview, May 4, 1992). The first tier of work was based on the information and data collected from the hearings. This was organized into side-by-sides of the original language and alternative language suggested by policy actors. The task of transforming this into a bill was taken on by Hatch, Kassebaum, Kennedy, and Pell's staff members. The four staffs worked out all of the noncontroversial issues and then cleared the agreements with the full subcommittee. If the agreement was acceptable to the full subcommittee, then that section of the bill was completed. If agreement could not be reached by the four staffs or cleared by the full subcommittee, then the sticking point was given to the entire subcommittee staff to resolve. This represented a second tier of work in which the subcommittee staffs attempted to resolve the sticking point. If this failed, then the point of disagreement was sent to the subcommittee members for their resolution. The purpose of this organization of work was to produce a bill that could be signed by all of the subcommittee members.

As in the House, personalities were important in the Senate and helped shape the bill writing. One of the key personalities in this regard was David V. Evans. One participant described Evans as a person who would say, "You told me what you wanted, now get out of here and let me write the bill. I can't be bothered with you people" (Personal interview, February 28, 1992). The Senate approach to writing the bill certainly mirrored this observer's impression of Evans.

The difference between the House and the Senate approaches reflects different histories and traditions. The Senate is much smaller than the House, thus collegial development of legislation is important not just for the sake of reaching agreement today, but for the operation of the body tomorrow. Blakey who had worked on both sides of Congress observed "they don't function alike, the Founding Fathers didn't intend for them to function alike. . . . [P]eople who expect the Senate to function like the House misunderstand the difference. . . . [T]here are a lot of people in this town who do misunderstand the difference" (Personal interview, February 26, 1992).

The description of the House as open and the Senate as closed should not obscure the fact that higher education policy actors were afforded considerable opportunity for input. Policy actors continued to send information, offer advice, and have representatives from the field contact subcommittee members even as the bills were being drafted. As the subcommittees drafted the bills, the members and their staffs had the recommendations of policy actors in front of them in the form of the "side-by-sides." Finally, the position papers, recommendations, and testimony of policy actors were available for review.

More important than the differences in style and approach were the policy issues considered by the subcommittees. If this was to be a historic reauthorization, then it would turn on the issues of direct loans and Pell Grant entitlement. Failure to deal with issues that could be distinguished in a word or phrase would mean that reauthorization was "going to be viewed as tinkering because beyond the beltway, nobody's going to be able to explain what the hell it was that was done" (Blakey, personal interview, February 26, 1992). How the subcommittees dealt with these issues is the focus of the remainder of this chapter.

The Pell Grant Program

As the subcommittees met to write the respective bills, a wide range of alternatives were available. One of the prime alternatives was the Pell Grant proposal presented by the higher education associations. As noted above, this proposal met the needs of the major higher education associations as well as meeting the stated goals of Chairmen Ford and Pell. Specifically, the proposal met the goals of increasing aid to middle-income students, increasing the size of individual awards, and providing the Pell Grant program with a de facto entitlement status.

The Bush administration also presented a Pell Grant proposal, but its proposal is more difficult to summarize because the proposal kept changing and because the administration simultaneously pursued changes through the budget process and the reauthorization process. In early 1991, the administration proposed major changes in the Pell Grant program as part of its budget recommendations. These came prior to Alexander's reauthorization testimony and closely followed former Education Secretary Cavazos's recommendations from late 1990. The budget called for increasing individual awards from $2,300 to $3,700, decreasing the number of middle-income participants, denying grants to students in the bottom 10 percent of their college classes, and creating a $500 Presidential Achievement Scholarship for Pell Grant recipients in the top 10 percent of their high school class or in the top 20 percent of their college class (DeLoughry, 1991, February 13). By targeting the neediest students, the administration claimed that its proposals would decrease loan defaults by increasing grants to high risk students. Finally, the administration projected that 227,000 low-income students would be drawn into higher education by the larger Pell Grant awards.

Like Cavazos' proposals in the Fall and Alexander's recommendations that followed, the Pell Grant changes in the budget proposal were dead on arrival. The administration seemed to be unaware of the changes its proposal would cause in a policy arena that placed a high premium on equal treatment of and balance between the different higher education sectors. If accepted, the administration proposals would have provided "a windfall for trade schools" (DeLoughry, 1991, January 23, p. A22). This provoked a considerable outcry from segments of the higher education community that would be adversely affected by the shift in grant aid. When the administration realized the impact of its proposals, it suggested limiting aid to trade school students by calculating grant aid based on community college costs (DeLoughry, 1991, February 13). In doing this, the administration violated the policy arena's principle of equal treatment of sectors, thus prompting almost as much criticism as the original proposal. In addition, the proposal would have reduced the number of Pell Grant recipients by some 627,000 students. This ran counter to the expressed desires of Ford, Pell, and other subcommittee members to expand grant aid to middle income students. While referring only to the fellowship segment of the budget proposal, Jerold Roschwalb of NASULGC could well have summarized the policy arena's feelings about the entire package when he called the proposals "a strange goulash" that did not stand "a snowball's chance in hell" (quoted in DeLoughry, 1991, February 13, p. A26).

In brief, Roschwalb was right. Congress rejected the administration's recommendations and waited for the subcommittees to come forward with reauthorization legislation. The House subcommittee passed its bill on October 8, 1991. On a straight party line vote, the subcommittee approved a bill that included generous changes in the Pell Grant program (Zuckman, 1991 October 12). The House version of the Pell Grant formula provided a base award of $2,750 for living expenses plus 25 percent of tuition up to $1,750 in 1994–95. In subsequent years, the grant would increase based on changes in the Consumer Price Index (CPI). Finally, the program would become an entitlement, thus mandating full funding at the authorized level.

The Pell Grant proposal drew heavy criticism from Republicans who claimed that the cost of the entitlement placed the bill on a "collision course" with the president (Zuckman, 1991, October 12, p. 2958). Emblematic of the administration's confusion over its education policy, President Bush had called on colleges to push Congress to make the Pell Grant program an entitlement and to expand aid to middle-income students approximately one month before the House subcommittee recommended legislation to do just that ("Washington Update," 1991). Of greater concern to Ford, than Bush and the House Republicans, were the reservations of House Democrats William H. Natcher and Leon E. Pannetta. In their respective positions on the appropriations and budget committees, they would decide which programs met the test of the budget agreement and the actual level of funding.

The Senate subcommittee bill quickly followed the House bill. The Senate bill provided a Pell Grant formula with a base award of $2,300 for living expenses plus 25 percent of tuition up to $1,300 in 1993–94. After that, the maximum would increase each year to reach $4,800 in 1999–2000. Drawing from the Big Six proposal, the Senate bill required the education secretary to borrow ahead to meet full funding needs in a current year. Finally, the program would become an entitlement in 1997–98 after the budget agreement had expired, thus avoiding any obstacles created by the agreement.

In response to the House and Senate bills, the administration threatened to veto any legislation that contained a Pell Grant entitlement. The veto threat came in a letter from Alexander to the committee members (DeLoughry, 1991, October 30). Chairman Ford strongly defended the bill, claiming it was "the first bold step this committee has taken in a decade to assert the importance of education" (quoted in DeLoughry, 1991, October 30, p. A27). Citing the uniform support of both public and private institutions for the House Pell Grant formula, Ford declared it to be "either the glue that holds this whole thing together or the Plastique that blows the thing apart" (quoted in DeLoughry, 1991, October 30, p. A30).

Chairman Ford's resistance to any change in the Pell Grant formula despite the reservations of two key Democrats, the obstacle of the budget agreement, the opposition of House Republicans, and a promised veto puzzled members of the policy arena. One participant suggested that Ford could be setting "things up in a way where he can lose what he's proposed, but still win more than he would have without proposing those things. . . . [H]e is very, very smart and has been around a long time and I won't be surprised if that's what he is doing" (Personal interview, February 28, 1992). Still, there were doubts given "that he is 64 years old, he has been doing this for 20 something years, this may be his last reauthorization. He still has a burn in his stomach from the last reauthorization where he felt like it was a waste of time. . . . [I]t may very well be that during this process, as it's gone on, the political reality has gone the other way" (Personal interview, February 28, 1992).

In contrast, Barmak Nassirian had no question about what was happening to Ford's political perspective. Nassirian believed "that Ford is losing touch with reality on this one" (Personal interview, February 27, 1992). The higher education community "always thought Ford was the savvy one who . . . understands realpolitik and knows what can and cannot be done," but as the process wore on there was less certainty about Ford's political savvy (Nassirian, personal interview, February 27, 1992). It seemed as if he might be heading into an unwinnable political showdown with Bush that could seriously disrupt and delay the flow of federal aid to students and institutions.

What was actually happening is that Ford was carrying out the policy decision of the House Democratic leadership. The Democrats wanted a higher education bill that would distinguish them as the "Education Party," while demonstrating that Bush was shallow and uncommitted to the issue. Ford, who had been in a defensive position during most of the Reagan-Bush years, needed little encouragement to go on the offensive. Working with a sense of history, Ford and the Democrats on the subcommittee drafted a generous bill with significant funding increases and several new programs. Ford forced a partisan bill through the subcommittee and committee despite opposition from Republicans and the threat of a presidential veto. Having done this, he looked to the Democratic leadership to help him push the bill through the House.

Due to concerns about the entitlement provisions and program cost, Ford had trouble obtaining cosponsors for HEA. To Ford's dismay and disappointment, the leadership's rhetoric was stronger than its action. While the leadership had encouraged Ford to write the bill, it did not support him by putting pressure on members to get in line behind the Democratic agenda. As the possibility for conflict over HEA grew, the House leadership became increasingly uncomfortable with the idea of a showdown with the administration. The leadership wanted Ford to use HEA to clearly delineate differences and distinctions, but was unwilling to accept the conflict that the challenge would bring.

In February 1992, House Speaker Thomas S. Foley publicly withdrew the leadership's support for making the Pell Grant program an entitlement. Speaking at NAICU's annual conference, Foley withdrew the support stating "that does not mean the program does not have strong support. We will demonstrate a strong commitment to Pell Grants in any event and increase resources" (quoted in "Ways & Means," 1992 February 12, p. A23). Without having consulted Ford, Foley had announced a major policy change on HEA. Wolanin summarized the leadership's behavior by stating this "leadership is pathetic" (Personal interview, May 7, 1992). In a private meeting with the leadership, Ford vented his anger, but Pell Grant entitlement was dead in the House.

In the Senate, Chairman Pell withdrew the provision for an entitlement to insure that the bill would pass with strong support. The Senate version of the Pell Grant entitlement had been designed to capture conservative support by placing the entitlement beyond the budget agreement expiration date. To be successful in its bid to capture conservative votes, the committee needed to generate lots of contacts by presidents of institutions to lots of senators. When the contacts failed to materialize, the window of opportunity on Pell Grant entitlement closed.

Staff members in the House and Senate blamed the failure to obtain a Pell Grant entitlement on a number of factors. A major factor was the administration's position on Pell. Once the administration failed to convince either the House or the Senate to adopt its proposals, it simply ceased to participate in the negotiations. In place of a dialogue aimed at problem solving, the administration constructed a roadblock promising to veto any bill with a Pell Grant entitlement, without offering an alternative for agreement or negotiation. This position, coupled with the retreat of the House leadership, virtually ended any hope of an entitlement.

Despite this, subcommittee staff members believed that an entitlement might have been possible if the higher education associations had put their full effort behind the cause. The view from the House was that "the associations never gave Pell entitlement the same priority that the committee did nor did they ever really buy into it" (Wolanin, personal interview, May 7, 1992). Instead, "the associations complained about what was in the bill without voicing support for Pell Grant entitlement" (Wolanin, personal interview, May 7, 1992). Because of this, it was "difficult to build support in the House for the idea since members could respond by noting that it was not important to the associations" (Wolanin, personal interview, May 7, 1992). In addition, "the associations never organized their campus presidents to call House members in support of Pell Grant entitlement" (Wolanin, personal interview, May 7, 1992).

In the Senate, "the associations never bought into and supported the proposal" for a Pell Grant entitlement (Senate staff, personal interview, May 6, 1992). Instead of supporting Pell, the associations "became obsessed with" institutional integrity (Personal interview, May 6, 1992). The associations could have complained about institutional integrity and still supported the entitlement. What they did was elect to "represent the interest of institutions over the interest of poor kids. This was very clear in their decision to abandon Pell Grant entitlement and spend time on state licensing" (Personal interview, May 6, 1992).

While the final legislation contained a Pell Grant formula that looked very much like the Big Six recommendation, the higher education associations cannot be considered winners in the struggle over the Pell Grant formula. Their failure to support an entitlement angered many congressional members and staff members. The associations were left with considerable fence mending to do over the entitlement issue. This can be seen in a staffer's musing:

> For the most part, we are kind to the associations. In D.C., you never know when you might need a job. We sometimes think what would we do if our member died or was not reelected. If that happened, then we might have to go to work for an association. That thought makes you realize that death is a reasonable alternative in some circumstances. (Senate staff, personal interview, May 6, 1992)

Direct Loans

The concept of direct loans is not a new idea in the higher education policy arena. Milton Friedman is credited with introducing the concept as early as 1945 (Bluestone & Comcowich, 1992). The basic concept is a simple one: students receive loans from the government to pay for higher education and then repay those loans after graduation with the repayment schedule being contingent on income. Robert Reischauer, director of the Congressional Budget Office (CBO), has championed the idea since the 1960s (Pear, 1991). In 1988, as a senior fellow at the Brookings Institution, Reischauer proposed a federal trust fund from which students could borrow and then repay the loan through their payroll taxes. Proponents of the concept were also able to cite federal experience with the concept of direct student loans. The NDSL program discussed in chapter 2 is one example of direct student loans while the Perkins loan program is still another.

The idea of "study now, pay later," or income contingent loans, already existed as a pilot program when a direct loan proposal was floated by the Bush administration (Byron, 1992, p. A23). Education Secretary Bennett had successfully pushed the Income Contingent Loan (ICL) program during the Reagan administration and the pilot was still running (DeLoughry, 1991, August 7). The reasoning behind the 10 school, $21 million pilot was that students making small, income contingent payments would be less likely to default and would not be deterred from entering low paying careers by the specter of large loan payments looming just beyond graduation. The Bush administration endorsed the program and asked that it be continued and expanded. In contrast, higher education officials opposed the program and recommended its extinction.

While neither new nor untested, a confluence of factors created an impetus for serious consideration of direct loans as an alternative to the GSL program. One factor was the continuation of high loan default costs despite different efforts to control rising GSL program costs. The HEAF crisis and the Nunn committee had focused national attention on the problem of defaults. The feeling in Congress was that the public was being robbed by defaulters while honest students were being denied the chance to attend college. This point was driven home with considerable force when the Nunn committee report predicted the "ultimate collapse" of the GSL program (quoted in DeLoughry, 1991, May 22, p. A25). The report also reinforced the sense that lenders and guarantee agencies were making money at the expense of students, were not performing as intended, and were unfairly sheltered from real risk by the federal guarantee of loans and profit rates.

The budget agreement was also a driving force in the considera-tion of direct loans. The agreement, specifically the Federal Credit Reform Act of 1990, changed the way in which loans were scored under the budget. The old system created a bias in favor of guaranteed loans while the new system allowed for a more equitable comparison between guaranteed and direct loans. Using the new rules, the General Accounting Office (GAO, 1991) estimated that the direct loan program would save the federal government $1 billion. The GAO report was consistent with a CBO report that estimated a savings of $900 million in the first year of operation (DeLoughry, 1991, October 2). The savings would result from the government no longer paying interest subsidies, special allowances, or the cost of defaulted loans.

As members of Congress viewed the projected savings, they also saw a way to boost aid for middle-income students, build political support for student aid programs, and increase aid support for low-income students. For middle- and upper-income students, direct loans would provide an avenue of support that simply did not exist under the GSL program. If these students were given access to aid, then it was less likely that their parents, the voters, would see student aid as a poverty program. The savings in the loan program could then be shifted to the Pell Grant program and other programs designed for low-income students.

A final factor that served as a driving force behind direct loans were a number of individuals and organizations problemizing direct lending as the solution to any number of student aid problems. As discussed above, the Bush administration gave the concept a major boost at the beginning of 1991 when a member of the administration leaked the proposal to *The New York Times*. Just as it had difficulty finding its voice in regard to its Pell Grant proposal, the administration had difficulty establishing its stance on direct loans. The leaked proposal was not included in the 1992 budget recommendations that the administration sent to the Congress. When Education Secretary Alexander testified in April, the administration did not have a proposal for the GSL program or direct loans, but promised that one would be forthcoming. In July, Alexander announced that he could not support the idea of direct lending. The next month, the administration announced its support of the ICL program asking not only that the program be renewed, but that it be expanded, too. Finally, in October, Alexander stated that Bush would veto the HEA if it included a direct lending program.

While the administration was uncertain about its position on direct loans for most of 1991, other policy actors were quite certain of their stance. The Big Six recommendations included a proposal for a direct loan pilot program that would be an addition to the existing GSL program. Under this proposal, students and institutions would have a choice of loan programs in which to participate. The net effect would be a withering away of the GSL programs as students and institutions voted with their feet. NASFAA, NASULGC, USSA, and other groups also presented loan proposals that varied in scale from a pilot program to the complete elimination of the GSL program.

The association proposals were joined by a host of proposals from members of the House and Senate. For example, Representative Thomas E. Petri, a Wisconsin Republican, and thirty-one co-sponsors presented an income contingent loan program that would be repaid through the payroll tax (DeLoughry, 1991, July 17). In the Senate, Paul Simon, an Illinois Democrat, and David Durenberger, a Minnesota Republican, also offered a direct loan program with IRS collection of income contingent payments.

As the subcommittees met to write the reauthorization legislation, it seemed almost beyond question that the bill would contain a direct loan program. What was unknown was the extent of the program and whether or not it would get past the larger Congress and the threat of a presidential veto. The House proposal came via a rather unusual route given that Representative Ford and Staff Director Wolanin were driving the process and had not initially indicated that a direct loan program would be part of the subcommittee bill. Making the proposal even more unusual was that it had come from NASULGC, which had already signed onto the more limited Big Six recommendations.

To fully understand the House proposal, some background is required. Thomas A. Butts, University of Michigan associate vice president for governmental relations, and Elizabeth A. Hicks, Harvard University coordinator of financial aid, were two people who, according to a NCHELP representative, had "made a career of speaking and saying this [direct lending] is the greatest thing since sliced bread" (Personal interview, February 25, 1992). In preparing for reauthorization, Butts was loaned to NASULGC by the University of Michigan. One of his primary tasks was to prepare a direct lending program proposal and help build support for the proposal.

In Representative Robert E. Andrews, a New Jersey Democrat, NASULGC and Butts found a legislative partner who shared their problematization. The direct loan proposal started when Butts came to Andrews with the NASULGC proposal. Andrews had identified a problem but had not crafted a solution. For Andrews, the problem was one of lenders making too much of a profit from students at the expense of the taxpayers. The proposal offered by Butts was a good solution for Andrews' problem. Butts, who had worked out much of the bill, meet five times with Andrews' staff to complete the final details of the Andrews' direct loan bill. One Dupont Circle associations were consulted to make sure that the final details were acceptable, then Butts, an Andrews' staff member, and a legislative services representative prepared the final draft.

When the House subcommittee staff began to write its version of HEA, staff director Wolanin included the Andrews bill with only minor changes. The direct loan provision, as written by Andrews and Butts, would mean an end to the GSL program. To build support for such a dramatic change, Representative Andrews went on a speaking tour of association meetings to encourage them to accept and support the proposal. In addition, he sent a number of "Dear Colleague" letters to educate fellow House members on the proposal and to encourage their support. While Andrews' actions were important to the success of the direct loan provisions, Ford was clearly the reason for its inclusion in the final bill. Without the support or approval of the chair, it is almost impossible for a low ranking member to successfully propose such a sweeping change.

Ford included the direct loan proposal in the bill that was reported out of committee. As written, the bill would have phased out the GSL program over a three year period and replaced all federal student loan programs with a single direct loan program. Before the bill reached the House floor, the Democratic leadership insisted that Ford make the bill meet the budget agreement's pay-as-you-go requirements by instituting student loan fees and scaling back the size of the program. The direct loan program became a demonstration project limited to $500 million and was to include a representative cross-section of institutions participating in the current student loan programs. Without a Pell Grant entitlement and with a limited direct loan program, there were no controversial issues to build opposition around on the House floor. The House version of HEA passed by a vote of 365–3 on March 26, 1992.

The situation in the Senate was more sensitive because of Pell's views on direct lending and the position he held in the legislative process. As a Senate staffer explained, "if you want to get in good with Chairman Pell, then you talk about how your proposal will help poor kids have an equal chance to attend college" (Personal interview, May 6, 1992). Since the Senate was unwilling to support a Pell Grant entitlement, Pell believed that it would then be wrong to "do something for well-off families at the expense of needy and deserving families" and that it would be "even worse if we do so by favoring loans over grants" (quoted in DeLoughry, 1992, March 4, 1992, p. A). The Simon-Durenberger Income-Dependent Education Assistance (IDEA) loan received a hearing, but was not part of the Senate bill.

The direct loan proposal produced several sharp exchanges in the Senate. Simon told Alexander, "I want to do something that really meets the national need. I know you want to do something that meets the national need" (quoted in Zuckman, 1991, April 13, p. 919). Instead of doing what was needed, Simon charged that what Alexander was doing was "putting his rubber stamp" on administration policy (quoted in Zuckman, 1991, April 13, p. 919) Alexander responded "I know what a rubber stamp is, and that is part of my job" (Zuckman, 1991, April 13, p. 919).

Senator Simon also clashed with college officials over whether or not their links to financial institutions created conflicts of interest in the debate over direct loans. In Simon's words, "someone who has an obligation to one special interest entity—especially a profit-making entity—should not be setting university policy on an issue that affects that special interest" (quoted in DeLoughry, 1992, February 19, p. A24). Referring specifically to direct loan critic William I. Ihlanfeldt, Simon questioned how anyone could be objective while serving as both Northwestern University's vice president for institutional relations and vice chairman of Sallie Mae. Lest anyone not understand the point, Simon staffer Robert M. Shireman claimed that Ihlanfeldt's opposition to direct loans was "a fiduciary responsibility to the shareholders of Sallie Mae" (quoted in DeLoughry, 1992, February 19, p. A24).

In defense of his position, Ihlanfeldt claimed that his relationship was well known and that his opposition was based on the fact that direct lending was a bad idea. William E. Trueheart, president of Bryant College, testified against direct loans without mentioning his relationship with the New England Marketing Corporation. Trueheart's explanation was that the relationship was a matter of the public record and he did think that it was relevant to his testimony opposing direct lending. While there is no evidence that Trueheart or other college representatives were intentionally deceptive or duplicitous, the revelations strained relationships between congressional supporters of direct lending and their opponents in the higher education lobby. The feeling among some representatives and senators was that they had been deceived while college representatives felt that their integrity had been unfairly impugned.

When the Senate and House bills went to conference, there was still considerable doubt as to whether or not the direct loan program would survive. The House leadership had already forced Ford to pare down the program and Pell had made his dislike of the program clear to all. If direct lending did survive the conference, it faced the presidential veto that Alexander had promised for any bill containing a direct loan program. Given these obstacles, it was surprising that the bill reported out of conference included a $500 million direct loan pilot with the potential for as many as 300 colleges and trade schools participating in the program (DeLoughry, 1992, June 24). Alexander lashed out at the committee members claiming that they had destroyed the HEA bill with the inclusion of the direct loan program and that it would be vetoed by the president. Ford reacted to Alexander's charge saying "I think it's one of the most irresponsible outbursts of petty childishness that I've seen in all my years on the committee" (quoted in DeLoughry, 1992, June 24, p, A 20). Alexander's outburst increased the uncertainty about final approval of the bill and about the ability of Democrats to override a veto. The uncertainty was removed when the administration, under pressure from congressional Republicans, reversed its position and announced that Bush would sign the bill. Alexander was placed in the embarrassing position of having to write a recommendation for a bill that he had just promised to terminate. Democrats did not let Alexander's awkward situation pass without comment. When Bush signed the bill, Evans, Pell's staff director, remarked that this "just proves that you can educate some of the people some of the time" (quoted in DeLoughry, 1992, July 29, p. A17).

The inclusion of a large, direct loan pilot program in the final HEA was something of a surprise. The early conventional wisdom was that direct lending would be considered, but eventually would be defeated by the powerful GSL lobby. Organizations such as CBA, NCHELP, and Sallie Mae were expected to either defeat the idea or limit it to a pilot of no greater size and significance than the ICL program. The expected failed to materialize for two reasons. The first is that arguments against direct lending were not grounded in the language and values of the policy arena. The proponents of direct lending were able to frame their arguments in a language that resonated with members of the policy arena.

As discussed in chapters 2 and 3, policy actors have developed a language, a logic, and a coherence that drives the higher education policy formation process. The supporters of direct lending were able to use the language and values of the policy arena to make direct loans more than a simple debate over loan delivery systems. Instead, the issue of direct loans was elevated into a struggle over values and principles. Once the debate shifted to this level, the supporters of direct lending were able to seize the high ground and gain a decisive advantage.

The use of language, principles, and values to frame the debate is nicely contrasted in the testimony of Phyllis K. Hooyman, Hope

College director of financial aid, and the CBA/NCHELP paper *Assessing the Impact of Direct Lending* (November 1991). Hooyman used her testimony to ground the direct lending concept in the experiences and values of the policy arena and to present direct loans as the solution to problems associated with the GSL program. Hooyman (1992) opened her testimony by congratulating the committee "on this landmark piece of legislation, which has indeed brought financial aid once again within the reach of middle-income families" (p. 1) and contrasted direct loans with the GSL program, which "is often a bureaucratic, time-consuming and frustrating for students, parents, institutions, and financial aid officers" (p. 1). If accepted, direct lending would "convert the savings into increased financial assistance for students" and "restore integrity to the student loan process" (Hooyman, 1992, p. 2). To remove the fear associated with the uncertainty of innovation, Hooyman linked direct lending to previous experiences such as the Perkins Loan program whose thirty-four years of operation could serve as a model for the future of direct lending. Finally, she reminded the committee that "direct financing for student loans worked in the past as an effective means of securing capital for Sallie Mae" (Hooyman, 1992, p. 3).

Lenders and guarantors found themselves in a defensive position making status quo claims for the GSL program, which had "provided a highly reliable source of on-time cash flow for institutions across the country" (Nicholson, 1991, p. 2). The response in *Assessing the Impact of Direct Lending* was primarily an attack on direct lending rather than a positive affirmation of the GSL program. CBA and NCHELP failed to use the paper to demonstrate how the GSL program could help low-income students, expand aid to middle-income students, answer concerns about program integrity, meet the demands for simplification, or save the federal government money. In addition, they found themselves in the uncomfortable position of arguing that members of the subcommittees, the CBO, and the GAO were all wrong in their analysis of the cost savings associated with direct loans.

Language can drive legislative issues to obligatory passage points. Language and the values, ideas, and beliefs represented by language can take problematizations up to these points in the policy process, but cannot move issues through passage points if resistance from the guardians of these points is too great. This is the second reason that a direct loan program was part of the final legislation. To borrow a phrase from a higher education lobbyist, no one guardian was willing to "fall on his sword" to prevent the creation of a direct loan program. Absent such a defense, the direct loan proposal was able to move forward.

In the case of HEA, the obligatory passage points are well known and stable. The first, and most important, passage points are the subcommittee chairs. In the House, Ford was supportive of the concept, thus it was safe at the subcommittee level. In the Senate, Pell was not a supporter, but had little reason to oppose the proposal in conference committee once he had made the best possible deal on the Pell Grant formula. Also, a successful direct loan program might improve Pell Grant funding in future years. The next passage point is with the committee chairs, namely Ford in the House and Kennedy in the Senate, both of whom supported the idea. The next point is the entire body, but the whole of the House or Senate seldom refuses a committee or subcommittee. After Ford had adjusted the proposal to meet the objections of the House leadership and the demands of the budget agreement, there was even less reason to expect a reversal by the full body. Once a proposal passes the two bodies, it then goes to conference committee. In this case, direct loans were well represented by a host of champions from both the majority and minority parties, thus it was almost certain to be part of the final legislation. The final passage point is the president. It is true that Bush had threatened a veto, but the administration had maintained an avenue of escape by signaling a willingness to accept a pilot program. Bush signed the legislation because he was unwilling to test the strength of his veto and was unwilling to block otherwise acceptable legislation in the midst of a presidential election campaign.

Taken together, language and the failure to block the obligatory passage points are the two reasons that a direct loan pilot was part of the final legislation. Language was used to build support for the concept and to drive the issue the issue toward the passage points. As the issue reached the various passage points, there was not enough opposition to block the policy development process, thus direct lending continued to move along. When it reached the last passage point, Bush was not willing to fall alone in the battle and allowed the issue to pass without challenge.

CONCLUSIONS

The above description of the social context of policy making fills in the broad outline presented in chapter 3. The internal complexity of the policy arena is low to moderate with a small number of participants, most of whom know each other personally. This personal knowledge and interaction plays an important role in the development and eventual acceptance of policy proposals. The use of trial balloons in the prelude to reauthorization helps policy actors gauge support for their proposals as well as map relationships within the arena. The size and internal complexity of the policy arena are also reflected in the development of position papers and recommendations. While ostensibly the product of an association or group of associations, the recommendations are in fact the mutually shaped and tested product of the larger community of higher education policy actors.

Some aspects of the social context illuminate more than one characteristic of the policy arena. For example, bidirectional lobbying reflects the complexity and size of the policy arena. Policy actors view the arena as a community in which conversation and exchange is the norm. In addition, bidirectional lobbying also reflects the functional autonomy of the policy arena. Since policies are largely formulated and implemented within the arena, it is seldom necessary to lobby in the traditional sense. Instead, policy actors can "do those kind of conversations and . . . find out what people are thinking . . . one-on-one" (Higher education association representative, personal interview, January 10, 1991).

With this reauthorization, as with past reauthorizations, there were threats to the functional autonomy of the policy arena. Specifically, the HEAF crisis, the Nunn committee, and the budget agreement seemed to pose serious challenges to the arena's autonomy. The primary impact was to problematize issues before the higher education policy arena could act, force consideration of a full range of policy issues, and encourage direct lending. In addition, the budget agreement created financial limits in which the higher education policy arena was forced to work in formulating and implementing policy making Pell Grant entitlement nearly impossible while encouraging consideration of direct lending.

The language of policy actors reveals the level of unity among participants. For example, the debate over Pell Grant entitlement was not a debate over the concept, but over the feasibility of implementing an entitlement in the face of the budget agreement restrictions. There was unity on the concept, but that unity broke down as the budget agreement impinged on the functional autonomy of the arena. The arena's unity suffered another blow when the House leadership reneged on its promise to support Ford in presenting a Democratic alternative to the Education President.

In contrast, there was not unity among policy actors on the issue of direct loans. Guarantors, lenders, and some educational institutions were strongly opposed to direct loans and were eventually joined in opposition by the Bush administration. The supporters of direct lending were successful, in part, because they were able to use language that grounded direct lending in the values and principles of the arena. In addition, direct loan proponents were able to persuasively identify their problem solution as being rooted in the policy arena's history and vital to its future. This approach appealed to the majority of the policy arena and disarmed the direct loan opposition.

The above description supports the definition of the higher education policy arena as a communication community. Communication was at the core of the community's collective action. Personal knowledge and interaction, mutual shaping and testing of policy recommendations, bidirectional lobbying, and language are specific aspects of the community's collective action that reinforce the concept of a communication community. The Pell Grant entitlement and the direct loan program demonstrate the dynamics of the community in action. They also represent cooperative activities in which "the pulls and responses of different groups reenforce one another and their values accord" (Dewey, 1927/1988). While the dynamic was at times conflictual, the shared activity helped create emotional, intellectual, and moral bonds.

On the issue of Pell Grant entitlement, the associations were willing to reach agreement well short of subcommittee proposals. This willingness to accept a lower point of agreement reduced the bargaining leverage of subcommittee members who wanted to test the limits of the budget agreement and the veto threat. The associations' lower settlement point may have contributed to the House leadership's withdraw of support for Pell Grant entitlement. In any case, the House proposals were not supported by other sectors of the community, thus there was no chance of their being accepted as policy. While Senate and House staffers blamed the failure of Pell Grant entitlement on the unwillingness of associations to lobby for the issue, it is at best speculation to claim that a stronger effort by associations would have produced a breakthrough.

The direct loan issue produced a different dynamic. The associations were willing to meet the Congress at a point much closer to the original House proposal. When the House leadership forced Ford to scale down the proposal, there were fallback positions that allowed supporters to keep much of the thrust of the Big Six proposal intact. This avoided the all or nothing situation that existed with the entitlement proposal. In addition, associations accepted and lobbied for direct loans in a way that they did not for Pell Grant entitlement.

On both issues, the administration withdrew from active participation once its proposals had been rejected. Rather than participate in negotiations directed toward reaching an agreement, the administration attempted to set the parameters for agreement with the threat of a veto. This was effective in denying entitlement status, but it was not the primary factor in blocking the Pell Grant entitlement. The budget agreement was much more important in establishing parameters than was the veto threat. With direct loans, the veto threat was withdrawn because the administration was uncertain about its ability to block a congressional override. While it claimed success, the administration was unable to keep the larger community from reaching a consensus on direct loans.

Finally, the social context of policy making provides some hints about the meaning of power. Rather than thinking in terms of a single definition or base of power, it might be better to think of power in terms of foundations on which influence is constructed. The interpretation and meaning of power in the higher education policy arena are the subject of chapter 5.

5

Power in the
Higher Education Policy Arena

The purpose of this project has been the reconstruction and reclamation of power as a concept for policy analysis and research. Restructuring power means understanding it as the thread that holds collective action together. Once power is understood in this way, then it can be reclaimed as a concept that helps explicate collective action. The sociology of translation provides a methodology for reconstructing and reclaiming power as a concept but neither defines nor interprets power. In fact, the methodological principles of the sociology of translation—agnosticism, generalized symmetry, and free association—require that any interpretation of the meaning of power be delayed until after the historical and social context in which power is situated is fully developed and presented. Now that this is complete, it is time to draw on that context to interpret the meaning of power in the higher education policy arena.

Any number of extant theories of power can be matched with parts of the historical and social context of the policy arena to make a case for that theory as *the* defining theory of power. For example, the existence of a large number of interest groups can be used to develop and support a pluralist theory of power. The participation of economic and social elites in the development of policy that benefits a small segment of society points to a power elite interpretation. Marxists would probably differ, noting that power elite theory is simply an indirect way of discussing class while avoiding the truth of power. While the case can be made for these and other theories, none of these theories matches exactly what was found in the case study of the higher education policy arena. This may be because their developers and proponents are seeking an overarching theory that explains power at all times and in all places. The interpretation of power offered below emerges from the historical and social context of the policy arena and is applicable only to the higher education policy arena. While it may be applicable to other arenas, it must be tested in those settings before broader claims can be made.

The interpretation of power developed in this chapter calls on earlier concepts of power developed in communicative action theories but goes beyond the work of Arendt, Dewey, Habermas, and others to search for the foundations of power. Power, defined in terms of the ability of policy actors to address problems, rests on three broad foundations. These foundations, suggested by the historical and social context of the higher education policy arena, interact to give form, shape, and meaning to power. One foundation of power is formed by society's defining institutions and structures. These visible structures of power are the products of decisions made in earlier policy arenas. A second foundation is formed by the personal and social relationships of the community. This includes the explicit rules that govern relationships among policy actors and programs, as well as, the personal relationships that develop between policy actors. The third foundation of power consists of the beliefs and values that policy actors draw on for guidance in making policy decisions and choices. Interaction between foundations generates power, regulates power, and provides the channels and boundaries of power in the communication community that is the higher education policy arena.

Communication communities, as defined by Arendt, Dewey, and Habermas, exist to solve problems. Problem solving in the higher education policy arena does not match the Habermasian ideal of communicative competence nor is it an irrational activity that produces problem solutions through some random or accidental confluence of events that results in a policy decision. Instead, problem solving rests on and is framed by an axiomatic system of beliefs, institutional relationships, personal relationships, and values that guide the community in the construction and design of student aid programs. Successful problem-solvers are those who build their solutions on these foundations and show how the community's past and future are linked to acceptance of those solutions.

Lest the idea of foundations of power present too neat and orderly a view of the community, it is important to recognize that problem solving in the policy arena is often a messy business. Structural and institutional foundations crumble, fall, shift, and are replaced as policy actors build new institutions and renovate existing ones to meet societal needs. Personal and social relationships change as new actors enter the community and new rules are created to govern the relationships of the community. Time and a changing world undermine some beliefs and values, renew others, and generate entirely new community beliefs and values as policy actors seek to make sense of a dynamic world. Always there are interactions as ideas, institutions, and individuals bump, clash, conflict, and join, creating the need for problem solving.

The remainder of this chapter is devoted to developing and defining power and its foundations in the higher education policy arena. Examples from the earlier discussion of the historical and social context of higher education policy making are used to develop and explain the meaning of power within the policy arena. Finally, since problem solving is central to the concept of power in a communication community, the chapter concludes with a discussion of problem solving and the basis of problem solving in the higher education policy arena. A discussion of the implications of this interpretation of power is reserved for the next chapter.

FOUNDATIONS OF POWER

In an intellectual era in which high theory is dedicated to the proposition that there are no foundations, it might be considered odd or out of step to call on foundations anchored in a historical and social context to explain power in the higher education policy arena. This might be a reasonable reaction if the interpretation that follows were a venture into traditional foundationalist epistemology but this is not the case here. The use and meaning of the term "foundations" here is consistent with the lay use of the term. That is to say that a foundation is simply a base on which a project is constructed. Even those who claim that there are no foundations, in the traditional sense, have the denial of foundations as the base for their project. Project builders might approach the task of foundation construction with the intent of building a base that will support their project for eternity, but the reality is that foundations weaken and deteriorate over time. When existing foundations cease to function or lose their integrity, new foundations replace the old ones or are built over them. This approach to foundations is Deweyan in that it does not seek reinforcement from some transcendental ideal or permanent reality, but instead it follows a pragmatic path by defining power through "a principled openness toward, and an enthusiastic search for, new and temporarily valid knowledge in a universe of constant change" (Hollinger, 1985, p. 31).

Institutional Foundation

The institutional and structural foundations of power consist of society's defining institutions. These institutions are the "structures [that] define interactions among individuals and groups" (Rorty, 1992, p. 10). They also house the persons and social relationships of the community. This description of the institutional foundation of problem solving answers the "where" of addressing problems while persons and social relationships represent the "who" and beliefs and values the "why" of policy making. As such, these structures represent the exercise of power in the past but are not generative sources of power in the present. Instead, these structures represent "the greatest achievement of power . . . its reification" (Clegg, 1989, p. 207). These monuments to past power form the relatively fixed obligatory passage points of power in the present. While they do not generate power in the present, problems must be addressed within these structures. Institutions become important when occupied and manipulated by humans who are addressing problems.

Social institutions represent ways society has devised to cope with the reality it faces. While defined and described as a foundation, the view of social institutions here is consistent with poststructuralist thought, which holds that social institutions and structures are neither products of nature, nor are they permanent. Social institutions have life only as long as they are recognized and accepted as legitimate structures by the community. School children learn about these structures and the relatively fixed obligatory passage points these institutions form early in their academic experience, but not necessarily in these terms. Instead, they learn about the Constitution as the document that binds and guides the nation in its governance and provides the authority for the institutions of governance. They also learn about the system of checks and balances such as presidential vetoes, congressional overrides, and judicial review. In addition, they learn about ways in which the system of governance can be changed through constitutional amendments as well as by revolutions and civil wars.

As noted above, institutional structures represent the reification of power. They are the products of decisions made in earlier policy arenas that have been continued into the present. Long-established institutional structures become highly resistant to change as they gain the weight of tradition. As new structures are moved into place, "the interdependence and intermeshing of each institution with others creates an institutional structure strongly resistant to serious reconstitution" (Connolly, 1987, p. 160). The interdependence and intermeshing of old and new structures forms the channels and boundaries within which communication communities function. Unless and until they fail to serve the needs of the community, the structures are removed from debate. While institutional structures can be added, deleted, or changed, they are not usually part of the policy problematization. Instead they form the seemingly natural background against which policy decisions are made within the communication community.

The Education Department

In the higher education policy arena, the Education Department (ED) represents reified power, as well as what happens when a structure fails to become fully interdependent and intermeshed with other institutional structures. Created during the Carter administration, the ED was designed to bring together all of the federal government's various education interests into one sharply focused cabinet level department. From the beginning, questions were raised about the legitimacy of an ED. Critics felt that the federal role in education was too limited to deserve a cabinet level department and that such a department would encourage the federal government to expand beyond its proper role in education. The higher education policy arena was especially concerned that the ED might limit the autonomy campuses enjoyed under federal programs. Despite questions about the legitimacy and need for an ED, the Carter administration and K–12 policy actors successfully pushed legislation through Congress enabling the creation of an ED. The ED seemed to be on its way to becoming an established institutional structure and an obligatory passage point for federal education policy decisions.

Before the ED became established as part of the institutional foundation of power, the Reagan administration entered office with an agenda that included elimination of the ED. In contrast to previous post–World War II administrations, which had sought to expand the federal role in education, the Reagan administration questioned whether or not the federal government had a legitimate role in education. While the Reagan agenda was clear, the ED was not eliminated, but actually grew in importance under the leadership of Terrell Bell. The publication of *A Nation At Risk* (1983) helped set the tone for the administration's policy of promoting excellence in education and helped establish the ED as a leader in the school reform movement. Thanks to Bell's problem definitions, the ED moved from being a target for elimination to becoming an important part of the Reagan domestic agenda.

The evaluation of American education that had started under Bell continued under William J. Bennett with the results forming the basis for his criticisms of higher education. As education secretary, Bennett became engaged in a running battle with the higher education community claiming among other things that it lacked coherence and cohesion, and that higher education had failed in its obligation to provide moral guidance to students. College students were another of Bennett's targets serving to further his criticism of higher education. Students, according to Bennett, were not only failing to meet the standards set by earlier generations, but were using student aid to buy cars, purchase stereos, and enjoy vacations in Florida. The message from Bennett was that colleges would have to reclaim their historical legacy and students would have to learn the meaning of sacrifice because the federal gravy train was coming to an end.

The ED, which had briefly appeared to be an established part of the structural layer of power, was now open to translation. The Reagan administration, which had once wanted to eliminate the ED, now found the ED to be an important part of its domestic agenda. Under Bell's leadership, the administration sounded the alarm of falling standards in K–12 and issued a call for excellence. Under Bennett's leadership, the administration cudgeled higher education, blaming professors for the moral decline of American civilization. In each case, the administration was able to define the solutions, and thus the costs, as resting with those who had created the problems. The role of the ED was open to translation because neither problem required the ED, as originally envisioned, for its solution.

While the Reagan administration no longer wanted to eliminate the ED and was happy to use it as a bully pulpit, members of the education community and Democratic members of the education committees in the Congress were unhappy that the ED was not fulfilling the mission it had been created to serve. Members of the House and Senate education committees did not want to eliminate the ED, but they no longer trusted its ability or willingness to carry out broad policy objectives. Increasingly, the education committees wrote into legislation the regulations and minute details usually left to the department or agency charged with implementing program and policy objectives. In the higher education policy arena, policy actors complained about micromanagement of student aid programs, but they were not the intended targets. Micromanagement affected campus student aid administrators, but it was aimed at limiting ED's administrative discretion by forcing it to meet specific congressional directives.

The ongoing struggle to define the role and mission of the ED prevented it from becoming an obligatory passage point in higher education policy making. The Reagan administration used it as a bully pulpit, but was not interested in the ED as an obligatory passage point. To a considerable extent, the Reagan administration's strategy of linking all social and domestic programs to the budget deficit meant that the Office of Management and Budget (OMB), not the ED, was the obligatory passage point for higher education policy decisions in the Executive. OMB, not ED, stood as the guardian of education policy decisions determining which passed through the administration and which met with resistance. Congress often bypassed the ED leaving it out of discussions on policy, then giving it highly detailed rules and regulations to implement. What could have been, seemingly should have been, an obligatory passage point for higher education policy making became superfluous to the process. John B. Lee, a higher education consultant, summarized the situation of the ED as being "like an autistic child. Did you ever watch an autistic kid work? Just real agitated, and they're doing all this internal stuff, but when you're outside you can't tell what they're about. . . . [I]t's a real, real heartbreaking process" (Personal interview, January 10, 1991).

ED Programs

In contrast to the struggling ED, some of its programs have gained institutional status. The GSL and the Pell Grant programs are two of the better known examples but they are not the only ones. State Student Incentive Grants (SSIG), TRIO programs, and other aid programs have also gained institutional status. While these programs are not obligatory passage points on a level with the education subcommittees or the OMB, they do form the institutional standards against which alternative policy proposals are judged. While alternative proposals might actually offer advantages over existing programs, the institutional status of existing programs makes them highly resistant to change. As a result, proposals for change usually produce either a tinkering with existing programs or the creation of new parallel programs.

The GSL program is an excellent study of how an institutionalized program grows and resists change. The original GSL program was a product of the tension that existed over aid to middle-income students. To forestall support for tuition credits and to undermine Republican opposition to the legislation, a guaranteed student loan program for the middle class was included in the original HEA. The 1972 HEA created Sallie Mae to serve as a secondary market for student loans

freeing lenders to increase student loan volume. The Middle Income
Student Assistance Act (MISAA) of 1978 opened the GSL program to
all students regardless of family income. The 1980 HEA reauthorization created a new GSL loan program for parents while restricting
eligibility requirements that had been expanded by MISAA. Coming
into the 1992 reauthorization, the GSL program had grown from a
defense against tuition tax credits to a $10 billion per year program
with three major loan programs supported by some fifty secondary
loan market organizations, over fifty state and private guarantee
agencies, numerous loan servicers, and Sallie Mae.

The institutional status of GSL moved decisions about the
program away from questions about the institutional legitimacy of the
GSL program and toward rules and regulations governing the
program. Rather than ask questions about the legitimacy of the GSL
as an institution, debate centered on the rules of the program. The
Nunn committee investigation of fraud and abuse in the federal
student aid program illustrates how the level of debate remained
outside the institutional foundation. After identifying a range of
problems in the GSL program and focusing on the seemingly ever
increasing volume of loan defaults, the Nunn committee report
recommended a number of rule changes. The institutional structure
and life of the GSL were not questioned but were treated as a given
structure that would continue to hold the GSL program as modified
by the rule changes. The impact of the recommendations, if fully
accepted, would have been a tinkering with the rules rather than a
change in institutional architecture.

In contrast to the Nunn committee, proponents of direct lending
presented a problemization that did question the legitimacy of the
GSL program. Direct lending, as defined by its supporters, was the
solution to any number of student aid problems including loan
defaults, middle-income aid, private sector profiteering, and structural
inefficiency. Direct loan advocates used the language and values of the
policy arena to elevate the debate from a simple discussion over loan
delivery systems to a struggle over values and principles. Once the
debate shifted, direct lending proponents gained the high ground and
what seemed to be a decisive advantage.

What direct lending advocates gained was a lesson in institutional
resistance to change. The GSL programs were not necessarily the best
solution to the problem of middle income student aid but they had
taken on the weight of tradition and still served, with some deficiencies, the needs of the community as a whole. Direct lending
proponents were unable to convince the larger community that a

complete reconstitution of the GSL program in the form of a direct lending program would solve the problems associated with the GSL program, retain the advantages, and not create a new set of problems. Faced with known questions about the existing structure and uncertainty about the proposed alternative, the policy arena elected the path of least resistance. The direct loan program was added as a new, parallel program creating an addition to the institutional foundation.

Unlike the debate over direct lending, the debate over Pell Grant entitlement did not broach the question of institutional legitimacy but focused on the rules governing student eligibility. Still, had it been achieved, entitlement status would have enhanced and strengthened the program's institutional status. As an entitlement, the Pell Grant program would have been removed from any debate over its legitimacy and over its funding level. The interaction of the institutional and social foundations of power would have made the Pell Grant program virtually immune to problematization.

The example of the ED highlights the fact that while institutional structures are highly resistant to change, they are not immutable. The discussion of the GSL and Pell Grant programs illustrates that in normal times, times of social stability, institutional structures are usually not subject to question. When established structures are questioned, as was the GSL program, they prove highly resistant to change. In the policy decisions that formed the HEA, the institutional foundations of power, with the exception of the GSL program, were not subject to problematization. Instead, the focus was on social relations and rules leaving the institutions and structures as an unobtrusive background to policy making.

The institutional structures that form the obligatory passage points for federal higher education policy were identified and discussed in the last chapter: the education subcommittees, the education committees, the conference committee, the House and Senate and the White House. Programs such as the GSL and Pell Grant are not obligatory passage points, but they are included as part of the institutional foundation because they form the standards against which alternative policy proposals are measured and because they house social relationships that help form the social foundations of power. While institutional structures form the channels and boundaries within which the higher education communication community functions, they alone are not generative of power. Without human occupants, the institutional structures are mere monuments to the past. Power in a communication community is generated through interactions between the foundations of power.

Social Foundation

The social foundation of power consists of the rules governing the relationships between policy actors and programs in a policy arena. In addition to the formal rules and relationships, it includes the personal relationships that develop between policy actors apart from any formal relationships created by the rules of the game. Over time, these relationships, formal and informal, become relatively fixed, but this stability should not be interpreted as permanence. Instead, what is being observed is adherence to customs, loyalties, and norms that have developed over the years and that guide the policy arena in the conduct of its affairs.

Which rules, relationships, and norms become institutionalized over time is a function of the ability of policy actors to gain acceptance of their problematizations. The basing of student aid on need rather than on merit, the requirement of a family contribution, and the favoring of students over institutions are examples of successful translations that have not been reopened. Some translations produce additions to the institutional foundation of power. The education subcommittees in the House and the Senate are examples of additions to the institutional foundation created by decisions to restructure the formal social structure in the two bodies. The creation of the direct loan program might be an addition to as well as a replacement for the GSL program, but the full impact of that decision is still uncertain.

When the social foundation is stable, it combines with the institutional foundation to make radical change difficult. This was a lesson learned by both the Reagan and Bush administrations when they sought to reshape HEA. Direct lending proponents learned the same lesson when they attempted to eliminate the GSL program and replace it with their direct lending proposal. Unless social relationships are seriously disrupted or destabilized, then "even dissident political movements are pressed to define objectives congruent with the established order" (Connolly, 1987, p. 166). This seemed to be implicitly, if not explicitly, understood by the Johnson administration when it added HEA titles with little or no funding for the purpose of shaping future debates. Since the early 1970s, the higher education policy arena has remained remarkably stable. The resistance to change produced by this stability has sometimes been presented as a model for policy making: incrementalism. Far from being a model, it is merely a byproduct of the interaction between the institutional and social foundations of power.

Formal Roles

The stability and longevity of policy actors in the arena has contributed to the definition of the policy arena as a higher education partnership. As discussed in chapter 3, higher education partnership is also used by policy actors to describe the social relations of the policy arena. The belief in a partnership is reinforced by participation in shared activities associated with reauthorization. The circulation of personnel within the policy arena also contributes to the sense of a higher education partnership. The community of interests produced by stability, longevity, shared activities, and circulation of personnel creates a common language, shared values, and shared experiences strengthen unity and reduce conflict within the policy arena. Policy actors think of themselves as working toward the same goals, but with different solutions that sometimes cause conflict and misunderstanding. This is not viewed as serious conflict, but as differences that can be eliminated through exchanges of information and ideas, bidirectional lobbying, and other communicative activities.

Implicit in the concept of a partnership are rules that govern the relationship and rights of the partners. This is certainly true of the higher education partnership with different rights, rules, and status for the various policy actors. The differences in status and rights between the associations and the Congress prompted NASULGC's Jerold Roschwalb to define the relationship not as a partnership, but as

> a medieval marriage. One all powerful partner who can beat you up when they want, if you run away, they'll bring you back to the house because the rules require that. That's not a partnership. It's incidentally legally a partnership, but in practice it's not. . . . We are cooperating bodies. The Congress uses us, often very wisely, because we are sources of information, sources of facts, sources of data and it is very useful to have us around to help out. (Personal interview, February, 27, 1992)

The rules that govern the creation of policy clearly favor some policy actors over others. The chairs of the education subcommittees are in the most favored positions within the Congress because they occupy obligatory passage points in the policy process and because the tradition of the House and Senate is to defer to the wishes of committee and subcommittee chairs in the drafting of legislation. The division of work in the House and the Senate also works to the advantage of the chairs and members of the education committees and subcommittees who can devote their time to education issues and become the experts in education policy. Other members are doing the same thing, but in different policy areas and arenas. The compartmentalization and division of work and knowledge means that members usually defer to their colleagues on the basis of expertise as well as on the basis of mutual self-respect of policy arena boundaries. In an act of self-defense and reciprocity, members do not cross into one another's areas of expertise and control.

While the relationship might seem to tilt entirely in favor of the education committees and subcommittees, this is not the case in practice. Members, especially House members with their two-year terms, have to be concerned about reelection. The higher education community can do little to influence the outcome of an election, but it is not helpful to be estranged from the education community if part of your reelection record is based on achievements in education policy. The demands of the job, especially in the much smaller Senate, are such that members are always short of time and knowledge as they quickly move from issue to issue with staffers attempting to keep them informed as they move. The demands of the job and the shortage of time and information creates an opportunity for association staff, higher education representatives, lobbyists, and others to become de facto congressional staff members. In an effort to assist and influence members, they provide research, draft legislation, prepare position papers, calculate Pell Grant formulas, identify witnesses, and lobby other members. To help create the illusion of public demand or need for a program, they promote members' proposals. Finally, knowledge provides access for policy actors who can inform and persuade as they provide knowledge.

The rules would seem to give the most favored position to the White House, but this has not been true in recent practice. The priorities and demands of the White House are such that higher education policy and legislation receive little attention from the president. The current status of the ED is such that it has little opportunity to influence the president's domestic policy agenda. The influence that has been exerted tends to be on K–12 policy rather than higher education. This may help explain why Presidents Reagan and Bush often communicated what they did not want in the HEA rather than articulating what they did want. Higher education policy was important enough to contain through a defense of the president's obligatory passage point, but not important enough to create through an active involvement in social and personal relationships and roles that form the social foundation of power.

The actions of the education subcommittees, the associations, and the White House demonstrate how the social and institutional foundations interact to produce relationships and outcomes that would not be expected if one examined only institutional or formal social relationships. If appearances were reality, then the White House would be institutionally positioned to exert the greatest influence on policy. In reality, the White House did not take advantage of its position to fully participate in the social relations of policy making. By default, the leading role went to the education committees and subcommittees but they also found themselves limited in their ability to take full advantage of their positions. Institutional resistance to change, the budget agreement, the contested principles of the arena, the inability to find change-oriented partners, and the nature of work in the Congress all combined to restrict the range of policy options available to the committees. The formal arrangement of institutions provides no role for the associations but they were able to use an active social involvement to influence policy. They expanded this influence by developing personal relationships.

Personal Relationships

An important part of the social foundations of power consists of developing and maintaining personal relationships. The nature of personal relationships often determines who interacts with whom in the policy formation process and how they respond to ideas, suggestions, and recommendations. A strong personal relationship can be more valuable in the consideration of policy proposals than reams of data. Since reauthorization is a cyclical event, relationships must be developed and maintained during and between reauthorizations. A NASFAA representative summarized the importance of social relationships:

> We're nice people. And that's a glib way of saying that on the Hill, if they don't like you, they're not going to open the door, and they're not going to open their minds and listen to you. So we try to be pleasant and we try to, you know, do the socially correct things that one does as a group that wishes to move federal policy in one direction or another. So I think that . . . social aspects . . . are important in building up the relationships with members of Congress, Senators, and their staffs. (Personal interview, February 24, 1992)

The combination of strong personal relationships combined with programs rich in the values of the policy arena and a history of success provides an enormous advantage to association representatives. Arnold L. Mitchem, executive director of the National Council of Educational Opportunity Associations (NCEOA), represents the TRIO programs (Talent Search, Upward Bound, Equal Opportunity Centers, and three other programs) whose origins date from the Johnson administration Great Society programs and the original HEA. The programs are highly regarded as efficient, effective contributors to the goal of equal educational opportunity. Building on this, Mitchem has worked diligently to develop strong personal relationships with congressional members and staffs. This helps explain why funding for the TRIO programs grew consistently faster than funding for other HEA authorized student aid programs during the 1980s.

In assessing the NCEOA record, it is difficult to overstate the importance of Mitchem's personal relationships. Mitchem's success in cultivating relationships on Capitol Hill is the object of both reverence and resentment. Describing characteristics of an effective lobbyist, Wolinanin noted that "one factor is long term credibility. Arnold Mitchem is a good example of this characteristic. If he asks for something on TRIO, then we usually just do it" (Personal interview, May 7, 1992). This view was repeated on the Senate side by a staffer who stated that "NCEOA recommendations are usually just accepted. This is probably because the proposals are from a group that is well respected and for programs that are well run. TRIO does things with equal educational opportunity that resonate with the members" (Personal interview, May 6, 1992).

The view of Mitchem on Capitol Hill is shared at One Dupont Circle. NASULGC 's Jerold Roschwalb described Mitchem's success:

> Arnie is doing something that Congress is very interested in. He's focused on poor kids with a large percentage of them being minority . . . because of the way he deals with those kids . . . those kids are doing better than other kids of their own category. . . . They graduate more frequently, they go on to graduate school more frequently, they go to professional schools more frequently. They have a Rhodes Scholar among their graduates. And so that's exactly what people want to see. And he seems to be doing that cleanly. . . . And that program has been growing like so, because everybody likes Arnie Mitchem for good reason. He's a solid guy, works hard as hell and is committed to his work, committed to his kids. . . . [H]e

knows what's happening out there. And I think people around trust him. Not only that he's TNT and honest and all the rest but he's smart. And you take that combination and that's power all by himself. Arnie Mitchem is a powerful man because he can talk to virtually any member of the committees or their staff and make his pitch. . . . [T]here's a form of power that is neither from money, neither from votes, and neither from pressure from back home, but because of the sheer reputation built on years of work and accomplishment. (Personal interview, February 27, 1992)

Not everyone in Washington was as impressed with Mitchem or with single issue groups as was this higher education association representative. Representatives from broad-based higher education associations felt that limited-issue and single-focus organizations sometimes received more credit than they deserved or earned because of the greater ease inherent in single issue lobbying. A representative from NCHELP lamented that

there are individuals or groups around from various schools, TRIO for example, where they can get almost anything they want but I mean you're talking literally dollars, small program. . . . I always thought it would be real neat to be hired, you know, on the one issue lobbies . . . basketball . . . I mean that's not hard. You could get "the Secretary shall spend this money," for you know, "including but not limited to." You could get the word basketball in if that's all your client's paying you to do, doesn't mean he gets any of it. And there are a lot of people who do that. (Personal interview, February 25, 1992)

While complaints about one-issue and limited-agenda associations might be discounted as sour grapes, there is considerable accuracy in the lament. One-issue and limited-agenda associations do find it easier to maintain their focus and their social relationships. Associations with larger, broader agendas face an inherently more difficult task in staying focused and on good terms with other policy arena participants. Simple probability means that the longer the list of issues being considered the greater the possibility of conflict, controversy, and disagreement. It is hard to stay on good terms with other policy actors when you have an opinion on everything.

ACE and NASFAA

The American Council on Education (ACE) and the National Association of Student Financial Aid Administrators (NASFAA) both faced difficulty maintaining their social relationships because they found it impossible to be in agreement with all policy actors at all times. ACE's problems with the issue of institutional integrity illustrates how difficult it can be for large associations to maintain social relationships. The institutional integrity issue was promoted by the State Higher Education Executive Officers (SHEEO) as a way to better regulate the use of federal student aid and to protect against the type of fraud and abuse that had been highlighted by the Nunn committee. In many states, the proposal would have also allowed state governing boards to exercise greater control over colleges and universities than was possible under current state law. The SHEEO proposal was introduced by Representatives William F. Goodling and Nita M. Lowey for the purpose of generating discussion on the issue. As the bill was being drafted, the majority staff accepted the proposal as part of the subcommittee bill, thus moving it from a discussion issue to a section of the bill.

When it became aware of the issue, ACE representatives met with Representatives Thomas Coleman and Goodling to negotiate a reduced role for state higher education boards in institutional oversight and review. After listening to ACE's concerns, Coleman and Goodling agreed to change the language to limit the role of the state boards. To confirm the agreement, ACE sent a letter to Coleman and Goodling indicating agreement and acceptance of the new language. A potentially contentious issue had apparently been resolved without any great conflict between the policy actors.

The deal unraveled when ACE began to hear complaints from its members expressing concern over the institutional integrity language. While it was questionable as to whether or not the provisions would ever impact ACE member schools, they were concerned with what they saw as state encroachment on their autonomy and academic freedom. Responding to member pressure, ACE attempted to again renegotiate the language, but instead of returning to Coleman and Goodling ACE took its concerns directly to the chair, Representative Ford. The response of Republican members and staff was a sense of bad faith bargaining and betrayal that clouded future negotiations (Republican staff, personal interview, May 5, 1992). Democratic members and staff saw it as nothing more than part of the ongoing negotiation process (Wolanin, personal interview, May 7, 1992). Whatever the reason for ACE's bypassing of Coleman and Goodling, the decision to do so damaged its relationship with Republican subcommittee members.

Apart from any problems that grew out of the institutional integrity negotiations, Democrats and Republicans from both the House and the Senate were critical of ACE's ability to interact on a personal level. A Republican staffer in the House went straight to the point claiming that

> ACE always seems to be a reauthorization behind. This time they were well prepared technically, but not personally. Personality helps drive policy and ACE had terrible interpersonal skills. They focus on the chair and ignore the members. They treat the staff, even some members, in a very pompous manner. This has caused some staff to remark, "If ACE is for it, then we are not." (Personal interview, May 5, 1992)

In fairness to ACE, staff members from both parties and both sides of Congress also gave the association high marks. Charles Sanders and Pat Smith of ACE governmental relations were praised for their technical skills, knowledge of issues, responsiveness to requests for information, and interpersonal skills. The diversity of views and reactions to ACE reflect the difficulty in trying to stay on good terms with a wide range of policy actors over a broad range of policy issues. This is something NASFAA learned as it attempted to broaden its traditional role and move into a whole new set of social relationships as an association concerned with broad policy issues.

Traditionally, NASFAA has been perceived as the premier association for technical advice and technical issues. Technical advice and issues concern the means used to achieve specific policy goals and objectives. For example, NASFAA was often looked to for advice on the needs analysis formula that determines the amount of student aid an individual is eligible to receive. NASFAA was also concerned with technical issues that impacted the day-to-day life of campus student aid officers. In preparing for the 1992 HEA reauthorization, NASFAA sought to expand beyond its traditional role as technical specialist to address broad policy issues.

In reality, it is impossible to separate technical and social policy issues. All technical questions and issues are intertwined with social questions and issues. Policymakers in medical science and nuclear arms, to give but two examples, have found that supposedly limited technical policy issues actually have broad social implications. Within the higher education policy arena, there are several examples of the unanticipated, unplanned political and social implications of technical amendments. The inclusion of proprietary schools was done without any understanding or anticipation of the impact on the GSL program or public reaction to the default problem. MISAA was well intended but the unanticipated results sparked sharp criticism and eventually the reversal of provisions for expanded participation in the GSL program.

NASFAA's desire to become a major policy actor speaking to broad policy issues moved the organization onto a different, more slippery terrain than that on which it was accustomed to operating. The organization ran into trouble almost immediately when Senator Kennedy introduced the NASFAA needs analysis formula prior to its finalization. While the mistake was Kennedy's, NASFAA received much of the criticism. NASFAA may not have been blameless, according to Nassirian:

> NASFAA struggles with the problem endemic to any organization with a diverse membership. The wise thing to do in such cases of real and irreconcilable differences within such a heterogeneous constituency is not to take sides with one segment of your membership against another. Some of my aid directors (from the public sector) complain that there is too much of a private-institution prejudice to NASFAA's policy priorities, which they view as the tail wagging the dog. I believe the need analysis that NASFAA put forth tends to support that view. It is geared towards privates with large amounts of institutional aid to guard, and would have resulted in a massive reduction in the public's share of Pell dollars. Selling a plan like this had to be based on either negligence or dissimulation. (Personal interview, February 27, 1992)

While Nassirian raised his questions in an interview, others went public with their concerns about NASFAA. One of these was the Advisory Committee on Student Financial Aid. The advisory committee, created by the 1986 HEA reauthorization, was charged with advising the Congress and making recommendations on the maintenance of higher education access for low and middle income students. Shortly after Senator Kennedy introduced the NASFAA needs analysis proposal in the form of S.1137, the advisory committee responded with a quick critique and a list of shortcomings it saw not just with the needs analysis proposal but also with NASFAA's larger set of reauthorization proposals. The advisory committee seemed to be competing for NASFAA's unofficial title of technical advisor to the education committees and subcommittees to add to its legislative mandate. In doing so, it was making its criticisms public for all to see.

In August 1991, some six weeks after the advisory committee critique, NASFAA President Dallas Martin responded to the advisory committee claims in a seven-page letter to advisory committee Chair Stanley Z. Koplik. Martin stated, "I am increasingly troubled by the Student Aid Advisory Committee's actions and characterization of NASFAA's *Plan for Reform*." Acknowledging that the advisory committee and NASFAA had addressed concerns that were not mutually shared, Martin charged that it was "unfair and misleading to infer that NASFAA does not care about these issues" simply because no recommendations were made. After rebutting the advisory committee charges from June, Martin closed with the hope that "you can now understand why I feel that the Advisory Committee has misrepresented our position, and since the committee elected to distribute their faulty analysis both on the Hill and in the community, I feel that I have no choice but to circulate this response so that people can have the chance to draw their conclusions."

The problems with the advisory committee were not the only difficulties NASFAA was encountering. In attempting to become a major policy actor on broad policy issues, NASFAA was moving beyond the social relations that it had carefully developed as a technical advisor. The policy actors were the same but the interactions and skills were different. NASFAA's behavior, while appropriate for assessing technical issues, was interpreted differently when associated with policy issues. For example, NASFAA eventually came to support a pilot direct loan program and attempted to build support for the proposal, but it was slow in coming to this decision. What might have been interpreted as prudence in technical decision making was perceived by some as political maneuvering. This was apparent in Ken Holdsman's, a House Democratic staff member, explanation for placing NASFAA in the same grouping as proprietary schools and associations representing lenders because "it is now funded by bankers. This may explain why it took them some eight months to take a stand on direct lending" (Personal interview, May 4, 1992).

Ironically, NASFAA's difficulty in mastering the social relations of broader policy issues opened it to criticism over its technical role. While the organization had once been praised for its technical expertise, some now criticized NASFAA for being too technocratic. Wolanin evaluated NASFAA's performance as

> less effective than it has been in the past. The reason for this is the increasing professionalization of student aid administrators. At one time you became a student aid administrator because you were driven, or at least moved, by a mission to help students, but this is no longer the case. Once their passion was students, but now their passion is forms and technical mechanisms. They are no longer the surrogate for parents and students in the policy process. They have lost their policy values and become technicians. (Personal interview, May 7, 1992)

As the above examples demonstrate, it is important to understand the rules and relationships of the policy arena. The customs, loyalties, and norms of the arena combine with institutional relationships to circumscribe what is possible. Institutional and social relationships also establish the behavior that is expected from policy actors. When policy actors violate community expectations, as NASFAA did, the result can be a disruption of social relationships. Failure to take full advantage of social relationships sometimes prevents policy actors from reaching their full potential as was the case with the White House. In contrast, the education committees and subcommittees were able to expand beyond what might be expected by institutional relationships but they too were restricted by social relationships. The associations used personal relationships to create an institutionally undefined role for themselves in the policy making process. For all policy actors, personal relationships are also important as policy actors seek other policy actors whose ideas, suggestions, recommendations, and reactions they can trust. ACE and NASFAA found it difficult to maintain good social relationships across a broad range of policy issues compared to limited-agenda associations that have the relative luxury of concentrating on a few policy issues. Social and personal relationships are the explicit, visible manifestations of problem solving activities and behaviors in the communication community. By observing these activities and behaviors, it is possible to see who is addressing problems and how they are being addressed but still not fully comprehend why problems are being addressed or why they are being addressed in a particular way. The why of problem solving is found in the community's foundation of beliefs and values.

Beliefs Foundation

The third foundation of power rests on the beliefs, principles, and values of the community. Many of the beliefs, principles and values that guide the arena are well defined but the community often works with a tacit understanding of its beliefs and values. At times, the values and beliefs that underlie student aid policies are unconnected, compartmentalized and even conflictual. The arena does not seek philosophical coherence nor does it have a mechanism for value clarification. Over the years, new programs and policies have been created to match policy actors' assumptions about problems without any concern over whether or not the guiding assumptions and beliefs mesh to form a coherent philosophy. This explains why supporters of seemingly contradictory policy proposals can each claim that their problem solution is grounded in the values of the arena and vital to its future. While the values and beliefs that guide the policy arena are not always well defined and articulated, and at times conflictual and contradictory, successful problem solving is dependent on solutions that are grounded in the beliefs and values of the higher education policy arena.

In addition to beliefs, principles, and values, traditions and emotional experiences serve as a basis for problem solving without first being developed into abstract principles or clearly articulated beliefs. As Roschwalb explained, the basis for a policy proposal often is that "we all feel good about it" (Personal interview, January 10, 1991). A student playing a Chopin polonaise may move congressional members to offer a policy position that becomes a belief or value statement over time but is a strictly emotional response when initially stated. A specific example of an emotional response resulting in a policy decision was from a "1986 hearing where a medical student that had over $100,000 in student loan debt testified, and you got the combined payment plan found in Section 45(b) as a memorial to that poor guy" (John Dean, personal interview, January 11, 1991). The Morrill Act probably earned support from a feeling that farmers and mechanics were being treated unfairly by higher education as much as from any well-articulated belief about the proper role of the federal government in higher education. These emotional reactions and responses to events are proto-beliefs that sometimes evolve into fully articulated beliefs, principles, or values. In considering the beliefs foundation, it is important to recognize that beliefs may follow from the actions of policy actors as much as their actions follow from beliefs.

Although the higher education policy arena often functions with a tacit understanding of its beliefs and values, a number of beliefs and principles that guide policy actors in the development of policy are well defined, articulated, and understood. The contested principles identified in chapter 2 represent beliefs and values that have evolved into clearly stated principles. One of these contested principles, dating from the earliest days of the nation, holds that it is a proper role of the federal government to provide grants to states for the support of higher education. A second principle is that the federal government can and should use the higher education system to meet national needs for specially educated and trained human resources while recognizing the independence of individual institutions. Federal use of the higher education system as an instrument for social reform is a third principle and is reflected in many HEA programs. The belief that higher education is both a public and private good whose cost should be shared between the federal government, state government, the student, and the family is a fourth principle. A fifth principle is that of nondiscrimination between private and public institutions in the awarding of federal grants and loans. A related principle, which played a major role in the 1992 reauthorization when proprietary schools were confronted with proposals for separate aid programs, is nondiscrimination between nonprofit and proprietary schools in the availability of student aid. The last principle is a preference for the use of private agencies in the delivery of student aid. This was evident in the direct lending versus GSL program debate.

In crafting policy proposals, it is important to recognize and respect these principles. By ignoring the principles or proposing policies that conflict with understood principles, a policy actor is not merely proposing a new policy course but is proposing that the beliefs of the community be rethought. As the Bush administration learned when it proposed changes that clashed with these principles, it is difficult to implement policy changes that ask policy actors not just to reallocate funds or restructure programs but to reconsider their assumptions and beliefs. To implement change, the Bush administration needed either to ground its proposals in the contested principles of the community and demonstrate how the proposals extended those principles into the future, or convince policy actors that their assumptions about the world were no longer congruent with reality. Since the Bush administration did neither, the merits of its proposals were never seriously considered even by members of its own party.

In addition to the contested principles, other basic beliefs and values are also well defined and understood by members of the higher education policy arena. One of the longest standing is the belief that the federal government has a positive role to play in promoting equal educational opportunity for the social and economically disadvantaged. This was a guiding belief of the original HEA and continues to be important today. It is clearly reflected in a Senate staffer's explanation that "if you want to get in good with Chairman Pell, then you talk about how your proposal will help poor kids have an equal chance to attend college" (Personal interview, May 6, 1992). The Pell Grant program, the Supplemental Educational Opportunity Grant, and the TRIO programs can be interpreted as tangible representations of the community's belief in equal educational opportunity.

Another belief that guides and shapes policy making is that student needs outweigh institutional needs. While this is a long held belief, it is one that many higher education associations still have difficulty understanding. The difficulty associations have with internalizing this belief may be due to the fact that they are largely organized by sectors. Blakey believed that this form of organization hurts associations because "I don't think people on the Hill want to hear about sectors and I don't think they want to hear about institutions. I think they want to hear about students" (Personal interview, January 17, 1991). Problem solutions may provide benefits to institutions but not before the needs of students or at the expense of students.

A third belief is the orientation toward need-based rather than merit-based aid. Rate of return studies indicate that the federal government reaps a handsome return on student aid and would benefit by investing in all students regardless of need (Leslie & Brinkman, 1988), but the dominant value orientation of the policy arena is one of providing need-based assistance. In return for federal assistance, parents are expected to contribute toward the cost of higher education, students are expected to take summer jobs and school year work-study jobs, and students and their parents are expected to take loans to pay for schooling. The Eisenhower administration's proposal for merit-based scholarships, discussed in chapter 2, confronted this value orientation and quickly faded. Democratic members of Congress supported a similar proposal for merit scholarships with the same results. Some success has been achieved in the creation of merit-based graduate scholarships but these are seen in a different light than undergraduate student aid. Graduate aid is not thought of as student aid but as human resource development. At the undergraduate level, the belief in need-based aid has been operationalized in programs such as the GSL program, the college work-study program, and Pell Grants.

Still another set of beliefs revolves around the issue of aid to middle income students. These beliefs are more difficult to summarize because they grow out of a broad set of assumptions that policy actors hold about aid and the need for aid to middle-income students. One of these is the assumption or belief that middle-income students are being squeezed out of the higher education because of the high cost of college and the lack of student aid. The claim accompanying this assumption is that low-income students qualify for and receive extensive federal student aid, high-income students go to college without aid, and middle-income students do not qualify for student aid and cannot afford the cost of college. It is this belief that helped produce MISAA and still creates support for tuition tax credits.

The last part of this set of beliefs is the assumption that without aid to middle-income students the student aid programs would not enjoy the support of middle-class voters. The argument for extending aid to middle-income students is that without it and the support it brings from middle-class voters the student aid programs would be relegated to status of poverty programs. Given the level of support for poverty programs, this would be the end of student aid as we know it. This assumption about aid to middle-income students is the basis for the various GSL program loans, the expansion of loan limits, SSIG, and the expansion of qualifying income limits under the Pell Grant program.

The three foundations of power provide a framework within which problems must be addressed. The foundations serve as a basis for problem solving only as long as the needs of the community are being met. In the policy arena, it is impossible to solve all problems, but a few unsolved problems are acceptable. It is when unsolved problems begin to multiply, institutions become unresponsive, social relationships strain, and beliefs are questioned that the communication community moves toward a crisis. If the foundations lose their ability to bind and organize the community's historical and social experience, then they must be repaired, rebuilt, or replaced if the community is to continue its existence. The higher education policy arena is not close to a crisis state. While some unresolved problems continue to plague the community, none come close to precipitating a crisis. Just the opposite, the community has used the framework to address problems that threaten its equilibrium and to maintain its balance.

PROBLEM SOLVING

At the core of the communication community is the concept of problem solving. Communication communities, as defined by Arendt, Dewey, and Habermas, and as defined here, exist to solve problems. Power is the ability to address and solve problems that arise within the community. Problem solving is the thread that binds the community and collective action. When the community loses its ability to solve problems, it unravels and ceases to exist as a communication community. The key to understanding the meaning of power in a communication community is in understanding what it means to solve problems.

The idea of problem solving as power in a communication community is directly attributable to John Dewey (1927/1988). This is also true of the belief that communication communities exist to solve problems. The interpretation of power and problem solving in the higher education policy arena is indebted to Dewey and other communicative action theorists, but because the interpretation is grounded in the social and historical experience of that arena it differs from earlier theorists in important ways. If these differences are found to apply to other communication communities, then they mark a significant expansion and improvement of communicative action theory.

One of the differences is the identification of the foundations of power in the community. The foundations of power form a framework within which problems are addressed and solved. While there are different ways to address problems in the arena, a common characteristic of successful problem solving is that the solution rests within the constraints of the framework created by the foundations. The most elegant, effective, efficiently designed and constructed problem solutions have little prospect of success if the solutions fall outside the boundaries of the framework.

The use of foundations also captures the dynamic, interactive nature of power in a communication community. This was missing from earlier communicative action theories. Arendt presents a rather static community bound by a social contract. Habermas offers a world so bound by rules that it is difficult imagining people despoiling his idealized society by engaging in the actual rough and tumble of communicative action. Dewey presents the most dynamic community of the three but also fails to fully capture the interactive nature of power in a communication community. Instead, Dewey focuses on the prerequisites of problem solving—common language, mutual experiences, shared symbolic meanings—without exploring the interactions inherent in problem solving.

The concept of foundations of power provides not only a framework for problem solving but also a framework for understanding the interactions that take place in problem solving. From a broad view, the interaction between the three foundations generates power, regulates power, and provides the channels and boundaries of power in the community. A closer look at the interactions reveals institutions struggling to expand or survive, policy actors supporting policy recommendations on the basis of friendship, and policy actors taking stands on their beliefs and values. The community is alive with persons and personal ties, ideas, beliefs, fears, and hopes stated in the form of policy proposals, recommendations, and objectives. Indeed, it is a dizzying view of a community in near constant motion seeking to maintain balance and control. The use of the concept of foundations of power allows the observer to look at and understand problem solving based on an interaction of social and personal relationships, institutional relationships, and the beliefs and values of policy actors.

Last, the concept of foundations of power improves on and goes beyond earlier communicative action theories by establishing the relationship between power and change in a communication community. Within the community, power, problem solving, is not exercised as long as a state of equilibrium exists. If there are no problems, there is no need for problem solving. Power becomes evident when the community sees an imbalance and seeks to return the community to a state of equilibrium. The need for change often comes from one of the foundations, for example, institutional change or challenge, personnel change or shifting beliefs. The reauthorization cycle forces the community to confront change on a regular basis.

Types of Problem Solving

Problem solving has several different meanings in a communication community. At its most basic, problem solving is simple problem solution. The proposal for direct lending as a substitute for the GSL program is an example of simple problem solving. One can make the case that the solution was not simple and that its impact would be complex and far reaching, but that misses the point. Direct lending is not simple problem solving because the solution is simple. It is simple problem solving because it is a direct response to a stated problem. The proposal for a Pell Grant entitlement falls into the same category of problem solving. How can the problem of shortfalls in Pell Grant program funding be solved? Make the Pell Grant program an entitlement.

Problem definition is a more complex form of problem solving in that one must identify and define a problem where none had existed before. The elements of a problem might exist, but they have not been crystallized and shaped into a clearly defined and accepted problem. One must convince the community that it is experiencing a problem. For example, loan defaults were an inherent feature of the GSL program because it provided unsecured loans to young men and women with no credit history and no viable means of repaying the loans should they fail to finish school. The potential for defaults increased as the GSL program opened to more students and schools. While the potential existed for a ballooning default rate, the default rate actually remained stable (Lee & Merisotis, 1990).

Several factors combined to give definition to the problem of defaults. One factor was the shift in federal student aid from grants to loans. The default rate, while stable, was overshadowed by the volume of loans in default. Indeed, much of "the furor over defaults that occurred in the middle 1980s appears to have been the result of total dollars defaulted" (Lee & Merisotis, 1990, p. 52). The short-lived MISAA added to the furor when the public learned that students and families without need had obtained low-interest loans that were then placed in high-interest-bearing accounts. The speculation in student loans was quickly stopped, but the stories lived on and on.

As researchers focused on who defaulted, they found that a high number and volume of loan defaults were from proprietary school students. The negative focus on proprietary schools increased as it became clear that unscrupulous schools had entered the sector merely to make money off the hopes and dreams of students leaving them with no labor market skills, large loans, and no way to repay their debts. The *Arizona Republic, Chicago Sun-Times, Cleveland Plain Dealer, Los Angles Times, St. Petersburg Times*, and a number of other major metropolitan newspapers published articles and series on proprietary school fraud and abuse. The loan default problem was being defined as the proprietary school problem.

Education Secretary William J. Bennett reinforced this definition of the problem with his steady criticism of proprietary schools and loan defaults. Bennett did identify traditional higher education as part of the problem, but most of the time he used proprietary schools and loan defaults interchangeably in discussing the problems of the GSL program. Legitimate proprietary schools, with long histories of excellence, found themselves having to make the case that they were not sleazy fly-by-night operations that existed only to use and abuse the federal student aid system.

Another important factor in the definition of the problem was the role played by traditional higher education associations. The associations could have defined the problem of defaults through any number of reasonable, acceptable definitions, but decided to define defaults in terms of the legitimacy of the proprietary sector. Part of their motivation was probably philosophical, but the steadily increasing share of federal student aid going away from traditional schools and to proprietary school students was almost certainly a factor in determining how associations defined the problem. Defining defaults as a proprietary school problem kept the focus away from traditional schools, limited the share of aid going to the proprietary sector, and held the potential for eliminating an entire sector from federal student aid programs. The traditional associations suggested that consideration be given to differentiating between the collegiate sector and vocational programs.

The proprietary sector attempted to respond but once the problem definition took shape it was very difficult to present an alternative not suggested by the emerging definition. Proprietary schools pointed to default rates in traditional schools, but the rates were lower and generally did not involve fraud and abuse. The case was also made that proprietary schools served a population not reached by traditional schools. The associations countered that community, junior, and vocational colleges served the same population and did it better than proprietary schools. Finally, the proprietary sector argued against different regulations on aid, but the traditional associations were willing to accept tough regulations for all schools, knowing that it would have a disparate impact on the proprietary sector.

As defined, the problem of loan defaults took on quite a different meaning than might have been expected by simply looking at the data. Various factors combined to define the problem of defaults as one of proprietary school participation in the GSL program. Once defined, the proprietary sector found it impossible to alter the debate because the alternatives were framed by the accepted problem definition. Proprietary schools were not the sole cause of the loan default problem, but even the alternatives offered by the proprietary sector saddled them with blame.

While simple problem solution and problem definition are more common, it is not unusual for policy arena participants to engage in problem avoidance as a form of problem solving. In problem avoidance, members of the policy arena either deny that a problem exists or claim that the problem definition is not legitimate. For example, during the debate over loan defaults, the idea of separate student aid programs for traditional and proprietary schools was offered as one possible solution. A related proposal involved transferring the proprietary sector to the Department of Labor (DOL) because the vocational programs offered by these schools fit with the DOL's training and development functions. Whatever the merits of such proposals, they were quickly squashed when Representative Ford and Senators Kennedy and Pell claimed that such proposals were not legitimate because they violated the principle of equal treatment for all education sectors. The traditional associations might have continued to define the problem solution as separate aid programs, but Ford, Kennedy, and Pell were also guardians of key obligatory passage points in the policy process—the House and Senate education committee and sub-committee chairs. Given the obstacles of principle and the positions of key policy actors, the associations let the problem solution drop and addressed other issues.

Communication communities that practice problem avoidance run the risk of undermining the basis of their community as other policy arenas look to solve the problems that they see going unaddressed. This gives license to those outside the community to address the problems being avoided. The Nunn committee report is a primary example of what can happen when problems are not addressed. Another example comes from the direct loan debate in the Senate, which found its way into the finance arena when the education subcommittee refused to address the issue.

Finally, there is problem solving that produces no visible change and appears to those outside the policy arena to be inaction rather than action associated with power and change. When the reauthorization cycle calls policy actors to review and renew the HEA, they sometimes find the status quo is more desirable than the available alternatives. As discussed in chapter 2, the higher education associations have at times asked the subcommittees to continue the HEA without any programmatic changes but with increases in the authorization levels. The White House has also called for programmatic continuation but with decreases in spending levels. In some reauthorizations, the subcommittees have reauthorized the HEA with little or no change. This gives the appearance that no problems were addressed when in fact they were but the solutions remained virtually the same.

Basis for Problem Solving

Problem solving in its different forms rests on an axiomatic system of beliefs, institutional relationships and personal relationships that guide the higher education policy arena in the construction and design of student aid programs. Problems are addressed on the basis of recommendations of a policy actor with whom another policy actor shares a personal relationship. The reason for following the recommendation is explained by policy actors in terms of knowledge, longevity, respect, trust, and other characteristics that define personal relationships. Institutions are defended because they are the institutions that policy actors know. Programs are created and defended on the basis of what a member believes to be right. As problems are addressed, there is an interaction between the foundations of power.

The interaction can be seen in the case of Arnie Mitchem and the TRIO programs. As discussed above, Mitchem is a good example of how personal relationships form a foundation for problem solving. As strong as his personal relationships might be, Mitchem must not violate institutional relationships or the guiding beliefs and values of the community. The position that Mitchem and TRIO hold is helped by the fact that the TRIO programs are fully interdependent and intermeshed with other institutions, and strongly reflect the values of the community. Policy actors who enjoy strong personal relationships and are aware of the limits and boundaries of these relationships are well positioned to be successful problem solvers. Those who can build on all three foundations are ideally positioned to address problems.

Institutional relationships and arrangements are a second basis for problem solving. Policy actors know and understand the existing arrangements and relationships and are reluctant to move toward unknown, untested alternatives. Institutional resistance also plays a role in shaping and determining problem solutions. Problem solving that meshes with existing institutional arrangements and relationships is less likely to meet with resistance and more likely to find supporters in the policy arena. The result is seen as conservatism and incrementalism in the policy process.

The debate over the State Student Incentive Grant (SSIG) program is a good example of problem solving shaped by institutional arrangements and relationships. Created by the 1972 reauthorization, SSIG was intended as a way to help students attend private schools and to provide the seed money for the creation of state-funded scholarship programs. By 1992, the program had achieved its goals and should have been discontinued on that basis. Supporters of early intervention programs saw SSIG as an opportunity to use the program as a template for a new program that would inherit the existing arrangements and relationships but for a new purpose.

The strategy was well conceived, the early intervention concept was popular, and success seemed imminent. Supporters were also encouraged by the strong level of support offered by Senators Kennedy and Pell. Despite the presence of all of the ingredients for success, the idea of substituting an early intervention mission for the SSIG's scholarship mission failed. Policy actors were unwilling to alter the existing institutional arrangements and relationships. SSIG supporters acted to reinforce this unwillingness and resisted ending a program on the basis of goal attainment. An early intervention program, based on the SSIG model, was created while the SSIG program was enlarged.

Institutional arrangements and relationships can also be thought of as problem solving that is based on maintaining the community. The same can be said of any set of social relationships and beliefs. Members of the community want to engage in problem solving that does not go beyond or against the culture of the community. This is represented in the institutional integrity problem and solution. The requirements of the language on institutional integrity did not go beyond the experience of policy actors, protected the arena against outside critics, and were consistent with the contested principles of the policy arena. Higher education associations opposed the language but were unable to define it as a solution falling outside the boundaries of the community. Many of the Reagan and Bush administrations' proposals can be viewed as conflicting with this pattern of problem solving. Policy actors were unwilling to embrace problem solutions that were not grounded in the history of the arena and which presented a future with institutional arrangements and relationships that were radically different from their current or past experiences.

ACE and Pell

The ACE orchestrated Pell Grant formula illustrates problem solving based on the community's beliefs, institutional relationships, personal relationships, and values. As discussed in chapter 4, the Pell Grant proposal was the product of extensive communicative interaction between first the associations and then the associations and the education committees and subcommittees. The proposal was a simple solution to the defined problem of the declining real dollar value of individual Pell Grant awards. Association representatives drew on personal relationships in crafting and presenting the proposal to the community. The proposal continued existing institutional relationships and was firmly grounded in equal educational opportunity and middle income concerns.

The final Pell Grant formula looked very similar to the initial ACE group proposal and was negotiated between the ACE group and the education committee, thus one might claim that the ACE was a powerful organization. The key to understanding ACE's success is not to think in terms of traditional power definitions of control over output but in terms of how ACE crafted and built its solution to the Pell Grant problem on the foundations of the community. First, by creating working groups that represented a broad cross section of higher education associations, ACE all but preempted any alternative problem solutions. The extensive communicative interaction with the subcommittee and committee staffs moved the proposal from its status as an ACE group proposal to that of a community proposal. Since the proposal continued the existing Pell Grant program, it was already well grounded in the beliefs and values of the community.

The most significant element in the success of the ACE proposal was its attention to institutional relationships. One reason that the formula had not been changed significantly during previous reauthorizations was the fear that any change would upset the balance between private and public institutions. Blakey summarized this fear:

> What everybody is really interested in doing is protecting their share of the money. For example, they wouldn't necessarily agree with it, but I think it is true nevertheless, for a period of time now, the independent colleges have opposed a Pell Grant entitlement to students, because they think if you give an absolute entitlement to students, most of them will go to public institutions rather than private institutions because they're less expensive. (Personal interview, January 17, 1991)

The ACE consensus proposal and the final compromise proposal addressed the fear of massive shifts in student populations between sectors. First, the formula provided an increase for low-income students so that a higher percentage of their need would be met. While this was a positive feature of the formula, it was not as generous as it might seem. While it would ease the financial burden of low income students, it would not alter the status quo. In addition, the formula responded to Congress's interest in expanding the Pell Grant program to include more middle-income students. Middle income student needs would only be met by fully funding the Pell Grant program, thus creating pressure for full funding and protecting the status of low income students. Finally, by including tuition sensitivity, the formula addressed the needs of private colleges. While everyone benefited from the changes, the new formula did not alter the relationship between sectors because the additional money was not enough to enable students to buy up to more expensive schools. This made it possible for the different associations to remain committed to a consensus that supported significant change in the formula but maintained the status quo in terms of institutional relationships.

While the ACE group can claim success in problem solving, a simple counting of accepted problem solutions is not an accurate way to access success. Instead, one needs to carefully examine claims of success to determine their validity. It could be that an organizational claim of success is actually an artifact of another group's success. The interaction of foundations might produce results that benefit a group without that group having any influence in or over the interaction. The Career College Association (CCA) claimed a number of reauthorization victories but this does not necessarily mean that the association was a successful problem solver.

CCA

The CCA represents private, for-profit trade and technical schools. Formed in 1991 by a merger between the National Association of Trade and Technical Schools (NATTS) and the Association of Independent Colleges and Schools (AICS), CCA is the Washington voice of the proprietary sector but a run of bad publicity was threatening to muffle that voice going into the reauthorization. The problems of loan defaults, GSL program fraud and abuse, the activities of the Nunn committee, calls for separate student aid programs, and a growing anti–trade school sentiment in Congress created an atmosphere in which trade school representatives believed that their worst policy fears might become reality in the new HEA.

CCA attempted to counter this negative atmosphere through lobbying, education of congressional members and staff, field trips, and campaign contributions. The primary goal of CCA was to reframe the reauthorization moving the discussion away from issues of fraud and abuse, loan defaults, and institutional integrity and toward the question of workforce preparation. Lee believed that for CCA to be successful it had to

> position this reauthorization around the questions of work-force preparation. So if, if the proprietary school guys had their way, the debate in this reauthorization would be . . . How are student aid programs contributing to preparation of tomorrow's workforce? Because the proprietary schools assume that they can win on that. (Personal interview, February 24, 1992)

The CCA's efforts failed for a number of reasons. One very important reason was that institutional relationships in the community are not based on workforce preparation. This would have been a good way to frame the discussion in a vocational education or a human resources development and training policy arena but it was out of place in the higher education policy arena. A second reason was that CCA's personal relationships had weakened and waned as the concern over proprietary school abuse and fraud in the GSL program had increased. Members of Congress and their staffs continued to interact with CCA representatives and most probably understood that the large majority of its members were sound schools but after the Nunn committee hearings and report no one wanted to champion the proprietary school cause. In addition, CCA was excluded from communicative activities such as the discussions that helped elevate the ACE group Pell Grant formula from an association proposal to a community proposal. A final reason for CCA's failure to reframe the reauthorization agenda was the difficulty in linking workforce preparation with community beliefs and values. The community has never equated equal educational opportunity with the production of engineers, teachers, or other specific occupations or job skills. What was always important was that students have access to higher education not that they choose particular majors or careers. The closest example of workforce preparation would probably be the National Defense Education Act (NDEA) but even the NDEA fell far short of the CCA agenda. In sum, the CCA just "couldn't sell their agenda, they couldn't sell their sensibility about what we ought to be thinking about as a nation in this reauthorization" (Lee, personal interview, February 24, 1992).

Despite CCA's unsuccessful attempt to reframe the agenda, CCA head Stephen Blair proclaimed "we won the war" (quoted in DeParle, 1992, A1). A senate staffer dismissed Blair's proclamation as "a case of claiming victory and going home" because "they were not active in the process nor were they very effective" (Personal interview, May 6, 1992). Blair's ability to claim success when CCA had actually failed to control the agenda is explained by the nature of problem solving in the community. The nature of problem solving in the community is such that problem solutions seldom single out one sector as a winner or loser. Instead, the entire community enjoys the success or suffers the pain of a problem solution. This approach to problem solving was of particular benefit to the proprietary sector CCA represented because these schools had been defined as the problem plaguing the student aid program. Blair could claim victory not because CCA had won but because they had been protected by the community. For example, while the institutional integrity provisions of HEA would have a major impact on the proprietary sector the provisions would apply to all schools. CCA schools could still qualify on the same basis as traditional schools even if fewer schools could qualify.

The clearest statement of this protection came when Representative Ford and Senators Kennedy and Pell declared that a two-track student aid system was not a feasible recommendation and would not be considered. Ford flatly declared that such a system would produce "a federal policy of class structure in post-secondary education that I am absolutely never going to support" (quoted in Cooper, 1991, p. A9). By defending the contested principles that guided the community, Ford, Kennedy and Pell protected CCA's place in that community.

Even without the protection provided by the Ford, Kennedy, and Pell proclamations on separate programs, the traditional associations would have faced considerable difficulty in fashioning problem solutions that defined the proprietary sector as the problem and created separate programs or standards for those schools as the solution. Any such solution would have violated the contested principles that guide the policy-making process in the higher education policy arena. It is also likely that any solution limiting student access to proprietary schools would have been successfully redefined by CCA as an attack on equal educational opportunity and as favoring institutional needs over student needs. Many CCA school students are low-income and/or minority students, thus the claim of an attack on equal educational opportunity might have carried some weight. In addition, by redlining CCA schools, Congress would be denying those students an educational opportunity that would help them climb the ladder of economic and social mobility. By reserving student aid money for select institutions, Congress would have given tacit approval to institutional aid after having rejected the concept some twenty years earlier when it decided that students should determine where their aid dollars would be spent and that institutions would have to compete for those dollars.

The effect of the beliefs, relationships, and values of the community was to protect the CCA and the proprietary sector. A House Republican staffer summarized the role of beliefs, relationships, and values in explaining that "what happened was that ACE carried their water. In working to protect ACE schools, ACE also protected CCA" (Personal interview, May 5, 1992). This is not to suggest an immutable basis for problem solving that always maintains the status quo. Instead, it is to say that this reauthorization did not revolve around some of the fundamental beliefs and values of the community in the way that the 1972 reauthorization did. If a future reauthorization alters the basis for problem solving, CCA might find itself excluded from the community, or at least shunted to the margin, unless it improves its problem solving ability.

Successful problem solvers, whether engaged in problem solution, problem definition, or problem avoidance, ground their solutions in the beliefs, institutional relationships, personal relationships, or values of the higher education community. If the problem solution is grounded in the community's beliefs and values, then the problem solver must demonstrate that its acceptance will advance or meet the goal of equal educational opportunity, economic need, middle-income concerns or student need. Problem solutions based on institutional arrangements must show a link to the past, a consistency with the present, and the promise of taking the community safely into the future. Finally, problem solving based on personal relationships rest on a history of personal trust and knowledge but must not violate the beliefs, values, and institutional relationships of the policy arena.

CONCLUSIONS

Chapter 5 returned to the question that initiated this project: What is the meaning of power in the higher education policy arena? The short answer is that power is represented by the ability of policy actors to successfully address problems within the policy arena. Power cannot be fully explained in a word or phrase but must take its definition and meaning from the social and historical context in which it is situated. More fundamentally, power must be understood in terms of the foundations on which the community rests and on which problem solutions are constructed.

The idea of problem solving is at the heart of both the communication community and the foundations of power concept. As defined by Arendt, Dewey, and Habermas, communication communities exist to solve problems. Problem solving in the higher education policy arena does not conform to the expectations of earlier communicative action theories. The social relationships that mark problem solving in the higher education policy arena do not meet Arendt's concept of a social contract nor do they resemble or aspire to some Habermasian ideal of communicative competence. Policy actors do not always state propositions in such a manner that they are cognitively true. While there is a degree of normative orientation, policy actors do intend to deceive, or at least interpret to their advantage, in communicative acts.

The different positions held by policy actors in relationship to one another means that uncoerced communication is an ideal that will never become a reality. Finally, there is no communicative reason embedded in the language of the policy actors. The language of the arena is an expression of beliefs, emotions, goals, values, and visions that policy actors hope to translate into policy.

Power, the ability of policy actors to address problems, rests on three broad foundations. These foundations, suggested by the historical and social context of the community, interact to give form, shape and meaning to power. One foundation of power is formed by society's defining institutions and structures. These visible structures are the products of decisions made in earlier policy arenas. A second foundation is formed by the personal and social relationships of the community. This includes the explicit rules that govern relationships among policy actors and programs, as well as, the personal relationships that develop between policy actors. The third foundation of power consists of the beliefs and values that policy actors draw on for guidance in making policy decisions and choices. Interaction between foundations generates power, regulates power, and provides the channels and boundaries of power in the policy arena.

Identifying problem solving as power in a communication community is not new. What is new is the effort to uncover the beliefs, institutional relationships, personal relationships, social relationships, and values that form the foundations of power and guide the policy arena in problem solving. Once uncovered, these foundational elements provide insight into the framework that policy actors use to address and solve problems. The use of the foundations concept also captures the dynamic, interactive nature of problem solving in the community. The framework allows the observer to look at and understand problem solving based on an interaction of social and personal relationships, institutional relationships, and the beliefs and values of policy actors. Last, the concept establishes the relationship between power and change in a communication community.

Finally, problem solving grounded in the beliefs, relationships, and values of the community is the thread that holds collective action together. Interpreting power as problem solving opens new ways to consider policy making in the higher education policy arena. The use of the foundations of power concept provides a new analytical tool for understanding and interpreting activity in the higher education policy arena. The next chapter considers the implications of this interpretation for policymakers and policy researchers. In addition, areas of continuing research are suggested.

6

Making History

Under ordinary circumstances, chapter 5 would have marked the end of this study followed by a chapter devoted to a discussion of the implications of the work and the direction of future research. Historically, neither Congress nor the administration have proposed major changes in HEA immediately following reauthorization. Some exceptions can be noted, 1973 for example, but these efforts have been unsuccessful. Instead, a period of consolidation and adjustment has followed each reauthorization as Congress fine-tunes HEA through a series of technical amendments. One could safely assume that the analysis presented in chapter 5 would hold at least until Congress reauthorized HEA sometime between 1997 and 1999, and possibly even beyond.

A brief scan of the political scene in late 1992 only served to reinforce this view. If reelected, President Bush, who had not exhibited a strong interest in higher education, could not be expected to reopen HEA. Candidate Bill Clinton had proposed a national service program coupled with direct student loans, but the details of the national service program were fuzzy and the promise to provide direct loans had already been met by the 1992 HEA. Activist members of Congress might want to enact major changes but they had just exhausted considerable energy on HEA and had learned how quickly dreams, such as a Pell Grant entitlement, can crumble against the firewalls of the Budget Enforcement Act of 1990 (BEA). In any case, the committees that had just reauthorized HEA were now set to focus on ESEA reauthorization. With the exception of the usual technical amendments to HEA, members of the higher education policy arena could look forward to a rest from legislative activity.

Two events helped produce activity and outcomes in the higher education policy arena that were far different from what could be predicted at the conclusion of the 1992 reauthorization. The first event was the election of Bill Clinton as president. The newly elected

Democratic president came to the White House intent on keeping a campaign promise to create a national service program that would allow students to exchange community service for student aid and on replacing existing student loan programs with an income contingent, direct loan program with IRS collection. For Bill Clinton, the national service and direct lending programs would make history and leave a legacy in the way that the Peace Corps had for his boyhood hero, President John F. Kennedy.

The second event was the 1994 midterm election. The midterm elections gave the Republican Party a majority in the House and Senate for the first time since the Truman administration. Congressional leaders who had worked to expand the student aid program since the days of the Johnson administration were replaced by leaders intent on repelling the Clinton student aid agenda and reopening the contested principles and assumptions that had guided the policy arena for almost thirty years. More than simply repealing the Clinton agenda, the new Republican majority with its "Contract with America" wanted to make its place in history and leave a legacy by eliminating the last vestiges of the Great Society.

Chapter 6 focuses on these events and their impact on the higher education policy arena. The first part of the chapter examines Clinton's effort to leave a historical legacy with his plan for direct lending and national service. This is followed by a discussion of the of the self-proclaimed "Republican Revolution." In these two events one sees the interaction of ideas, institutions, and individuals as they bump, clash, conflict, and mesh creating the need for problem solving discussed in chapter 5.

LEAVING A LEGACY

"Opportunity for all, means giving every young American the chance to borrow the money to go to college and pay it back. Pay it back as a percentage of income over several years, or with years of national service here at home—a domestic G.I. Bill" (Clinton, quoted in Waldman, 1995, March/April, p. 34). With those words presidential candidate Bill Clinton presented his plan to widen access to higher education, reform the GSL program, and fight cynicism with the idealism of volunteerism. Democratic nominee Clinton's promise was captured in the party's 1992 platform statement that "a Domestic GI Bill will enable all Americans to borrow money for college, so long as they are willing to pay it back as a percentage of their income over time or through national service addressing unmet community needs" (quoted in Zook, 1994, June 8, p. A20). The campaign promise would become AmeriCorps, a centerpiece of Clinton's domestic policy agenda, a program that he believed would be his legacy to future generations (Gerstenzang, 1995).

Ironically, what Clinton saw as the crown jewel of his domestic policy and as his legacy to future generations had not been fully embraced by his campaign staff, nor had the promise been carefully scrutinized during the campaign. James Carville, one of Clinton's chief political advisors, saw the national service idea as a distraction from the campaign's main theme, but noted that "every candidate has one of these things. You humor him and you move on" (quoted in Waldman, 1995, p. 13). Candidate Clinton's claims about national service and revolutionizing student financial aid were overlooked as the press focused on economic issues, health care reform, welfare reform, and other campaign themes.

Clinton frequently mentioned his service plan but the focus of the campaign and the attention of campaign observers was the economy. While some may have viewed it as a side issue, Clinton's commitment to national service and student aid reform was real and deep. If there had been any doubts during the campaign, the questions were removed with the appointment of Eli Segal to run the White House Office of National Service. Segal (1994) was a trusted friend who had served as chief of staff of the Clinton-Gore campaign and as chief financial officer during the presidential transition. Noted as a man who got things done, Segal's project was to move the idea of national service from a campaign promise, to legislation, to law, and into a successfully functioning program by 1996.

While Segal enjoyed a history of political and entrepreneurial success, it did not include experience with national or community service programs (Waldman, 1995). If he was to succeed in this new arena, he needed able assistants who knew the policy issue and who knew how to get things done on Capitol Hill. In that vein, Shirley Sagawa, a former aid to Senator Kennedy, was convinced to leave her position as vice chair of the Commission on National and Community Service to help guide the project (Waldman, 1995). As a Kennedy staffer, she had been responsible for drafting the National and Community Service Act of 1990 (Waldman, 1995). Segal also tapped Jack Lew, who had previously worked for House Speaker Tip O'Neill (Waldman, 1995). Lew's expertise was not in the area of national service or student aid but in crafting legislation that could attract a majority in the House.

The president had promised national service, direct lending, and IRS collection of student loans. Segal, Sagawa, and Lew were faced with the task of drafting legislation that spanned several policy arenas while meeting the legal requirements of the BEA. They quickly learned that the reform project, as envisioned could neither be fully funded nor could it be navigated through Congress with its fragmented committee structure. The bill would have to pass through too many committees with each committee and committee hearing becoming an opportunity for opponents of the project to question its wisdom, budget, structure, and need. By March 1993, the decision was made to split the idea into its component parts (Kennedy, 1994). The administration would present national service as an amendment to the National Service Act of 1990 and the Domestic Volunteer Act of 1973 (Segal, 1994). Direct lending took the form of the Student Loan Reform Act of 1993 which was incorporated into the Omnibus Budget Reconciliation Act (Ford, 1993).

Segal, Sagawa, and Lew retained responsibility for the national service legislation. Kennedy (1994) took responsibility for introducing and guiding the service amendment through the Senate. For Kennedy, it was a labor of love that built on his earlier legislative work in the area and reflected his family's long commitment to service. Secretary of Education Richard Riley and Deputy Secretary Madeleine Kunin (1994) were given responsibility for the direct lending legislation. Representative Bill Ford (1994) agreed to be the bill's sponsor and floor manager in the House. For Ford it was one last chance to leave an education legacy after being frustrated by the Reagan and Bush administrations, as well as, by his own Democratic leadership during the 1992 reauthorization. In Clinton, Ford saw an education partner whose ambitions were as great as his own.

The administration had moved quickly on its campaign promise and seemed poised to deliver the legislation. The congressional sponsors controlled important obligatory passage points in the House and Senate. The staff behind the two bills were more than able with a history of legislative success. National service was an idea that resonated with the public and with members of Congress. The administration's service proposal could build on legislation and programs that had been previously approved by Congress. In contrast, the GSL programs had been the subject of increasing criticism in recent years. The banks, secondary markets, and guarantee agencies that earned considerable profits off the student loan programs found it harder and harder to justify their role in the system. These criticisms and questions had helped start the move away from the complex GSL system with the creation of a pilot direct loan program in the 1992 HEA. The administration could use this dissatisfaction with and movement away from the GSL program to build support for its direct lending proposal.

National Service

In May 1993, Kennedy (1994) and nineteen co-sponsors introduced the administration's national service bill. True to the history of bipartisan support for education issues, Kennedy's cosponsors included four Republican Senators. The bill was designed to accomplish four legislative objectives:

1. Create a National Service Trust which would fulfill Clinton's vision of national service linked to education benefits;
2. Expand the Serve-America service learning program, thus fulfilling Kennedy's vision of service learning;
3. Reauthorize other domestic service programs such as VISTA and the Older American Volunteer Programs, and
4. Bring all national service programs under the direction of a new administrative structure to be called the Corporation for National and Community Service. (Kennedy, 1994)

While separate from the direct loan bill, the two were clearly companion pieces of legislation intended to form a complete vision when joined together.

Once introduced the legislation was referred to Kennedy's Committee on Labor and Human Resources (see table 4) were it was then assigned to Christopher J. Dodd's Subcommittee on Children, Family, Drugs and Alcoholism (see table 5). As the bill moved through hearings, it attracted programs that were not envisioned by either Clinton or Kennedy when the legislation was introduced. The new programs represented the pet projects and interests of committee members. Jeff Bingaman of New Mexico wanted a program for historical and cultural preservation (Kennedy, 1994). A program to convert military installations into community centers was proposed by Howard Metzenbaum (Kennedy, 1994). Other Senators added their service related projects to the legislation as it moved through the markup process. The bill was reported to the full Senate from the Labor and Human Resources Committee by a vote of 14–3 on June 16, 1993 (Kennedy, 1994).

Conspicuous by her absence from the majority vote was the ranking Republican member of the committee, Nancy Kassebaum.

TABLE 4
Senate Committee on Labor and Human Resources, 103rd Congress

Democrats	Republicans
Edward M. Kennedy (Mass.) *Chairman*	Nancy Kassebaum (Kans.) *Ranking Member*
Claiborne Pell (R.I.)	James M. Jeffords (Vt.)
Howard M. Metzenbaum (Ohio)	Dan Coats (Ind.)
Christopher J. Dodd (Conn.)	Judd Gregg (N.H.)
Paul Simon (Ill.)	Strom Thurmond (S.C.)
Tom Harkin (Iowa)	Orrin G. Hatch (Utah)
Barbara A. Mikulski (Md.)	Dave Durenberger (Minn.)
Jeff Bingaman (N.Mex.)	
Paul D. Wellstone (Minn.)	
Harris Wofford (Pa.)	

TABLE 5
Senate Subcommittee on Children, Family, Drugs, and Alcoholism,
103rd Congress

Democrats	Republicans
Christopher J. Dodd (Conn.) *Chairman*	Dan Coats (Ind.) *Ranking Member*
Claiborne Pell (R.I.)	Nancy Kassebaum (Kans.)
Barbara A. Mikulski (Md.)	James M. Jeffords (Vt.)
Jeff Bingaman (N.Mex.)	Judd Gregg (N.H.)
Edward M. Kennedy (Mass.)	Strom Thurmond (S.C.)
Paul D. Wellstone (Minn.)	Dave Durenberger (Minn.)
Harris Wofford (Pa.)	

Historically, education legislation in the Senate Labor and Human Resources Committee has enjoyed bipartisan support. The subcommittee on education, arts, and the humanities was dominated for many years by the strong Stafford-Pell relationship. Kassebaum (1994) supported the idea, claiming that "the concept of community-based volunteerism is the most important aspect of service" (p. 35), but questioned the legislation designed to move the concept into reality. Earlier, Kassebaum (1994) had urged Segal to split the national service program into two pieces of legislation. Now that she had seen the piece devoted to national service, Kassebaum (1994) was concerned about the rate of expansion and projected costs, its bureaucratic structure, the lack of state and local autonomy, and the use of scarce higher education dollars for a new program while the Pell Grant program continued to be seriously underfunded.

Ironically, higher education associations privately shared some of Kassebaum's concern about the use of scarce education dollars being diverted to a new program while existing programs were wanting for funds. The BEA would force the programs to compete with one another for a limited number of dollars. As proposed, the program would accelerate the move away from grants and toward loans. This would be true regardless of whether or not students participated in the national service program. The direct loan program would enjoy entitlement status, thus any qualified student would be entitled to a loan. Loan volumes would explode just as they had exploded under MISAA. In contrast, qualified students receive a Pell Grant if, and only if, Congress provided funds for the program. Barmak Nassirian, AASCU's director of federal relations, claimed that "this whole national service thing is a bunch of ideological garbage. Combine it with income-contingent loans and it's a real piece of shit" (quoted in Waldman, 1995, p. 61). Nassirian's view may have expressed rather bluntly the feelings of the higher education associations' toward direct lending, but it did not matter because Clinton was the first president in more than twelve years to offer higher education anything new. The higher education associations could oppose their new friend, the president of the United States, or they could get on board with his program. They chose to get on board.

As a senator, Kassebaum had other alternatives available. On July 1st, she introduced S.1212 National Service and Community Volunteers Act of 1993 as an alternative to the administration's bill. She also went to work preparing a series of amendments to be offered during the floor debate on the administration's bill. During the floor debate, Kassebaum's amendments were defeated, but helped focus opposition to the administration's bill. After a series of defeated amendments, the Republicans had identified enough votes to sustain a filibuster. Once it became clear that the Democrats could not break the filibuster, Kennedy moved to satisfy opposition to the bill. On July 28, the Kennedy-Durenberger-Wofford bill was introduced as a substitute for the administration bill (Kennedy, 1994). On August 3, the Senate passed the bill on a vote of 58–41 with only 7 Republicans joining 51 Democrats. The bill now headed toward conference where the House bill had been waiting since July 28.

The House version of national service was controlled by Ford. The bill would have to pass first through his subcommittee on education and training (see table 7). Next, it would be reported to the house floor by his committee on education and labor (see table 6). Although Democrats enjoyed a majority in the House, the administration worked

TABLE 6
House Committee on Education and Labor, 103rd Congress

Democrats	Republicans
William D. Ford (Mich.) *Chairman*	William F Goodling (Pa.) *Ranking Member*
William Clay (Mo.)	Thomas E. Petri (Wis.)
George Miller (Calif.)	Marge Roukema (N.J.)
Austin J. Murphy (Pa.)	Steve Gunderson (Wis.)
Dale E. Kildee (Mich.)	Richard K. Armey (Tex.)
Pat Williams (Mont.)	Harris W. Fawell (Ill.)
Matthew G. Martinez (Calif.)	Paul B. Henry (Mich.)
Major R. Owens (N.Y.)	Cass Ballenger (N.C.)
Thomas C. Sawyer (Ohio)	Susan Molinari (N.Y.)
Donald M. Payne (N.J.)	Bill Barrett (Nebr.)
Jolene Unsoeld (Wash.)	John A. Boehner (Ohio)
Pasty T. Mink (Hawaii)	Randy Cunningham (Calif.)
Robert E. Andrews (N.J.)	Peter Hoekstra (Mich.)
Jack Reed (R.I.)	Howard P. McKeon (Calif.)
Tim Roemer (Ind.)	Dan Miller (Fla.)
Eliot L. Engel (N.Y.)	
Xavier Becerra (Calif.)	
Robert C. Scott (Va.)	
Gene Green (Tex.)	
Lynn C. Woolsey (Calif.)	
Ron Klink (Pa.)	
Karan English (Ariz.)	
Ted Strickland (Ohio)	
Scotty Baesler (Ky.)	

with Ford to build a broad base of support for the bill. Working with Republicans Christopher Shays of Connecticut, a former Peace Corps volunteer, and Steve Gunderson of Wisconsin, a moderate Republican, the administration sought to create bipartisan support that would cut the ground out from under the opposition before it could start a campaign against the national service bill. Shays and Gunderson responded with a "Dear Colleague" letter that claimed national service as nothing less than a Republican idea (Waldman, 1995). As the bill's prime sponsor and floor manager, Ford's strategy was to sign on so many co-sponsors that passage of the bill would seem inevitable when it was formally introduced.

Opposing the bill represented a difficult choice for would be opponents. The idea of national service was a bit like campaigns against waste and fraud. If you dared to claim that such a campaign

TABLE 7
House Subcommittee on Postsecondary Education and Training,
103rd Congress

Democrats	*Republicans*
William D. Ford (Mich.)	Thomas E. Petri (Wis.)
Chairman	*Ranking Member*
Pat Williams (Mo.)	Steve Gunderson (Wis.)
Thomas C. Sawyer (Ohio)	Randy Cunningham (Calif.)
Jolene Unsoeld (Wash.)	Dan Miller (Fla.)
Pasty T. Mink (Hawaii)	Marge Roukema (N.J.)
Robert E. Andrews (N.J.)	Paul B. Henry (Mich.)
Jack Reed (R.I.)	Peter Hoekstra (Mich.)
Tim Roemer (Ind.)	Howard P. McKeon (Calif.)
Dale E. Kildee (Mich.)	Richard K. Armey (Tex.)
Robert C. Scott (Va.)	
Ron Klink (Pa.)	
Karan English (Ariz.)	
Ted Strickland (Ohio)	
Xavier Becerra (Calif.)	
Gene Green (Tex.)	

was ill-designed, then you might look like a defender of waste and fraud. If you opposed national service, especially with Ford lining up so many co-sponsors, then you ran the risk of looking like an opponent of access to college, service to meet unmet community needs, and in favor of helping greedy banks make money at the expense of needy students. Still, the bill was not without its opponents. Veteran's groups opposed the bill in the House, as they had in the Senate, claiming that it gave too much to those who had never truly served, thus insulting veterans who had risked their lives for the country (Waldman, 1995). To satisfy the veterans, the amount of aid for service was reduced. Republican's attempted to introduce means-testing in the House, as they had in the Senate, but it was defeated. ACE found itself at odds with Ford when it offered a letter of support for the means testing amendment in the House. Ford had long favored expansion of student aid to middle-income families, claiming that this helped maintain political support thus keeping the programs alive for the poor. When Ford saw the letter, he exploded, telling his staff to "tell Terry Hartle never to darken my goddamn doorway again" (quoted in Waldman, 1995, p. 196). Ford demanded and received a new letter from ACE that supported the national service bill in its entirety (Waldman, 1995). Finally, IRS collection was quietly dropped to avoid conflict with the Ways and Means Committee.

While Ford was able to handle these and other challenges to the bill, he was unable to bring Representative Bill Goodling, the ranking Republican on the House Education and Labor Committee, on board in support of the bill. Goodling (1994) had opposed direct lending during the 1992 reauthorization and his relationship with Ford had been bruised during the reauthorization process. One year later, he was no more enamored with a national service program that would be linked to a direct lending program designed to accomplish what its supporters had failed to achieve during the 1992 reauthorization. Goodling publicly expressed what some of the higher education associations had been saying in private—national service coupled with direct lending would take education dollars from the many to give to the few. Without dollars to fully fund existing programs at their authorized levels, Goodling found it difficult to support a new program that would compete for the same limited funds, thus leaving existing programs poorer still.

Goodling had serious questions about the bill, but was also concerned that Ford had moved away from the bipartisan tradition associated with education legislation. This movement had started during the 1992 reauthorization and continued under the Clinton administration. Ford did not need Republican votes in the House the way Kennedy did in the Senate. Without a need for these votes, the committee was starting to take on the more partisan atmosphere of the larger House. Goodling's anger and hostility over not being treated as a full partner finally broke open during the House-Senate conference on national service. In response to a remark by Ford about his being a good friend, Goodling retorted "Oh! it was fun when I was *needed* [emphasis in original]. Some kind of friendship" (quoted in Waldman, 1995, p. 232). Bill Goodling, the ranking Republican on the committee, would not support his old friend Bill Ford on the national service bill, nor would he get on board for the upcoming direct lending bill. Ford delivered the bill 270–156 without Goodling's support and over his opposition.

The conference committee proved to be a relatively tame affair with less than twelve hours being spent on reconciling the differences between the House and Senate versions of the national service bills (Kassebaum, 1994). The conference committee meet briefly on August 5 to approve the bill and the House passed it on August 6 (Kennedy, 1994). The calendar in the Senate forced a delay until after the August recess, but the bill was passed on September 8 and sent to the president. Clinton signed the National and Community Trust Act on September 21, 1993, on the White House lawn in front of youth corps members from around the nation (Segal, 1994). The administration had moved national service from a campaign idea to legislation in less than nine months.

Direct Lending

National service was relatively unimportant compared to the struggle that would take place over the administration's direct lending proposal. This is not a statement about the merit or worth of national service but rather recognition of the financial importance of the GSL program to a large number of stakeholders. National service was about principles but direct lending was about money. Commercial banks enjoyed more than $1 billion in profits from their student loan portfolios each year, a profit that is nearly 100 percent guaranteed by the federal government (Bluestone & Comcowich, 1992). Sallie Mae, with some $46 billion in total assets, reported some $394 million in profits in 1993, making the federally created organization one of the 100 largest U.S. corporations (Konigsberg, 1993). National service would create new revenue opportunities while direct lending would end a revenue source that produced billions of dollars in government guaranteed profits for the GSL industry. Sallie Mae, the banks, the state and private guarantee agencies, the secondary loan markets, the loan servicers, and the collection agencies could not be expected to quietly relinquish their interests.

Defeating the direct lending proposal would not be an easy task. In Congress and in the larger policy arena, there was a strong feeling that the lenders and guarantee agencies were making money at the expense of needy students, were not performing as intended, and were unfairly sheltered from real risk by the federal guarantee of loans and profit rates. Public policy concerns over high default rates had not been assuaged. The budget agreement and credit reform continued to favor direct lending over the GSL program. Democrats still controlled the obligatory passage points in the Congress and were now joined by a president and a secretary of education who were committed to direct lending. In sum, the changes that had occurred since 1992 advantaged the proponents of direct lending and disadvantaged its opponents.

It may have been the long odds and the threat to its continued existence that moved the members of the GSL industry to respond with such a ferocious lobbying campaign. The campaign prompted Clinton to complain that "no sooner had I even mentioned this system than Congress was deluged with lobbyists" (quoted in Konigsberg, 1993, p. 15). Many of the lobbyists were well-connected Democrats who were signing with the GSL industry to help defeat their president's proposal. Key GSL industry lobbyists included: Akin, Gump, Robert Strauss's firm; Patton, Boggs & Blow, home to a number of major Democratic party players, and once the home of Ron Brown and Vernon Jordan; Powell Tate, a firm that took part of its name from Jody Powell, President Carter's former press secretary; Walker/Free Associates, with Free being former Carter White House official James Free; and, Williams & Jensen, which employed David Starr, a former Metzenbaum staffer (Konigsberg, 1993; Boot, 1993). Sallie Mae used their usual lobbyist, Williams & Jensen, while also adding several new lobbyists to work on direct lending. A key addition was Jerry Hultin, who had managed the Clinton campaign in Ohio and had helped with the cost analysis of the national service program (Waldman, 1995). The GSL industry lobbyists would be able to open doors, but there was no guarantee that the policymakers behind those doors would be inclined to cooperate.

Despite the wealth of lobbying talent, the GSL industry got off to an impressive start. When the CBA offered to endorse a cut in loan subsidies, Andrews proposed simultaneously phasing in direct lending and cutting subsidies for existing loans (Waldman, 1995). Andrews mocked the CBA's embrace of proposals it had rejected in 1992 as "a death-bed conversion" (quoted in Jaschik, 1993, March 10, p. A28). Simon set the debate in stark either or terms stating "we subsidize students or we subsidize banks" (quoted in Jaschik, 1993, March 10, p. A28).

In March 1993, direct lending proponents turned a CBA-sponsored lobbying day into a major news event reported almost entirely from a pro–direct lending perspective. The CBA had brought a number of number of local bankers to Washington for a lobbying workshop to be followed by visits with congressional members. Simon staffer Robert Shireman and press secretary David Carle convinced the media to cover the workshop as an attack on national service and an effort by greedy bankers to maintain profits at the expense of needy students. The CBA lost control of any message that it might have wanted to deliver as the media turned its attention to GSL profits and the large salaries of senior GSL officials.

The CBA event did not go as planned, but the CBA was on target with its understanding of the need to involve the grassroots in lobbying committee and subcommittee members and staff. Congressional members and staff can become immune to the message of lobbyists, but the same message takes on a freshness and newness when it comes from the grassroots. In the absence of a groundswell of public support, lobbyists often create grassroots organizations to deliver their message from the hinterlands. When the public failed to rally to the cause of protecting the GSL industry, the industry created a grassroots to defend the current GSL system.

In Ohio, Andrew M. Goldner, a student at the University of Cincinnati, expressed student concerns about the possible demise of the GSL program. Goldner was speaking as president of the newly formed Ohio Students for Loan Reform. The organization presented the case against direct lending through newspaper ads, campus posters, and a toll-free line that students could use to call their senators (Jaschik, 1993, June 2). It did not help the GSL cause when Goldner admitted that his wages and the organization's expenses were paid by the Cincinnati-based Student Loan Funding Corporation (Jaschik, 1993, June 2). At almost the same time, two University of Wisconsin student leaders revealed that Sallie Mae had flown them to Washington as part of a failed effort to convince the students to establish a similar grassroots organization in Wisconsin (Konigsberg, 1993).

Instead of building support for the GSL program, the grassroots campaign seemed to strength the position of direct lending proponents. Andrews, Durenberger, Petri, and Simon strongly criticized the industry in a joint press conference that also demonstrated bipartisan support for direct lending (Jaschik, 1993, March 10). Discussing the Ohio Students for Loan Reform, Simon charged that "special interests are using students as fronts" (quoted in Jaschik, 1993, June 2, p. A18). Deputy Secretary of Education Kunin charged the industry with " a deliberate effort to raise uncalled-for fears" (quoted in Jaschik, 1993, June 2, p. A18). The salaries of GSL industry executives became a special target for criticism. In one press conference, Simon made the point by using charts to compare the salaries of Sallie Mae officials with the salary of the president of the United States (Waldman, 1995). The president's salary was represented by one small coin on the chart while the Sallie Mae salaries were represented by tall stacks towering high above the small coin. The best lobbyists that money could buy seemed to be doing little to help the GSL cause while doing a great deal to give aid and comfort to its opponents.

If the industry was to have any success, then it would have to look for help in the House or Senate rather than in the court of public opinion. In the House, Ford seemed to remain firmly in control and devoted to the president's proposal. The direct lending bill was easily included in the Omnibus Budget Reconciliation bill. More important than its inclusion was the way the bill was scored by the Congressional

Budget Office. Thanks to credit reform, the direct lending bill was scored as a budget savings item. Under the BEA, this meant that any critic of the proposal would have to substitute a proposal with savings equal to the $4 billion plus direct lending savings. The same rules that had prevented Ford and others from realizing a Pell Grant entitlement during the 1992 HEA reauthorization were now protecting the direct lending proposal.

With the House seemingly out of reach, the Senate represented the last opportunity for opponents of direct lending to derail the administration's proposal. As in the House, the Senate version of direct lending was to be included in the budget resolution. It looked as if the proposal would pass quietly through the Senate until Kassebaum focused attention on the proposal with the introduction of an amendment to alter the bill (Kunin, 1994). As with national service, she had doubts about the federal government's ability to administer the program. Kassebaum also worried because "its an enormous change. I'm only pausing because if it can be shown to be successful, then no, I wouldn't have a problem" (quoted in Zuckman, 1993, May 8, p. 1153). The purpose of the Kassebaum proposal was to scale down the direct lending program and to recapture the lost savings from other domestic programs.

Kassebaum was not alone in questioning the wisdom of substituting direct lending for the current GSL program. Pell also voiced "concerns over the ability of the department and many institutions to administer a direct lending program" (quoted in Zuckman, 1993, May 8, p. 1153). Jeffords supported direct lending but was also uneasy about dismantling the GSL program without first testing the reliability and validity of a direct lending program. The Kassebaum amendment failed by a vote of 51 to 47, but it revealed the weakness of the administration's position in the Senate with five Democratic senators voting against their president (Kunin, 1994).

The Kassebaum amendment had failed in large part because it would have required real cuts in existing education programs to replace the paper savings created by the CBO scoring of direct lending. The administration had prevailed on the amendment but a final victory looked less certain. Kennedy was willing to carry the administration's water on direct lending but he did not want to roll his old friend Pell and he would need Kassebaum and Jeffords' support. Something less than a complete replacement of the GSL program would have to be offered as a compromise.

Uncertainty about the legislation in the Senate created an opportunity for the GSL industry to redefine the problem and to offer a new solution. John Dean had tried to redefine the relationship between national service and direct lending during the CBA's ill-fated lobbying day but the point was lost in the media reports. The point that Dean had attempted to make that day was that national service could go forward without direct lending (Jaschik, 1993, March 3). Students who participated in a qualified service program could be given a certificate or voucher for a loan that would be repaid by the federal government. The existing GSL industry could make and service the loans thus eliminating the need for a new loan program.

Unable to gain support for decoupling the two programs, the GSL industry played on questions about the Education Department's ability to administer a massive direct lending program. Failure would mean that students who depended on loans would be denied access to higher education. Colleges that depended on students' having loans would be facing a financial crisis. Once the banks left the program, it would be impossible for them to return on short notice, thus higher education would be facing a catastrophe. Rather than risk this disaster, the GSL industry proposed a phase in of direct lending while maintaining the current system as a safety net. An additional advantage of this approach would be the opportunity to test the two systems in a direct competition.

Pushing this approach, the GSL industry worked hard to fashion an alternative with "unusual direct assistance from a member of Congress" (Dean, 1994, p. 168), Representative Bart Gordon. Gordon, with the help of Representatives Earl Pomeroy and Goodling, worked with the industry including "actively participating in meetings with banks, guaranty agencies, secondary markets, and Sallie Mae" (Dean, 1994, p. 169). The industry also worked with the staffs of Jeffords, Kassebaum, and Pell to develop an alternative to direct lending in the Senate. Despite these efforts, an industry consensus was not forthcoming "largely because of Sallie Mae's refusal to accept any package containing a user fee on its holdings or new financing" (Dean, 1994, p. 169).

To everyone's surprise, the alternative to the administration's proposal came not from the GSL industry or Kassebaum, but from Pell (Waldman, 1995). The Pell proposal called for a phase-in of direct lending until 30 percent of schools were under the program. At that point, a commission would review the program and Congress would vote on continued expansion. To recapture money lost by the scaled-down program, Pell's proposal reduced fees to banks. The proposal appealed to those with concerns about direct lending while still allowing them to move the president's plan forward. The proposal formed the basis of a compromise between Kennedy, Pell, Kassebaum, and Jeffords. As approved by the committee, the new bill called for 5 percent of schools to participate in 1994–95 increasing to a maximum of 50 percent in 1997–98 (Senate Panel, 1993, June 11). At that time, a bipartisan commission would review the program and make recommendations to the Congress. Finally, fees to bank would be sliced.

The senate bill's passage set the stage for an interesting conference committee. Participants such as Ford, Kennedy, and Pell, normally allies, found themselves on opposite sides of the issue. Ford entered the conference committed to a complete direct lending plan while Kennedy had to have a phased-in plan to maintain bipartisan support in the Senate. Without that support, the bill would not reach the floor for a vote. Republicans found themselves divided along similar lines. In the midst of the conference committee's work, Gordon released a letter opposed to direct lending with the signatures of 282 House members (Boot, 1993). Kennedy could do little to help Ford because he would face a rebellion in the Senate if he attempted to move away from the Senate consensus . The GSL industry found itself lobbying for a bill that would reduce its profits and eliminate as much as 50 percent of its market.

Fearful that its plan for student loan reform might be slipping away, the administration maintained pressure on the participants throughout the week of the conference. The administration strongly endorsed the house plan and gave full backing to Ford. As a show of support, Riley and Kunin sat in on one of the conference committee meetings (Zuckman, 1993, July 31). In addition, they met privately with conference members to encourage support for the president's position. Clinton moved to silence critics and build support by nominating Donald R. Wurtz to be the Education Department's (ED) chief financial officer (Zook, 1993, August 11). Wurtz, the director of financial integrity issues for the GAO, had been a strong critic of the ED's student loan programs.

The key players in the conference committee were Ford and Kennedy. Ford was committed to making 100 percent direct lending a reality. Kennedy supported Clinton's plan but did not have the votes in the Senate to pass a complete direct lending plan. As a result, the conference committee meetings were "combative, frustrating, tedious" (Zook, 1995, August 11, p. A23), and intense as the members met several times over the week and four times on the last day of the conference (Zuckman, 1993, July 31). The final language on direct lending looked more like the Senate proposal than the House proposal but it was hardly cause for celebration by the GSL industry.

The conference committee bill was built on the blueprint provided by the Pell proposal. The program would start with 5 percent of new loan volume in 1994–95 (Zuckman, 1993, July 31). Loan volume would then increase to 40 percent in 1995–96 and 50 percent in 1996–97. In 1997–98, the formula for participation would change to 50 percent plus any additional schools followed by 60 percent plus any additional schools in 1998–99. Depending on the number of schools participating after 1996–97, the volume of loans provided by the direct lending could exceed 50 percent of all loans within three years of the program's origination. To capture the savings lost by the scaled down program, the bill reduced fees paid to bankers and others in the GSL industry. The industry was not pleased with the final legislation, but at least it was alive. Roy Nicholson, chairman of the USA Group probably summarized the feelings of the industry when he said "we're very excited they made the decision not to implement 100 percent direct lending, but the cost-saving provisions may drive us out of the program" (quoted in Boot, 1993, p. 3).

With the passage of direct lending, Clinton had successfully implemented most of his student aid reform agenda during his first year in office. For the committees involved in higher education policy making, August 1993 marked the end of an intense and productive period of legislative activity. The committees had started work on reauthorization in 1990 and had been working, with little rest, on higher education policy issues for almost four years. With the Labor Day recess just ahead, the committee members could look forward to the vacation knowing that higher education was taken care of for the immediate future. In the meantime, they could tell the voters at home about their record of accomplishment.

THE REPUBLICAN REVOLUTION

In September 1994, Republican members of Congress and Republican congressional candidates gathered on the steps of the Capitol to offer a promise and present a contract to the American people. If the electorate voted the Republican party into a majority in the House, then the leadership would bring to a vote the ten items that formed its "Contract with America." The contract items called for cutting spending, getting tough on crime, encouraging personal responsibility, strengthening the family, giving a break to middle-class families, strengthening the military, letting senior citizens earn more, helping business create more jobs, limiting lawsuits against corporate America, and placing term limits on members of Congress. The intent of the Contract was nothing less than a revolution aimed at dismantling the social structures of the New Deal and Great Society and the regulatory structures created by the Nixon administration.

In November, the voters responded giving Republicans a majority on Capitol Hill for the first time in forty years. The architect of the Contract with America, Newt Gingrich, was elected Speaker of the House. The new leaders of the 104th Congress moved quickly to translate campaign promises into legislation. The new leadership also acted to reorganize committees, hire new staff, and award committee and subcommittee chairs. The new Congress looked very different from the 103rd Congress, which had so recently enacted national service and direct lending for an eager President Clinton, and from the 102nd Congress, which had sent the HEA reauthorization to a reluctant President Bush.

Among the changes enacted by the new Republican leadership was the renaming and reorganizing of the House Committee on Education and Labor. The committee was renamed the committee on economic and educational opportunities (see table 8). After years of toiling in the minority, the 67 year old Bill Goodling finally took the committee chair. He quickly acted on the Republican promise to reduce the size of government by consolidating the subcommittees and reducing the size of the staff by one-third (Stanfield, 1995). This reflected the Republican agenda of reviewing, consolidating and reducing the role of government.

The new tone and direction may have made some senior Republicans and staff uneasy but it fit well with Goodling's desire to revisit direct lending and national service (Sanchez, 1995, January 10; Stanfield, 1995). It also fit well with the political philosophy of Victor F. Klatt, the committee's education coordinator, who was described as "fervently conservative" (Stanfield, 1995, p. 1487). Even if the change had not suited Goodling, a political moderate, and the senior staff, they were receiving their orders from Speaker Gingrich and he was calling for "a double-time march to the right" (Stanfield, 1995, p. 1487). The entire policy arena was open to reconsideration and change.

The chair of the subcommittee on postsecondary education, training, and lifelong learning, another new name, was Howard P. "Buck " McKeon, a second-term member from California. McKeon was neither reluctant nor hesitant to admit that he did not know enough about the key higher education issues to discuss those issues in an interview with *The Chronicle of Higher Education* (Zook, 1995, February 10). When asked, McKeon "said he had no opinion on the

TABLE 8
House Committee on Economic and Educational Opportunities,
104th Congress

Republicans	Democrats
William F. Goodling (Pa.)	William L. Clay (Mo.)
Chairman	*Ranking Member*
Thomas E. Petri (Wis.)	George Miller (Calif.)
Marge Roukema (N.J.)	Dale E. Kildee (Mich.)
Steve Gunderson (Wis.)	Pat Williams (Mont.)
Harris W. Fawell (Ill.)	Matthew G. Martinez (Calif.)
Cass Ballenger (N.C.)	Major R. Owens (N.Y.)
Bill Barrett (Nev.)	Thomas C. Sawyer (Ohio)
Randy Cunningham (Calif.)	Donald M. Payne (N.J.)
Peter Hoekstra (Mich.)	Pasty T. Mink (Hawaii)
Howard P. McKeon (Calif.)	Robert E. Andrews (N.J.)
Michael N. Castle (Del.)	Jack Reed (R.I.)
Jan Meyers (Kans.)	Tim Roemer (Ind.)
Sam Johnson (Tex.)	Eliot L. Engel (N.Y.)
James M. Talent (Mo.)	Xavier Becerra (Calif.)
Jim Greenwood (Pa.)	Robert C. Scott (Va.)
Tim Hutchinson (Ark.)	Gene Green (Tex.)
Joe Knollenberg (Mich.)	Lynn C. Woolsey (Calif.)
Frank Riggs (Calif.)	Mel Reynolds(Ill.)
Lindsey Graham (S.C.)	
Dave Weldon (N.C.)	
David Funderburk (N.C.)	
Mark Souder (Ind.)	
David McIntosh (Ind.)	
Charlie Norwood (Ga.)	

role of the new State Postsecondary Review Entities, the proposed privatization of the Student Loan Marketing Association, or whether the federal government should continue to focus its higher education efforts on insuring student access to colleges" (Zook, 1995, February 10, p. A33). If Republicans were to review, consolidate, and reduce the role of government in education, then much of the effort would have to flow through McKeon's subcommittee (see table 9).

The Senate had also changed but the changes were less dramatic than those in the House. The Senate had moved from Democratic to Republican control and back again in recent years, thus it was not the same historic shift that shook the House. Republican members of the Senate had experience as both the majority and the minority party, while the House Republicans had experience only as members of the

TABLE 9
House Subcommittee on Post Secondary Education, 104th Congress

Republicans	Democrats
Howard P. McKeon (Calif.)	Pat Williams (Mont.)
Chairman	*Ranking Member*
Steve Gunderson (Wis.)	Robert E. Andrews (N.J.)
David McIntosh (Ind.)	Jack Reed (R.I.)
William F. Goodling (Pa.)	Tim Roemer (Ind.)
Thomas E. Petri (Wis.)	Xavier Becerra (Calif.)
Marge Roukema (N.J.)	Gene Green (Tex.)
Frank Riggs (Calif.)	Lynn C. Woolsey (Calif.)
David Funderburk (N.C.)	
Mark Souder (Ind.)	

minority. In addition, Senate members and candidates had not been part of the Contract with America. Finally, the Senate had a better record of bipartisanship on education issues. This was especially true when Pell and Stafford had moved between the roles of subcommittee chair and ranking minority member.

While the changes in the Senate may not have been as dramatic, the changes in the Senate should not be understated. The committee on labor and human resources (see table 10) was now chaired by Kassebaum. She was the first women in Senate history to hold such an important position. Absent from the new committee were key members such as Bingaman, Durenberger, Hatch, Metzenbaum, and Wofford. When it reached the Senate, the House Republican revolution in education would have to come through Kassebaum's committee were much of it would be referred to the Subcommittee on Education, Arts and Humanities (see table 11).

Setting the Agenda

In the first heady days of the 104th Congress, the flurry of activity surrounding the Republican ascendancy seemed to obscure the focus of their agenda for change. At first, the agenda seemed to focus on cosmetic and symbolic changes. For example, changing the names of committees and reducing the size of committee staffs. The many and various Republican voices calling for change also made it difficult for observers to be certain what changes might be forthcoming as part of the Contract with America. In February, Goodling and Gunderson announced plans to combine the Equal Employment Opportunity Commission with the Education and Labor Departments to create a

TABLE 10
Senate Committee on Labor and Human Resources, 104rd Congress

Republicans	*Democrats*
Nancy Kassebaum (Kans.) Chair	Edward M. Kennedy (Mass.) Ranking Member
James M. Jeffords (Vt.)	Claiborne Pell (R.I.)
Dan Coats (Ind.)	Christopher J. Dodd (Conn.)
Judd Gregg (N.H.)	Paul Simon (Ill.)
Bill Frist (Tenn.)	Tom Harkin (Iowa)
Mike DeWine (Ohio)	Barbara A. Mikulski (Md.)
John Ashcroft (Mo.)	Paul D. Wellstone (Minn.)
Spencer Abraham (Mich.)	
Slade Gorton (Wash.)	

TABLE 11
Senate Subcommittee on Education, Arts and Humanities, 104rd Congress

Republicans	*Democrats*
James M. Jeffords (Vt.) Chair	Claiborne Pell (R.I.) Ranking Member
Nancy Kassebaum (Kans.)	Edward M. Kennedy (Mass.)
Dan Coats (Ind.)	Christopher J. Dodd (Conn.)
Judd Gregg (N.H.)	Paul Simon (Ill.)
Bill Frist (Tenn.)	Tom Harkin (Iowa)
Mike DeWine (Ohio)	Barbara A. Mikulski (Md.)
John Ashcroft (Mo.)	Paul D. Wellstone (Minn.)
Spencer Abraham (Mich.)	
Slade Gorton (Wash.)	

Department of Education and Labor (Wells & Tin, 1995). By May, a Republican task force was calling for the elimination of a number of higher education programs and the relocation of other programs into the Department of Health and Human Services (Wells & Tin, 1995).

Observers might have been confused, but the Republican leadership in the Congress was certain of the agenda it was setting. A major part of that agenda was focused on reducing the size of the federal government's budget and its role in American life. That meant examining each federal program to determine whether the responsibility should be continued by the federal government, left to the state and local governments, or turned over to the private sector. It also meant reducing the level of domestic spending. Spending on higher education would have to be reduced as part of higher education's contribution toward the reduction of the federal budget.

The agenda was also driven by an almost "reflexively negative" (McCarthy, 1995, p. A13) Republican response to any Clinton administration success. This placed AmeriCorps and direct lending high on the agenda for elimination. Ironically, in the case of AmeriCorps, this put the Republican leadership at odds with a number of its business allies. Corporations as diverse as Anheuser-Busch, General Electric, Nike, and Shell viewed AmeriCorps as a positive factor in reviving the economic and social life of communities (McCarthy, 1995). Corporations not only praised AmeriCorps, but supported it with equipment and supplies, money, and volunteers. Erie Chapman, CEO of U.S. Health Corp and a loyal Republican, commented that "it's tragic to cut these programs. Why shoot a bunch of innocent kids to get at the president?" (quoted in McCarthy, 1995, p. A13).

Part of what *The New York Times* called ''political animus carried to an extreme'' (Reneging on AmeriCorps, 1995, p. A24) reflected a sincere difference in political philosophy between Clinton and the new Republican leadership. Even accounting for the difference in views over the proper role of the federal government, AmeriCorps was a target for elimination largely because Clinton claimed it as an accomplishment. Shays summarized the Republican attitude, stating ''we have a wounded President. AmeriCorps is something the President deserves to be proud of, but it's a target for those people who don't even want to give him that'' (quoted in Manegold, 1995, p. A25).

The debate over the future of AmeriCorps and direct lending was marked by sharp ideological divisions that were uncharacteristic for the higher education policy arena. The divisions grew sharper as 1995 progressed with Republicans repeatedly stating their intent to reduce student aid, eliminate various higher education programs, and to eliminate AmeriCorps and direct lending. Clinton repeatedly stated his intent to defend the centerpieces of his domestic policy agenda with all the resources of his office, including the veto. The two sides offered no ground for compromise.

The summer of 1995 was spent debating the budget numbers and political philosophy, but the debate did nothing to alter the fact that the Republicans controlled a majority of votes in the House and the Senate. The chairs of the key committees had opposed national service and direct lending when they were in the minority and had not changed views with the move to the majority. College officials such as Edmond Vignoul of the University of Oregon could claim that "direct lending is the finest thing to hit financial aid in the 29 years that I've been in it" (quoted in Burd, 1995, October 27, p. A30), but his claim and pleas from colleges and students to keep the direct lending program alive fell on deaf ears. The agenda was set.

By the fall of 1995, leaders in the House and Senate had agreed on a series of changes to HEA programs and budgets. The net impact of the changes were less than colleges students and officials had feared in large part because of the intense lobbying of school and student representatives. The 0.85 percent tax per college on student loan volume, the elimination of the six-month loan waiver, the increase in PLUS loan interest rates, and the elimination of the direct loan program were no longer part of the budget bill (Burd, 1995, November 3). Still, the direct lending program was capped at 10 percent of total student loan volume (Burd, 1995, November 17). The cap would force the ED to eliminate almost 75 percent of the institutions participating in the direct lending program.

The House and Senate leaders were less kind to AmeriCorps. The budget bill eliminated all funding for the program (Gray, 1995). While disappointing, the decision could hardly have been a surprise to the administration. Speaker Gingrich had publicly stated that he was "totally unequivocally opposed" to a program he saw as "coerced voluntarism and gimmickry" (quoted in Wartzman, 1995, p. A18). Clinton promised to veto any budget bill that did not include funding for AmeriCorps, but no one in the congressional leadership seemed to be listening. If they were listening, then they were not believing what they were hearing from the White House. The budget bill that was sent to the president included caps on direct lending and the complete elimination of Clinton's beloved AmeriCorps.

As promised, Clinton vetoed the budget bill. The veto was the start of a seven month budget battle that included two federal government shutdowns and numerous temporary spending resolutions. The Republican leadership seemed to think that the president, weakened by the midterm elections, would fold and accept their budget. Instead, the president seemed to draw strength from the battle increasing his resolve to stand firm with each passing month. In late April 1996, the Republican Congress gave in to the president and public opinion. The battle that had started with such sound and fury when the Republicans had first ascended to leadership "ended with a whimper" (Rosenbaum, 1996, p. A1). There would be no revolution in 1996.

The AmeriCorps program was continued under the 1996 budget (Gray, 1996). The program received $400 million in funding for the fiscal year. While this was a $69.5 million cut from 1995 and $417 less than the administration's request, it was far from the planned elimination. The Corporation for National Service, which runs AmeriCorps, announced the results of the budget deal with a press release under the headline "AmeriCorps Lives!" (Burd, 1996, May 3, p. A23).

Direct lending also survived the battle of the budget with little impact or change (Burd, 1996, May 3). Under the budget agreement, colleges retained the freedom to choose which loan programs they would enter. The 40 percent cap that the House had wanted and the 10 percent cap that had been in the earlier budget bill were gone from the final 1996 budget. The budget did limit the administrative costs of the program to $436 million but this did not impose a significant limitation on the continued growth of direct lending (Gray, 1996). Vignoul probably spoke for the majority of the higher education community when he claimed "this is a huge victory for higher education and for students" (quoted in Burd, 1996, May 3 , p. A23). Not sharing in his joy were members of the GSL industry who had probably lost their best, last chance to limit the impact of direct lending on their market share.

CONCLUSION

While the 1996 budget battle was seen as a victory by Vignoul and others, too much attention to the details of the budget agreement obscures the larger more significant changes in the higher education policy arena. The arena was in a period of flux and transition. Institutional relationships were being realigned. Social relationships were changing as new leaders emerged and long time leaders and policy arena participants were leaving the field. The beliefs and values that had guided the arena for so long were being questioned from without and from within. The stability that had marked the arena for nearly three decades was crumbling.

History was made in the late 1990s but it was neither the legacy that Clinton had hoped to leave nor the revolution that the Republicans had hoped to lead. The   real historical events the end of the communication community that characterized the higher education policy arena. The meaning of power and the understanding of how to address problems in the arena had fundamentally changed in a very short period of time after having evolved over some thirty years.

CONCLUSION:
Flux and Transition

The higher education policy arena changed dramatically between 1992 and 1996. Many of these changes, and hints of changes to come, were visible in 1992–93, but were too subtle to be noticed against the bright success of the 1992 reauthorization and the flush of the Clinton administration's success with direct lending and national service. While these legislative successes were being triumphed, the institutional, social, and beliefs foundations of the policy arena were shifting. The social foundation of power was heavily impacted by the departure of several senior policymakers and the arrival of a new class of policy actors. Policy actors who had held or had helped defend key obligatory passage points, some for almost three decades, were leaving the policy arena. Some left voluntarily, others by retirement, and still others were called home by the voters. In addition, the formal rules of the arena changed at the very same time the informal rules and relationships were shifting. The relationship between the different institutional structures that housed the persons and relationships of the arena were also changing, with the budget taking on an increasingly important role. Last, the beliefs, principles and values which had guided the arena from the 1960s through the first years of the Clinton administration were being challenged. Critics might maintain that the arena's beliefs in theory were always inconsistent with its beliefs in action, but now its beliefs in theory were being openly questioned. Finally, the meaning of power in the higher education policy arena was changing.

The first part of the chapter reviews the changes that took place in each of the three foundations of power in the 1990s. This is followed by an examination of the policy arena's beliefs in theory compared to its beliefs in action. Finally, the concept of foundations of power is used to reinterpret the meaning of power in the higher education policy arena in the late 1990s.

INSTITUTIONAL FOUNDATION

The easiest changes to identify in the institutional foundation were among the actors and social relationships housed in the institutions. While this discussion more properly fits in the social foundation discussion, a brief summary is necessary to fully understand what follows. The White House changed from Republican to Democratic with the new occupant believing that government could and should play a positive social role in American life. The new secretary of education and his leadership team expressed similar views about the ED's role and function. The ED bureaucracy, which had been under siege, was asked to come out of its defensive posture and to go on the offensive with new ideas and programs for American education. In contrast, the Congress changed from Democratic to Republican with the new leadership believing that the role of the federal government was strictly limited by the Constitution. Education was a right reserved for the states. These changes in the social and beliefs foundations made institutional conflict inevitable.

The ED, which had been a point of conflict from its creation, was once again at the center of controversy. Unlike the Reagan and Bush administrations, the Clinton administration wanted the department to be an integral part of education policy making. The administration wanted to use the department to expand the federal role in education at all levels. The seriousness of the administration's intent was reflected in the quality of its appointments. The appointment of Richard Riley as secretary, Madeleine Kunin as deputy secretary, Leo Kornfeld as senior advisor to the secretary, as well as individuals such as Elizabeth Hicks, David Longanecker, and Thomas R. Wolanin moved the ED toward becoming an established institutional structure and an obligatory passage point for federal education policy decisions.

This movement was reinforced with the rapid growth and development of the direct loan program. The program grew faster than its supporters could have hoped for when they agreed to a dual track loan system. In October 1995, nearly 40 percent of total student loan volume had been captured by the direct lending program (Burd, 1995, October 6). Institutions that had enrolled early were full of praise for the program and for the department. Colleges that had been hesitant to enter the program because of questions and doubts about the department's administrative abilities were now enrolling in large numbers as schools abandoned the GSL program for direct lending (Burd & Schoenberg, 1995, November 24). During the congressional debate over ending the direct lending program, ACE provided a letter of support with the signatures of 470 college presidents (Burd & Schoenberg, 1995, November 24). Unlike the GSL, which established a status separate from the ED, direct lending was helping establish institutional status for the department. Direct lending, administered by the ED, was becoming the institutional standard against which policy alternatives would be judged.

The change in status can be seen in the reaction to problems the department experienced in processing financial aid applications in the spring of 1996. The ED was tardy in reporting some 1.5 million student financial aid applications to colleges and universities which needed the data to construct individual student aid packages (Burd, 1996, March 8). Public institutions were severely impacted because of their dependence on the data from the ED analysis for awarding student aid. Private institutions were also hurt by the delay, but many also used other data sources to collect and analyze student aid information, thus they could still prepare aid packages. The delay was blamed on numerous factors including computer problems experienced by the data processing contractors, two government shutdowns, and harsh winter storms. Departmental turf battles between Elizabeth Hicks, deputy assistant secretary for student financial-assistance programs, and Leo Kornfeld, special assistant to the secretary for direct-loan programs, may have exacerbated the problem (Burd, 1996, March 15). Whatever the exact source of the delay, 900,000 aid applications remained unprocessed in mid-March 1996.

The delay sparked sharp criticism from those who had questioned the direct lending program and the ED's ability to administer the program. Victor F. Klatt III, the House Committee on Economic and Educational Opportunities education coordinator, criticized the ED leadership as "a gang that can't shoot straight" (quoted in Burd, 1996, March 15, p. A29). Even friends and supporters of the program questioned the department's slowness in responding to the early warning signs that a serious problem was looming just ahead in the absence of immediate corrective action. Questions about the ED's failure to act took on a greater immediacy given the political climate in the spring of 1996. The Republican leadership in Congress wanted to end the direct lending program and eliminate the department. The delays in processing student aid applications strengthened the arguments for doing both as Congress prepared the new budget. For such a new program with so many powerful enemies, this could well have been a fatal failure.

Instead of finding itself in a losing struggle for survival, made even worse by the aid application delays, the direct lending program emerged from the budget process stronger than even. Under the new budget, the 1,400 institutions that had been participating could continue and the door was open to any and all qualified institutions that wanted to participate. Vignoul called it a "huge victory for higher education and for students" (quoted in Burd, 1996, May 3, p. A23). The CBA expressed disappointment, but the cap and any possibility of limiting the growth of the direct lending program were gone. Direct lending and the ED were now firmly established as part of the institutional architecture.

The lesson in institutional resistance that had been taught to direct lending advocates in 1992 was learned by GSL industry advocates in 1996. The direct lending program, with some deficiencies, served the needs of the community as a whole, thus the majority of the policy arena saw no need to change the program. The GSL advocates had made a mistake in thinking that the direct loan program could be added as a new, parallel program creating an addition to the institutional foundation without actually altering the foundation. As the direct lending program grew, it reduced the community's need for the GSL program and the industry brought into existence by the program. The institutional status of the GSL program, which had seemed unquestionable in 1992, was crumbling in 1996. This was confirmed by the actions of industry members who were seeking to leave the student loan business, or at the very least, to diversify their operations away from student loans.

Another addition to the institutional foundation was the budget supported by the BEA. Historically, the budget has not been thought of as an obligatory passage point in higher education policy making on a level with the president, the Congress, or the courts. Indeed, the budget was often overlooked as policy analysts and policymakers focused on the authorization process without much concern or consideration for the appropriations process. As some House and Senate staffers explained during interviews, the authorization and appropriations process are different, thus the authorization actors do not worry about costs because funding is decided in a different policy arena. This was consistent with the logic of the policy arena prior to the passage of the BEA when appropriations committees were free to appropriate whatever had been authorized. The passage of the BEA changed the rules of the game and created a new institutional structure with a status equal to the earlier obligatory passage points. When considering legislation in the mid-1990s, authorization committees had to ask: Will the entire Congress pass the bill? Will the president sign the legislation into law? Will the courts uphold the law? Is the expenditure possible under the BEA?

While its impact was not fully comprehended, the evolving status and importance of the BEA was visible in 1992. Policymakers and analysts understood that the budget had made a Pell Grant entitlement impossible. They also understood that the BEA and Credit Reform had made direct lending an attractive alternative to the GSL program. Still, this was seen in the context of budget scoring and bookkeeping. The higher education policy arena as a whole did not fully understand the changing relationship between the budget and policy making in 1992. By 1996, the relationship was impossible to ignore as the budget impacted both the institutional and social foundations creating new obligatory passage points and new rules.

The importance of the BEA and credit reform were apparent for all to see during the debate over the Clinton administration's direct lending proposal. Opponents of the proposal were limited by the budget in their search for an alternative to the direct lending proposal once it had been scored as a $4 billion plus savings. Without a similar savings, opponents could not get an alternative proposal past the obligatory passage point of the budget. Unable to find an alternative proposal with the same savings, the BEA required new domestic spending to be offset by cuts in existing domestic spending. Opponents could neither find the savings nor could they marshal support for more real cuts in existing domestic programs.

The reality of the budget's new status was acknowledged by both sides during the debate over direct lending. Kassebaum lamented that the need for savings, not the quality of the idea, was pushing direct lending to the point that "it just seems to me that we have lost track of the reality of the situation" (quoted in Zook, 1993, August 11, p. A23). Other members of the policy arena readily agreed that the need for savings was a key point in the debate over direct lending. Ford was blunt and to the point about the change stating that "it's a maddening way to make policy, because the accountants are making policy for us" (quoted in Zook, 1993, August 11, p. A23).

The impact of the budget as a new obligatory passage point was felt again when the Republican leadership in the 104th Congress attempted to undo the Clinton student aid agenda. To eliminate the direct loan program, the Republican leadership had to find savings or cuts in domestic spending programs equal to the direct lending savings. While this may have been possible, direct lending enjoyed support among a number of Republicans, thus the idea of capping the program to limit its growth and to protect the GSL program. This plan unraveled with Clinton's veto of the budget. As the battle of the budget raged, public opposition to deep cuts in education, the environment, and other domestic expenditures increased. With little room to reduce spending and declining public support for their agenda, the Republican leadership found itself forced to accept direct lending because it counted as a savings in their effort to review, consolidate, and reduce the role of the government by reducing the size of the federal budget.

In some ways, the institutional structures that form the obligatory passage points for federal higher education policy making retained an expected consistency in the 1990s, for example, the education subcommittees, the education committees, the conference committee, the House and Senate, and the White House. Other parts of the institutional foundation changed with the addition of obligatory passage points that had not existed at the beginning of the decade. The ED changed from a neglected, battered stepchild to become an obligatory passage point for higher education policy making that was valued and respected by the White House. The direct lending program which had been a mere demonstration program in 1992 emerged as part of the institutional foundation becoming the standard against which policy alternatives were measured. The GSL program and its supporting industry which had seemed firmly entrenched at the beginning of the 1990s were crumbling. Finally, the budget, helped by the BEA, became an important part of the institutional foundation.

SOCIAL FOUNDATION

As noted above, the most visible changes were those that took place in the social foundations. From 1992 to 1996, there was a tremendous turnover of personnel in the higher education policy arena. Among those leaving or announcing plans to leave included Representatives Coleman, Ford, Gunderson, and Williams. In the Senate, Durenberger, Kassebaum, Metzenbaum, Pell, Simon, and Wofford left or announced plans to retire. DiNapoli, Flanagan, Hartle, and Wolanin, key staff members for the education committees, left the Congress but remained in the arena, moving to other education-related positions. Important personnel also left the associations with one of the most notable being Charles Saunders the longtime ACE governmental relations representative. In a brief four year span, the community lost the personal and social relationships that had developed over a period of almost three decades. In the Congress, Kennedy was perhaps the last member of either education committee who could recall and explain HEA's history and purpose to other members. The arena had lost most of its institutional memory.

The rapid change in community membership worked to undermine the use of the partnership metaphor to describe the social relations of the policy arena. New and old members of the arena were increasingly becoming advocates of positions instead of community members striving together to solve problems. They were becoming adversaries bent on winning. Indicative of the erosion of the partnership metaphor is the change in language used to describe events and relationships in the arena. The metaphors of war were replacing the metaphors of partnership, problem solving and community. A quote from Laura McClintock, USSA legislative director, illustrates this change:

> As soon as the Republicans came into power, they threatened to eliminate the in-school interest subsidy for students, kill direct lending, and gut a number of student-aid programs.
> And now we have succeeded in turning them back on every front. (quote in Burd, 1996, May 3, p. A23)

While not using violent descriptors such as "kill" and "gut," the erosion of personal relationships as a basis for policy making was also apparent in the language that House and Senate members used in the various student aid debates. If language is a guide, then members no longer trusted one another. Goodling's sharp retort to Ford during the conference committee on national service is one indication of the crumbling partnership and the shift in language. Other examples are readily available and are not limited to one political party or segment of the policy arena. Gingrich accused the administration of "coerced voluntarism" and "gimmickry" (quoted in Wartzman, 1995, p. A18). Kennedy lamented that the Republican attacks on national service "just defies logic and good sense" (quoted in Zuckman, 1993, September 11, p. 2397). Simon became so impassioned in his promotion of direct lending that he violated the unwritten Senate rule of never making a personal attack on another Senator (Waldman, 1995). Goodling claimed that the Democrats used a "smoke and mirror method" to reach the savings claimed for direct lending (quoted in Wells, 1995, p. 3741). Riley countered that "Goodling had cooked the books to make direct lending look more expensive than it is" (quoted in Wells, 1995, p. 3741). The change in personal relationships may have been captured best by Riley when he lamented that "education seems to be becoming a political target" (quoted in Wells & Tin, p. 1512). Higher education was no longer a policy arena in which problem solving was paramount.

The decline in community and partnership was also visible in the limited bipartisan support for direct lending and national service. The history of the arena had been one of bipartisan support for higher education programs, but the sense of bipartisanship faded quickly after the 1992 reauthorization. Some of this had actually started with the way reauthorization was handled in the House subcommittee. Goodling and other Republican members felt that Ford was moving away from the traditions of the subcommittee to advance a more partisan Democratic education agenda. This feeling only intensified with the debate over direct lending and national service. The size of the Senate and its traditions blunted the move toward partisanship, but did not entirely prevent it . The debate over national service and direct lending looked more like a debate in the House than in the traditional Senate. Kennedy had to work hard to build Republican support for the Clinton student aid agenda and achieved only limited results. The final votes in the House and Senate were far closer than what had come to be expected for higher education legislation.

The changes in the makeup and nature of the higher education policy arena worked to the disadvantage of the higher education associations. From Green through Ford, the chairs in the House had insisted that the associations work primarily with the chair in pursuing their legislative agendas. This was not the case in the Senate, but in both bodies the associations had worked primarily with the majority party, the Democratic Party, to advance their legislative agendas. With the changes in the House and Senate, the associations lost their partners and their contacts. After years of working with people who shared similar beliefs about higher education and the federal role in helping students achieve equal educational oppor- tunity, the associations found themselves seeking to build new relationships with new people who did not share their beliefs. Even worse, the associations, as recently as the 1992 reauthorization, had found themselves in conflict with key policy actors as such Goodling and his staff.

The rapid change in membership was but one of several reasons for the decline of community in the higher education policy arena. With the change in policy actors came a change in beliefs about the proper role of the federal government in higher education. As noted above, one of the driving purposes of the Republican revolution was to review, consolidate, and reduce the role of the federal government.

This was especially true in education. This was directly at odds with the beliefs of both the Clinton administration and many longtime members of the policy arena. Personal relationships can be developed without the benefit of shared beliefs, but it is difficult when beliefs are in conflict. It is impossible when the policy actors share neither widely understood signs and symbols that convey shared meanings nor the emotional, intellectual, and moral bonds that grow from collective action.

The change in beliefs reduced the need for communication within the community. In the early 1990s, the norm of the community was communication for problem solving with a concern for helping students achieve equal educational opportunity. After the 1994 elections, there was less need for the various policy actors to discuss programs to assure that student aid programs were well conceived, planned, and implemented. Instead of a need for communication, there was a chasm as the Republican leadership sought to end student aid in the form in which it had evolved over some thirty years, while longtime members of the arena sought to maintain the status quo. The pattern of communication for problem solving was replaced by rival camps plotting attacks and counterattacks in a battle for domination.

The change in the budget process also helped undermine the social relationships of the community. The budget process increased the internal complexity of the arena by introducing new rules and restrictions and by implicitly and explicitly increasing the number of policy actors involved in the authorization process. At the same time, the unity of participants decreased while conflict increased. The new rules of the game also impacted the functional autonomy of the arena. Earlier threats to the arena's autonomy had been successfully avoided or co-opted, but there was no escaping the BEA. This meant that policies which had once been formulated and implemented within the higher education arena were now open to control and influence by the appropriations arena.

As the higher education policy arena quickly moved toward a new reauthorization, members found themselves seeking to build a new social foundation for policy making. Most of the original members of the community were gone and their replacements were functioning without an institutional memory. The partnership that had guided and characterized the community was crumbling leaving the members without a sense of what would come next in the life of the arena. Finally, the rules of the arena, both formal and informal, had changed.

BELIEFS FOUNDATION

The beliefs, principles, and values that form the beliefs foundation can also be thought of as the culture of the higher education policy arena. The principles discussed in chapters 2 and 5 are part of that culture. The metaphor of partnership developed from that culture as policy actors created the world in which they work and live. The HEA is the enactment of the shared reality of the participants. While there were tensions and conflicts, the community was guided by a dominant vision of providing equal educational opportunity for all students.

The changes in the institutional and social foundations impacted the beliefs, principles, and values that form the beliefs foundation. The culture of the higher education policy arena was experiencing stress and strain in the mid-1990s. For the first time in recent years, the beliefs that had guided the policy arena were being contested. Earlier attempts to reopen the contested principles of the arena had failed, but now the challenge was coming from those in the majority who controlled key obligatory passage points in the House and Senate. Since this contest is yet to be resolved, the arena finds itself in search of the beliefs, principles, and values that will the guide federal higher education policy arena as it moves into the next century.

One of the principles being contested is the federal use of the higher education system as an instrument for social reform. HEA programs such as TRIO and Pell Grants represent the operationalization of that principle. National service and direct lending are the most recent examples of that principle in action. These programs reflect the Clinton administration's strong belief in the ability of the federal government to use education to promote social reform.

In contrast, the new Republican leadership in the Congress saw a limited role for the federal government in education and did not subscribe to the notion that education should be an instrument for federally directed social reform. Goodling moved into the chair once held by the activist Ford with a promise to review all education programs for possible reduction or elimination. During the 1995–96 budget battle, the Republican leadership in the House and Senate attempted to reduce education funding, end Goals 2000, eliminate AmeriCorps, and cap direct lending. The Clinton administration was successful in defending most of its legislative achievements, but the principle in dispute remained unsettled.

The belief that higher education is both a public and private good whose cost should be shared between the federal government, the student, and the family also came into question in the mid-1990s, but in a more subtle way. When it was addressed, it took the form of a question about the loan-grant balance. Questions about public versus private goods were not raised in debates over the continuation of HEA programs, but were apparent in the way in which programs were allowed to evolve. An increasing share of the cost of higher education was being shifted to students and their families. From a policy perspective, higher education was being treated as a private good that benefited only the student.

The change in beliefs is apparent in the trends in student aid. In 1994–95:

- The Pell Grant continued a decade long decline in real dollars and as a percentage of the average cost of attendance
- The average PLUS loan increased 14 percent as parents took on a greater loan burden
- Loans comprised 56 percent of all available aid while Pell Grants comprised 12 percent
- Unsubsidized loans increased 178 percent from 1993–94 to 1994–95. (The College Board, 1995)

These represent long-term trends rather than recent radical changes in the culture of the community. Yet the changes took place with little discussion beyond the question of the loan-grant balance. The movement away from principle remained largely unexamined.

The movement continued with the direct lending program and AmeriCorps. The two programs took money that might have gone to Pell Grants or other student aid grants. Direct lending held the potential for increasing student debt burden while making it look lighter because of the income contingent repayment schedule. When direct lending was first floated by the Bush administration, USSA opposed the idea because it would shift more of the cost of higher education to students. Pell expressed doubts about the idea in 1992 and again in 1993 for the same reason. In addition, Pell was concerned that money that should go to low-income students would be absorbed by direct lending becoming loans of convenience for middle-income students. Pell supported direct lending only after he had obtained all he could for other student aid programs and after obtaining modifications in the Clinton administration's proposal. Goodling expressed many of the same doubts and questions in the House, but was less effective in producing change.

The debate over direct lending also reopened discussion of principle that favored the use of private agencies for the delivery of student aid. In favoring direct lending administered by the ED, the Clinton administration broke with the principle of using private providers to deliver federal student aid. For the time being, the administration seems to have prevailed with direct lending having achieved institutional status. The dual-track system leaves the issue unresolved and open to continued debate.

The principle of nondiscrimination between private and public institutions in the awarding of federal grants and loans was also reopened in the 1990s. An effort was made to reopen the principle during the 1992 reauthorization but this was quashed by Ford and Pell's rejection of any consideration of separate systems. As the 1990s moved forward, the issue continued to reappear in policy debates. David A. Longanecker, assistant secretary for postsecondary education, reopened the issue for the Clinton administration (Separate regulations, 1995). Unlike past efforts, this one was not immediately rejected by the chairs of the education committees. Pamela Devitt, staff director of the senate education subcommittee, welcomed the opportunity to discuss the idea with the administration. ACE and NAICU also welcomed the possibility of change. Like the above-contested principles, this one remains unresolved and open to continued debate.

While the above principles were reopened, a number of the basic beliefs and values that guided the community remained firmly established in the late 1990s. For example, it was still an accepted belief in the community that the federal government has a positive role to play in promoting equal educational opportunity for the socially and economically disadvantaged, that student needs outweigh institutional needs, and that middle-income students must be included as a way to build support for aid to the disadvantaged. Still, the changes in the community and the challenges to contested principles produced an uneasiness in the policy arena about the direction of federal higher education going into the next century. Goodling captured part of this uneasiness when he expressed a desire not "to continue to go through the same old habit here of reauthorizing all of those programs year after year" (quoted in Sanchez, 1995, January 10, p. A13).

This uneasiness was increased as scholars and researchers questioned the direction and effectiveness of federal student aid programs. Some of these questions focused on the loan-grant balance, but others touched upon the core belief of the arena. Specifically, if the policy objective of federal student aid is to achieve equal educational opportunity, then are the programs helping economically and socially disadvantaged students achieve equal educational opportunity. Another way to think of the question is whether or not the policy arena's beliefs in theory conform with its beliefs in action. That question will be considered before turning to the meaning of power in the higher education policy arena in the late 1990s.

BELIEFS IN THEORY, BELIEFS IN ACTION

The belief in theory that has dominated the HEA has been that the federal government should help finance, with needs tested student aid, the individual pursuit of higher education as a means for achieving equal educational opportunity. This was the primary purpose of the 1965 HEA. Any doubts about the policy objectives driving HEA were removed with the resolution of the institutional versus student aid debate in the 1972 HEA. Congress made it clear that the first priority of federal policy was to aid students in their pursuit of higher education. Students who had previously been unable to attend college because of costs would be able to carry their federal financial aid with them to an institution of their choice. A student might not be able to attend the most expensive of schools, but with federal aid, state aid, institutional support, and family contributions a wide avenue of quality choices would be available. Institutions would benefit to the extent that they could respond to the needs and interests of those students.

While the beliefs in theory are not subject to question, the beliefs in action have been and remain subject to debate. In retrospect, one can see that the beliefs in theory and in action began to diverge in 1978 with the passage of MISAA. This was the Carter administration's response to the claimed financial squeeze on middle income students and to the growing support in Congress for tuition tax credits as a policy response to the perceived squeeze. MISAA shifted the HEA from a policy objective of equal educational opportunity to an objective of universal access with the uncapping of the GSL program and the expansion of eligibility for BEOG's. As the bill came due, Congress found that it could not afford to meet the student aid needs of both middle- and low-income students.

Unable to make a choice between the two, Congress dealt with the competing policy objectives through the appropriations process. Loans cost less than grants, thus the shift from Pell Grants as a student aid floor to a reliance on loans as the foundation of federal student aid. From the late 1970s forward, total loan aid has increased while total grant aid has decreased. The political argument to support this has been that without middle-class student aid and the support it engenders the federal student aid programs would not be able to fulfill their equal educational opportunity objective. This reasoning was the primary argument used to defeat Reagan and Bush administration proposals to target student aid toward the "truly needy."

Ironically, the effort to protect HEA programs targeted toward low-income students by expanding middle-income student eligibility has produce a policy bias against low-income students. Loans are a vehicle to opportunity for the middle-income student but an obstacle to opportunity for low-income students. Unlike middle-income students, low-income students tend to be loan-adverse (Leslie & Brinkman, 1988; St. John & Noell, 1989). Low-income students are more likely to respond to financial aid packages that are built on a grant floor (Mortenson, 1990).

Higher education participation rates among historical disadvantaged groups decreased as the reliance on loans as the foundation for student aid increased, (Mortenson, 1990). This decrease in participation rates was congruent with the increased dependence on loans. The decrease followed a period of increased participation for these groups that started in 1965 and continued until 1980. During that time period, grants formed the floor for student aid. Given the number of factors that influence participation rates, a direct causal linkage cannot be drawn, but the congruence between the increased reliance on loans and the deterioration of equal educational opportunity is unmistakable.

The 1992 HEA reauthorization continued the trend of shifting aid from the low-income to the middle-income in the name of equal educational opportunity. The Clinton administration's student aid agenda, while aimed at access, reflected a similar bias against low-income students. The administration followed this with a proposal for a tuition tax-credit as a means of increasing access (Lederman, 1996). AASCU's Elmendorf summarized the proposal for tuition tax-credits as "good politics, but lousy policy" (Lederman, 1996, p. A23).

The claims by Clinton, Ford and others that they were defending HEA programs for the low income by expanding middle-income eligibility were not true. This is not to suggest that Clinton, Ford or others are knowingly dishonest. Indeed, the proponents of equal educational opportunity were sincere in their beliefs. They actively sought to promote equality of opportunity for disadvantaged students. Unfortunately, their beliefs in action worked to undermine their beliefs in theory. While this conflict between theory and action was raised in the community, it was not resolved. The continuing shift of funds from programs targeting low-income students to programs benefiting middle-income students worked against equal educational opportunity and eroded the beliefs foundation of the community.

POWER AND CONFLICT

As the late 1990s unfolded, the communication community that had existed was quickly fading into history. The institutional, social, and beliefs foundations on which it had rested no longer existed. The beliefs in theory that had guided the arena were increasingly in conflict with arena's beliefs in action. Power in the arena was no longer related to problem solving. While the foundations on which the communication community was constructed were crumbling, the concept of foundations of power remained a valid framework for interpreting the meaning of power in the higher education policy arena.

In reviewing the above discussion of the foundations of power, no one thread seems to hold collective action together for the entire policy arena. Instead, the policy arena has fragmented into two major groups with various subgroups that cut across the two larger groups. The temptation is to identify the two groups by their political party affiliation, but this oversimplifies the division. The two groups should not be identified simply as Republican and Democratic because members of the two parties have worked across the major divisions in various subgroups. Direct lending, for example, attracted support from members of both parties. Rather than thinking about the two groups in terms of party affiliations, it is easier to identify and discuss the groups in terms of their beliefs about the proper role of government in education.

The first group can be defined by their shared belief in limited government. Members of the group, such as Coats, Goodling, Gordon, Kassebaum, Petri, and Gregg believe that the federal government has a legitimate, but limited, role to play in the lives of its citizens. While there is a wide range of philosophies within this group about the proper role of government, the members share a common belief that the federal government should play a limited role in education. In the area of higher education, primary responsibility should remain with the states and with individuals. Since individuals are the primary beneficiaries of higher education, they should be assisted with loans not grants. Government does have a role to play in helping the least advantaged in society and for the truly needy grants should be available. This last belief may seem inconsistent with the strong belief in a restricted government role in education, but is in fact consistent with the true conservative belief that government should remove the shackles from the oppressed.

The 1994 elections brought this group into the majority in the House and Senate where they now control the key obligatory passage points for higher education and for all legislation. Since coming into control of these points, they have shown a much greater willingness to block passage in order to affect change in higher education legislation. Prior to this recent change in positions, members of this group had worked in a problem solving framework affecting change, but not engaging in conflict designed to stop legislation or force a proposal on the arena. This started to change with the debate over Clinton's student aid agenda and reached fruition with the budget debates. The limited government group is willing to engage in conflict to force its view on those who might disagree.

The changes in the budget and budget process have assisted this group. Existing student aid programs can be cut in the name of the budget. Loans can be favored over grants because of the budget implications. New programs cannot be considered because of the limits on domestic spending. The budget does protect unfavored programs like direct lending but in most cases the budget prevents rather than allows program expansion or creation.

The willingness to engage in conflict and to use the budget as a tool in that conflict may be due to social relationships. The limited government group was in the minority for many years, for forty years in the House, and finds itself separated by its beliefs from the old majority and from the higher education associations. The new members are anxious to push their agenda after having waited for so many years for the chance to change policy. The rapid turnover in the policy arena means that they are not limited by old relationships or by an institutional memory of how and why higher education policy is made. Indeed, the changes in the budget rules make conflict a reasonable alternative as members struggle over how to allocate limited resources.

The second group is bound by their belief in an expanded government role in the lives of its citizens. This group, once the majority, has been diminished in recent years. It includes Andrews, Kennedy, Pell, and Williams. President Clinton can also be identified as a member of this group. Like the limited government group, this group believes that government should play a role in assuring equal educational opportunity for economic and socially disadvantaged citizens. Unlike that group, this group believes that government has a larger, legitimate role to play in education. Higher education can and should be used to bring about social reform. Federal student aid dollars can and should be targeted to historically disadvantaged groups. Federal funds should be spent on grants to individual students because higher education is a public good that returns the investment to government and to society in the form of taxes, higher wages, and human capital. These and other beliefs bind this group.

The expanded government role group had some success in the 1990s with direct lending, AmeriCorps, and expanding aid to middle-income students. Most of the 1990s represented a retreat for this group, as the higher education policy moved from being a community characterized by stability and longevity to one characterized by flux and transition. Its beliefs in theory continued to diverge from its beliefs in action as more aid was shifted to middle-income students reducing equal educational opportunity for low-income students. After its passage, AmeriCorps was under almost constant legislative assault and has yet to achieve the status envisioned for it by the Clinton administration. Direct lending has achieved institutional status, but still faces threats from the GSL program it was designed to replace. The proposal for a Pell Grant entitlement crashed against the budget firewalls. Finally, loans continued to replace grants as the floor for student aid.

After controlling the key obligatory passage points in the Congress for decades, the group now controls none. They do control the White House, but the president cannot force legislation through the Congress. The president can only block legislation once it leaves the Congress. The expanded government group has not been socialized in the ways of conflict having entered in the policy arena when problem solving was the norm, thus they have not responded quickly to the new social relations of the arena. It may be impossible for them to adjust regardless of their socialization. The budget makes any expansion of higher education programs very difficult. At the same time, they do not share enough of a common beliefs foundation with members of the limited government group to build alliances aimed at taking control of the obligatory passage points. They do share common beliefs and experiences with the higher education associations, but the associations have no votes in Congress and have limited influence with the new majority.

Each group is strongly bounded by its belief in the proper role of government, but there is no one thread that unites the two in collective action. Even in what seems like an area of common belief, equal educational opportunity, the groups are divided by different definitions of who is disadvantage and how they should be assisted. The differences in the arena are more ideological than at any time since the 1950s. The sharp ideological divisions increase the potential for conflict as the groups unite around and defend their beliefs. Just as beliefs unite members in collective action within their respective groups, beliefs separate the two groups from one another making unity across the arena difficult to achieve.

Power in this social context has devolved from problem solving to something that looks like the first face of power. To paraphrase Dahl (1957), power in the higher education policy arena looks something like this: the limited government group has power over the expanded government group to the extent it can impose its will on the expanded government group. The limited government group is united by its beliefs, controls the key obligatory passage points in the Congress, is not bound by previous social and personal relationships, is supported by the budget, is willing to engage in conflict to achieve its policy goals, and is limited by public opinion and the president's ability to sustain a veto.

To invoke Dahl in defining power as force and coercion is not the same as agreeing with Dahl. While his definition of power is helpful in describing the current state of affairs in the arena, his concept of power is too simple to capture the dynamics of a policy arena in flux and change. The foundations on which the arena rests will continue to change over the next several years as the participants seek to move toward a stable state of policy making. The policy arena, influenced by larger society, will continue to reassess its beliefs just as the K–12 arena has done in recent years. The social relationships of the arena will develop again as new policy actors work together and against one another. Ideological divisions in the arena, coupled with the budget, almost guarantee that the new social relationships will not replicate the previous social relationships of the arena. The arena appears to be headed toward a period of prolonged conflict.

Finally, the newly developing foundations of the policy arena will eventually crumble and fall just as the foundations that supported the policy arena as a communication community crumbled and fell. Marked by coercion and conflict, the developing arena will not be characterized by an expansion of federal student aid. Indeed, any change, including program elimination, will be difficult to achieve because there are no common bonds that span the entire policy arena, and because the groups are willing to engage in conflict. Policy analysts will see this as incrementalism characterized by multiple pressure groups. Such analysts misunderstand what is happening in the arena because they refuse to confront power. To understand federal higher education policy making, one must understand the meaning of power in the policy arena. To understand power, one must understand the institutional, social, and beliefs foundations on which the arena rests.

BIBLIOGRAPHY

Alexander, J. C. (1987). The centrality of the classics. In A. Giddens & J. H. Turner (Eds.), *Social theory today* (pp. 11–57). Stanford, Calif.: Stanford University Press.

Alexander, L. (1991, April 11). Testimony before the Senate Subcommittee on Education, Arts and the Humanities on the reauthorization of the Higher Education Act of 1965.

America 2000: The President's education strategy. (1991, April 18). Washington, D.C.: The White House

American Council on Education. (1989, November). *Background papers on HEA reauthorization issues*. Washington, D.C.: Author

Arendt, H. (1968). *Between past and future: Eight exercises in political thought*. New York: Viking Press.

Arendt, H. (1969). *On violence*. New York: Harcourt, Brace & World.

Arendt, H. (1986). Communicative power. In S. Lukes (Ed.), *Power* (pp. 59–74). New York: New York University Press.

Armstrong, A. (1990). How the Hill sees higher education. *Educational Record, 71,* 6–12.

Babbidge, Jr., H. D., & Rosenzweig, R. M. (1962). *The federal interest in higher education*. New York: McGraw-Hill.

Bachrach, P., & Baratz, M. S. (1962). Two faces of power. *American Political Science Review, 56,* 947–52.

Bachrach, P., & Baratz, M. S. (1970). *Power and poverty*. Oxford: Oxford University Press.

Bacon, K. H. (1993, July 30). House and Senate reach compromise on student loans. *The Wall Street Journal*, p. A4.

Bailey, S. K. (1975). *Education interests groups in the nation's capital*. Washington, D.C.: American Council on Education.

Ball, T. (1992). New faces of power. In T. E. Wartenberg (Ed.), *Rethinking power* (pp. 14–31). Albany: State University of New York Press.

Bauman, Z. (1987). *Legislators and interpreters.* Cambridge: Polity Press.

Bellah, R. N., Madsen, R., Sullivan, W. M., Swidler, A. & Tipton, S. M. (1985). *Habits of the heart: Individualism and commitment in American life.* New York: Harper & Row.

Bloland, H. G. (1985). *Associations in action: The Washington, D.C. higher education community.* Washington, D.C.: Association for the Study of Higher Education.

Bluestone, B., & Comcowich, J. M. (1992, February 3). The time has come to establish income-contingent student loans. *The Chronicle of Higher Education,* pp. B1, B2.

Bond, J. R. (1979). Oiling the tax committees in Congress, 1900–1975: Subgovernment theory, the overrepresentation hypothesi, and the oil depletion allowance. *American Journal of Political Science, 23,* 651–64.

Boot, M. (1993, August 5). Behind the student loan deal. *The Christian Science Monitor,* p. 3.

Bottoms, R. G. (1990, October 17). Sure we need beauticians. . . . *The New York Times,* p. A23.

Brademas, J. (1987). *The politics of education: Conflict and consensus on Capitol Hill.* Norman: University of Oklahoma Press.

Breneman, D. W., & Nelson, S. C. (1980). Education and training. In J. A. Pechman (Ed.), *Setting national priorities: Agenda for the 1980s* (pp. 205–46). Washington, D.C.: Brookings Institution.

Bresnick, D. (1979). The federal educational policy system: Enacting and revising Title I. *Western Political Quarterly, 32,* 189–202.

Brubacher, J. S., & Rudy, W. (1976). *Higher education in transition: A history of American colleges and universities, 1636–1976.* New York: Harper & Row.

Burd, S. (1995, October 6). Student-loan fury. *The Chronicle of Higher Education,* pp. A29–30.

Burd, S. (1995, October 13). Senators debate plan for cash transfer to loan agencies. *The Chronicle of Higher Education,* p. A33.

Burd, S. (1995, October 13). Defining the needy. *The Chronicle of Higher Education,* pp. A31, A33.

Burd, S. (1995, October 27). Colleges fight to keep semblance of direct-lending program. *The Chronicle of Higher Education,* p. A30.

Burd, S. (1995, November 3). Reprieve for student loans. *The Chronicle of Higher Education*, pp. A37, A45.

Burd, S. (1995, November 17). Compromise on loans. *The Chronicle of Higher Education*, pp. A25, A31.

Burd, S. (1995, December 1). Agreement on federal budget leaves college officials pleased but wary. *The Chronicle of Higher Education*, p. A38.

Burd, S. (1996, March 8). Education Department says 1.5 million student-aid applications have been delayed. *The Chronicle of Higher Education*, p. A27.

Burd, S. (1996, March 15). Sorting out a foul-up in student aid. *The Chronicle of Higher Education*, pp. A29, A31.

Burd, S. (1996, March 22). Senate moves to increase spending for some student aid programs. *The Chronicle of Higher Education*, p. A29.

Burd, S. (1996, May 3). A big win for direct lending. *The Chronicle of Higher Education*, p. A23.

Burd, S., & Schoenberg, T. (1995, November 24). Debate over direct lending mystifies supporters on the campus. *The Chronicle of Higher Education*, pp. A22–23.

Byron, W. J. (1992, April 8). Study now, pay later: A good idea. *The Washington Post*, p. A23.

Callon, M. (1980). Struggles and negotiations to define what is problematic and what is not: The socio-logic of translation. In K. D. Knorr, R. Krohn, & R. D. Whitley (Eds.), *The social process of scientific investigation* (pp. 197–219). Dordrecht, Holland: D. Reidel.

Callon, M. (1986). Some elements of a sociology of translation: Domestication of the scallops and the fishermen of the St. Brieuc Bay. In J. Law (Ed.), *Power, action, and belief: A new sociology of knowledge* (pp. 196–233). London: Routledge and Kegan Paul.

Callon, M., & Latour, B. (1981). Unscrewing the big Leviathan: How actors macrostructure reality and sociologists help them do so. In K. D. Knorr-Cetina & A. Cicourel (Eds.), *Advances in social theory and methodology: Toward an integration of micro- and macro-sociologies* (pp. 227–303). London: Routledge and Kegan Paul.

Carnegie Commission on Higher Education. (1973). *Governance in higher education*. New York: McGraw-Hill.

Champlin, J. R. (1971). *Power*. New York: Atherton Press.

Clegg, S. R. (1989). *Frameworks of power*. London: Sage.

Clifford, F. (1968). Washington outpost: More schools find use for a man in the capital. *Science, 159*, 1334–40.

Cohen, M. D., & March, J. G. (1974). *Leadership and ambiguity: The American college president*. New York: McGraw-Hill.

College Board. (1990). *Trends in student aid: 1980 to 1990*. Washington, D.C.: College Board.

College Board. (1993). *Trends in student aid: 1983 to 1993*. Washington, D.C.: College Board.

College Board. (1995). *Trends in student aid: 1985 to 1995*. Washington, D.C.: College Board.

Connolly, W. E. (1987). Appearance and reality in politics. In M. T. Gibbons (Ed.), *Interpreting politics* (pp. 148–74). New York: New York University Press.

Cooper, K. (1992, February 4). Hill chairman wants to reshape student aid. *The New York Times*, p. A9.

Dahl, R. A. (1956). *A preface to democratic theory*. Chicago: University of Chicago Press.

Dahl, R. A. (1957). The concept of power. *Behavioral Science, 2*, 201–5.

Dahl, R. A. (1958). Critique of the ruling elite model. *American Political Science Review, 52*, 463–69.

Dahl, R. A. (1961). *Who governs?*. New Haven, Conn.: Yale University Press.

Dahl, R. A. (1966). Further reflections on "the elitist theory of democracy." *American Political Science Review, 60*, 296–303.

Dahl, R. A. (1968). Power. In *International encyclopaedia of the social sciences* (pp. 405–15). New York: Macmillan.

Dahl, R. A. (1971). *Polyarchy*. New Haven, Conn.: Yale University Press.

Dahl, R. A. (1986). Power as the control of behavior. In S. Lukes (Ed.), *Power* (pp. 37–58). Oxford: Blackwell.

DeLoughry, T. J. (1990, August 1). Crisis at nation's largest guarantor raises fears for the soundness of student-loan programs. *The Chronicle of Higher Education*, pp. A16, A17, A19.

DeLoughry, T. J. (1990, August 8). $200-million in short-term aid enables student-loan fund to avert bankruptcy. *The Chronicle of Higher Education*, pp. A1, A18.

DeLoughry, T. J. (1990, October 3). Administration eyes linking student aid to academic record. *The Chronicle of Higher Education*, pp. A1, A28.

DeLoughry, T. J. (1990, October 10). U.S. says it will dissolve troubled loan guarantor, transfer $9 billion portfolio to stable agencies. *The Chronicle of Higher Education*, pp. A20, A21.

DeLoughry, T. J. (1990, October 17). Long-term effects of Senate student-loan investigation debated. *The Chronicle of Higher Education*, pp. A23, A28.

DeLoughry, T. J. (1990, November 7). Deficit-reduction plan could tighten budgets for student aid and research. *The Chronicle of Higher Education*, pp. A27, A28.

DeLoughry, T. J. (1990, December 19). Cavazos resigns as secretary of education; White House reportedly asked him to go. *The Chronicle of Higher Education*, pp. A1, A19.

DeLoughry, T. J. (1991, January 9). Colleagues expect Education nominee will be savvy and forceful secretary. *The Chronicle of Higher Education*, pp. A17, A20.

DeLoughry, T. J. (1991, January 23). Bush's budget asks for major increase in '92–93 Pell Grants. *The Chronicle of Higher Education*, pp. A1, A22.

DeLoughry, T. J. (1991, February 13). More aid proposed for neediest students; Middle-income Pell grants would be cut. *The Chronicle of Higher Education*, pp. A18, A19, A26.

DeLoughry, T. J. (1991, March 27). Preparation pays off as students impress lawmakers with testimony on aid. *The Chronicle of Higher Education*, pp. A23, A24.

DeLoughry, T. J. (1991, April 3). Bush asks Education Dept. officials to quit; Xerox chief nominated as deputy. *The Chronicle of Higher Education*, p. A21.

DeLoughry, T. J. (1991, May 1). Lawmakers, college officals focus on Pell Grants in effort to revise nation's student aid programs. *The Chronicle of Higher Education*, pp. A17, A22.

DeLoughry, T. J. (1991, May 22). Senate study sees "ultimate collapse" of U.S. loan program unless reforms are made. *The Chronicle of Higher Education*, p. A25.

DeLoughry, T. J. (1991, July 17). Lawmakers face challenge of revamping $11-billion-a-year student-loan system. *The Chronicle of Higher Education*, pp. A15, A18.

DeLoughry, T. J. (1991, August 7). White House backs income-contingent loans, but many colleges say the program is flawed. *The Chronicle of Higher Education*, pp. A15, A16.

DeLoughry, T. J. (1991, September 18). CUNY ex-official picked for higher-education post. *The Chronicle of Higher Education*, p. A35.

DeLoughry, T. J. (1991, October 30). Lawmakers clash over 2 versions of education bill. *The Chronicle of Higher Education*, pp. A1, A27, A31.

DeLoughry, T. J. (1991, December 4). Top U.S. higher-education official says he'll resign. *The Chronicle of Higher Education*, p. A21.

DeLoughry, T. J. (1991, December 11). U.S. student-aid official attributes resignation to management dispute. *The Chronicle of Higher Education*, p. A26.

DeLoughry, T. J. (1992, February 19). College officials' ties to financial institutions prompt questions about conflict of interest. *The Chronicle of Higher Education*, pp. A21, A24, A25.

DeLoughry, T. J. (1992, March 4). Four Senators introduce a bill to test direct federal loans at 300 colleges. *The Chronicle of Higher Education*, pp. A30.

DeLoughry, T. J. (1992, April 22). College officals say politics and budgetary constraints have doomed reauthorization bill's promise of reform. *The Chronicle of Higher Education*, pp. A29, A34, A35.

DeLoughry, T. J. (1992, May 13). College officials urge Congress to adopt a new Pell Grant formula. *The Chronicle of Higher Education*, pp. A25, A29.

DeLoughry, T. J. (1992, June 24). Final draft of higher education bill draws veto threat over student loans. *The Chronicle of Higher Education*, pp. A20, A21, A22.

DeLoughry, T. J. (1992, July 29). College officals say reauthorization law benefits some students, but that aid funds will be scarce. *The Chronicle of Higher Education*, pp. A15–A17.

DeParle, (1992, March 25). Trade schools near success as they lobby for survival. *The New York Times*, pp. A1, A21.

DeWitt, K. (1991, January 6). Education lobby getting crowded. *The New York Times*, Section 4A, pp. 38–39.

Dewey, J. (1988). *The public and its problems*. Athens, Ohio: Swallow Press.

Doyle, D. P., & Hartle, T. W. (1985). Facing the fiscal chopping block. *Change*, 17, 8–10, 54–56.

Doyle, D. P., & Hartle, T. W. (1986). Student-aid muddle. *Atlantic*, 257, 30–34.

Dreyfus, H. L. (1987). Beyond hermeneutics: Interpretation in late Heidegger and recent Foucault. In M. T. Gibbons (Ed.), *Interpreting Politics* (pp. 203–20). New York: New York University Press.

Duryea, E. D. (1981). The university and the state: A historical overview. In P. G. Altbach & R. O. Berdahl (Eds.), *Higher education in American society* (pp. 13–33). Buffalo, N.Y.: Prometheus Books.

Dye, T. R. (1980). *Understanding public policy*. Englewood Cliffs, N.J.: Prentice Hall.

Eddy, Jr., E. D. (1956). *Colleges for our land and time: The land grant idea in American education.* New York: Harper & Brothers.

Education policy: Chronology of action on education. (1981). *Congress and the nation: A review of government and politics (vol. 5), 1977-1980,* (pp. 657-77). Washington, D.C.: Congressional Quarterly.

Falkemark, G. (1982). *Power, theory and value.* Kungalv/Goteborg, Sweden: C. W. K. Gleerup.

Finn, Jr., C. E. (1977). *Education and the presidency.* Lexington, Mass.: Lexington Books.

Finn, Jr., C. E. (1978). *Scholars, dollars, and bureaucrats.* Washington, D.C.: Brookings Institution.

Finn, Jr., C. E. (1980, September). The future of education's liberal consensus. *Change,* 25-30.

Fischer, J. L. (1987). College costs and student debt: Will families bear the burden? *Educational Record, 68,* 18-22.

Ford, W. D. (1994). The direct student loan program: Acknowledging the future. In J. F. Jennings (Ed.), *National issues in education: Community service and student loans* (pp. 101-13). Bloomington, Ind.: Phi Delta Kappa International.

Foucault, M. (1980). *Power/knowledge: Selected interviews and other writings 1972-1977* (C. Gordon, Ed.). Brighton, Sussex, (U.K.): Harvester Press.

Foucault, M. (1986). Disciplinary power and subjection. In S. Lukes (Ed.), *Power* (pp. 229-42). New York: New York University Press.

Fraas, C. (1990). *Guaranteed student loans: Defaults.* Washington, D.C.: Congressional Research Service.

Fraser, N. (1989). Foucault on modern power: Empirical insights and normative confusions. In N. Fraser (Ed.), *Unruly practices* (pp. 17-32). Minneapolis: University of Minnesota Press.

Geertz, C. (1973). *The interpretation of culture.* New York: Basic Books.

Gerstenzang, J. (1995, September, 27). Senate looks high and low for final cuts. *Los Angeles Times,* p. A11.

Gibbons, M. T. (1987). Introduction: The politics of interpretation. In M. T. Gibbons (Ed.), *Interpreting Politics* (pp. 1-31). New York: New York University Press.

Giddens, A., & Turner, J. (Eds). (1987). *Social theory today.* Stanford, Calif.: Stanford University Press.

Gillam, R. (Ed.). (1971). *Power in postwar America.* Boston: Little, Brown.

Gillespie, D. A., & Carlson, N. (1983). *Trends in student aid: 1963 to 1983.* Washington, D.C.: College Entrance Examination Board.

Gladieux, L. E. (1977). Education lobbies come into their own. *Change, 9,* 42–43.

Gladieux, L. E. (1978). Appraising the influence of the education lobbies: The case of higher education. In E. K. Mosher & J. L. Wagoner, Jr. (Eds.), *The changing politics of education: Prospects for the 1980s* (pp. 266–73).

Gladieux, L. E. (1980). What has Congress wrought? *Change, 12,* 25–31.

Gladieux, L. E. (1983). The use, misuse, and non-use of policy research in student aid policy-making. *The Journal of Student Financial Aid, 13,* 13–17.

Gladieux, L. E. (1986). Student financial assistance: Past commitments, future uncertainties. *Academe, 6,* 9–15.

Gladieux, L. E. (Ed). (1989). *Radical reform or incremental change: Student loan policy alternatives for the federal government.* New York: College Board.

Gladieux, L. E., & Wolanin, T. R. (1976). *Congress and the colleges.* Lexington, Mass.: D. C. Heath.

Gladieux, L. E., & Wolanin, T. R. (1978). Federal politics. In D. W. Breneman & C. E. Finn, Jr. (Eds). *Public policy and private higher education* (pp. 197–230). Washington, D.C.: Brookings Institution.

Goodling, B. (1994). Direct student loans: A questionable public policy decision. In J. F. Jennings (Ed.), *National issues in education: Community service and student loans* (pp. 115–30). Bloomington, Ind.: Phi Delta Kappa International.

Government Accounting Office. (1991). *Student loans: Direct loans could save money and simplify program administration.* Washington, D.C.: U.S. Government Printing Office.

Graham, H. D. (1984). *The uncertain triumph: Federal education policy in the Kennedy and Johnson years.* Chapel Hill: University of North Carolina Press.

Gray, J. (1995, September 27). Senators refuse to save national service program. *The New York Times,* p. D22.

Gray, J. (1996, April 26). Both Congress and Clinton find cause for cheer in the final budget deal. *The New York Times,* p. A12.

Habermas, J. (1979). *Communication and the evolution of society.* Boston: Beacon Press.

Habermas, J. (1984). *Theory of communicative action.* Vol. 1: *Reason and the rationalization of society.* Boston: Beacon Press.

Habermas, J. (1986). Hannah Arendt's communications concept of power. In S. Lukes (Ed.), *Power* (pp. 75–93). New York: New York University Press.

Habermas, J. (1987). *The theory of communicative action*. Vol. 2: *Lifeworld and system: A critique of functionalist reason*. Boston: Beacon Press.

Hall, R. L., & Evans, C. L. (1990). The power of subcommittees. *Journal of Politics, 52*, 335–55.

Hamm, K. E. (1983). Patterns of influence among committees, agencies, and interest groups. *Legislative Studies Quarterly, 8*, 379–426.

Hamm, K. E. (1986). The role of "subgovernments" in U.S. state policy making: An exploratory analysis. *Legislative Studies Quarterly, 11*, 321–51.

Hartle, T. (1990, January/February). Federal support for higher education in the '90s: Boom, bust, or something in between? *Change*, 32–57.

Herbert, B. (1995, May 24). Good works? Bah! *The New York Times*, p. A21.

Herzlinger, R. E., & Jones, F. (1990). Pricing public sector services: The tuition gap. In L. L. Leslie & R. E. Anderson (Eds.), *ASHE reader on finance in higher education* (pp. 240–55). Needham Heights, Mass.: Ginn Press.

Higher Education Amendments of 1980: What do they mean for colleges and students. (1986, June 11). *The Chronicle of Higher Education, 12*, 14–15.

Hobbes, T. (1651/1991). *Leviathan* (R. Tuck, Ed.). Cambridge: Cambridge University Press.

Hollinger, D. A. (1985). Historians and the discourse of intellectuals. In D. A. Hollinger (Ed.), *In the American province: Studies in the history and historiography of ideas* (pp. 130–51). Baltimore: Johns Hopkins University Press.

Honey, J. C. (1972). The election, politics, and higher education. *Science, 178*, 1243.

Honey, J. C. (1979). Higher education's great opportunity. *Educational Record, 60*, 329–35.

Honneth, A. (1987). Critical theory. In A. Giddens & J. C. Turner (Ed.), *Social theory today* (pp. 347–82). Stanford, Calif.: Stanford University Press.

Hook, J. (1980, September 15). Senate rejects higher-education bill; Opponents cite costs of student loans. *The Chronicle of Higher Education, 21*, pp. 15–16.

Hooyman, (1992, February 25). Testimony before the Senate Committee on Labor and Human Resources.

Hrebenar, R. J. & Scott, R. K. (1990). *Interest group politics in America*. Englewood Cliffs, N.J.: Prentice Hall.

Hume, D. (1748/1920). *Enquiry concerning human understanding* (L. A. Selby-Bigge, Ed.). Oxford: Clarendon.

Hunt, S. (1977). NAICU's growing pains. *Change, 9,* 50–51.

Hunter, F. (1953). *Community power structure.* Chapel Hill: University of North Carolina Press.

Hyatt, J. C. (1991, January 2). Sallie Mae to buy Chase portfolio of student loans. *The Wall Street Journal,* p. A3.

Jaschik, S. (1993, March 10). Popularity of direct-lending proposal blunts banking lobby's assault on Capitol Hill. *The Chronicle of Higher Education,* pp. A28.

Jaschik, S. (1993, May 19). First 1,500 participants to be selected for service program . *The Chronicle of Higher Education,* pp. A21

Jaschik, S. (1993, June 2). Opponents of loan plan are said to use students as fronts. *The Chronicle of Higher Education,* pp. A18, A20.

Jaschik, S. (1993, June 30). Senate ready to compromise on direct lending. *The Chronicle of Higher Education,* pp. A21–22.

Jaschik, S., & Mercer, J. (1993, June 2). House backs direct lending to students as it passes president's budget. *The Chronicle of Higher Education,* pp. A18, A20.

Johnstone, D. B., Evans, S. V., & Jerue, R. T. (1990). Reauthorization: What's important, what's not. *Educational Record, 71,* 29–33.

Joseph, S. (1988). *Political theory and power.* New York: E. J. Brill.

Kassebaum, N. L. (1994). National service: A watchful concern. In J. F. Jennings (Ed.), *National issues in education: Community service and student loans* (pp. 31–50). Bloomington, Ind.: Phi Delta Kappa International.

Kennedy, E. (1991, March 18). Congress will shape future of student aid with Higher Education Act. *Roll Call,* pp. 13, 15.

Kennedy, E. (1994). Enacting the National and Community Service Trust Act of 1993. In J. F. Jennings (Ed.), *National issues in education: Community service and student loans* (pp. 13–29). Bloomington, Ind.: Phi Delta Kappa International.

Keppel, F. (1987). The Higher Education Acts contrasted, 1965–86: Has federal policy come of age? *Harvard Educational Review, 57,* 49–67.

King, L. (1975). *The Washington lobbyists for higher education.* Lexington, Mass.: Lexington Books.

Konigsberg, E. (1993, July 12). Sallie Maen't. *New Republic,* pp. 15–16.

Kunnin, M. M. (1994). Student Loan Reform Act of 1993. In J. F. Jennings (Ed.), *National issues in education: Community service and student loans* (pp. 87–99). Bloomington, Ind.: Phi Delta Kappa International.

Latour, B. (1986). The powers of association. In J. Law (Ed.), *Power, action, and belief: A new sociology of knowledge* (pp. 264–80). London: Routledge and Kegan Paul.

Lazarsfeld, P. F. (1972). *Qualitative analysis: Historical and critical essays.* Boston: Allyn and Bacon.

Lederman, D. (1996, February 2). Aid for whom? *The Chronicle of Higher Education*, pp. A23, A25.

Lee, J. B. (1983, Fall). Reauthorizing the Higher Education Act. *The Journal of College Admissions*, 27–31.

Lee, J. B. & Merisotis, J. P. (1990). *Proprietary schools: Programs, policies and prospects.* ASHE-ERIC Higher Report No. 5. Washington, D.C.: George Washington University, School of Education and Human Development.

Leslie, L. L. & Brinkman, P. (1988). *The economic value of higher education.* New York: Macmillan.

Locke, J. (1689/1959). *An essay concerning human understanding* (A. C. Fraser, Ed.). New York: Dover.

Lowi, T. J. (1969). *The end of liberalism: Ideology, policy, and the crisis of public authority.* New York: W. W. Norton.

Lowi, T. J. (1971). American business, public policy, case-studies, and political theory. In J. R. Champlin (Ed.), *Power* (pp. 132–66). New York: Atherton Press.

Lu, H. (1965). *Federal role in education.* New York: American Press.

Lukes, S. (1974). *Power: A radical view.* London: Macmillan.

Lukes, S. (1978). Power and authority. In T. Bottomre & R. Nisbet (Eds.), *A history of sociological analysis* (pp. 633–76). New York: Basic Books.

Lukes, S. (Ed.) (1986). *Power.* New York: New York University Press.

Machiavelli, N. (1513/1977). *The prince.* (R. M. Adams, Ed. & Trans.). New York: W. W. Norton.

Manegold, C. S. (1995, March 31). Clinton's favorite, AmeriCorps, is attacked by the Republicans. *The New York Times*, p. A25.

Meranto, P. (1967). *The politics of federal aid to education in 1965: A study in political innovation.* Syracuse, N.Y.: Syracuse University Press.

McCarthy, C. (1995, July 29). The assault on AmeriCorps. *The Washington Post*, p. A13.

McCarthy, T. (1992). The critique of impure reason: Foucault and the Frankfurt School. In T. E. Wartenberg (Ed.), *Rethinking power* (pp. 121–48). Albany: State University of New York Press.

McClelland, C. A. (1971). Power and influence. In J. R. Champlin (Ed.), *Power* (pp. 35–65). New York: Atherton Press.

McCool, D. (1990). Subgovernments as determinants of political viability. *Political Science Quarterly, 105,* 269–93.

McCool, D. (1989). Subgovernments and the impact of policy fragmentation and accommodation. *Policy Studies Review, 8,* 264–87.

McGuinness, Jr., A. C. (1981). The federal government and postsecondary education. In P. G. Altbach & R. O. Berdahl (Eds.), *Higher education in American society* (pp. 157–79). Buffalo, N.Y.: Prometheus Books.

McNamara, W. A. (1976). The wallflower dances: Education lobby steps out. *CASE Currents, 2,* 4–7.

Meltsner, A. J. (1972). Political feasibility and policy analysis. *Public Administration Review, 32,* 859–67.

Mills, C. W. (1956). *The power elite.* Oxford: Oxford University Press.

Mills, C. W. (1959). *The sociological imagination.* New York: Oxford University Press.

Moore, Jr., B. (1988). Review essay [Review of *The sources of social power. Vol. I: A history of power from the beginning to A.D.1760*]. *History and Theory, 27,* 169–77.

Morgan, (1981). Academia and the federal government. *Policy Studies Journal, 10,* 70–84.

Morgenthau, H. J. (1971). Power as a political concept. In J. R. Champlin (Ed.), *Power* (pp. 19–34). New York: Atherton Press.

Mortenson, T. G. (1990). *The impact of increased loan utilization among low family income students.* ACT Research Report No. 90–91. Iowa City, Iowa: ACT.

Mortenson, T. G. (1991). *Equity of higher educational opportunity for women, black, Hispanic and low income students.* ACT Research Report No. 91-91. Iowa City, Iowa: ACT.

Moynihan, D. P. (1971). On universal higher education. In W. T. Furniss (Ed.), *Higher education for everybody: Issues and implications* (pp. 233–54). Washington, D.C.: American Council on Higher Education.

Moynihan, D. P. (1975). The politics of higher education. *Daedalus, 104,* 128–47.

Munger, F. J., & Fenno, Jr, R. F. (1962). *National politics and federal aid to education.* Syracuse, N.Y.: Syracuse University Press.

Murray, M. A. (1976). Defining the higher education lobby. *Journal of Higher Education, 57,* 79–92.

Myers, C. (1990, October 3). Lenders assailed in Senate investigation of student loan programs. *The Chronicle of Higher Education,* p. A29.

National Association of Student Financial Aid Administrators. (May, 1991). *Recommendations for reauthorization.* Washington, D.C.: Author.

National Commission on Excellence in Education (1983). *A nation at risk: The imperative for educational reform.* Washington, D.C.: The Commission.

National Council of Higher Education Loan Programs and the Consumer Bank Association. (1991). *Assessing the impact of direct lending.* Washington, D.C.: Author.

Newton, K. (1969). A critique of the pluralist model. *Acta Sociologica, 12,* 209–43.

Nicholson, R. A. (1991, October 28). Cover letter to *Assessing the impact of direct lending.*

Ozer, K. A (1986). Congress and the politics of financial aid: A student view. *Academe, 72,* 25–27.

Parsons, T. (1951). *The social system.* New York: Free Press.

Parsons, T. (1963). On the concept of political power. *Proceedings of the American Philosophical Society, 107,* 232–62.

Parsons, T. (1967). *Sociological theory and modern society.* New York: Free Press.

Pear, R. (1991, January 7). Administration seeking to bypass banks in student loan program. *The New York Times,* pp. A1, A13.

Permanent Subcommittee on Investigations. (1991). *Abuses in federal student aid programs.* Washington, D.C.: U.S. Government Printing Office.

Pitsch, M. (1990, August 11). E.D. declines to rescue student-loan guarantor. *Education Week,* p. 42.

Polsby, N. W. (1980). *Community power and political theory: A further look at problems of evidence and inference.* New Haven, Conn.: Yale University Press.

Popiel. L. A. (1995, June 27). Student-loan plan creates controversy. *The Christian Science Monitor,* p. 9.

Poulantzas, N. (1986). Class power. In S. Lukes (Ed.), *Power* (pp. 144–55). New York: New York University Press.

Rasmussen, D. M. (1990). *Reading Habermas.* Cambridge, Mass.: Basil Blackwell.

Reneging on AmeriCorps. (1995, March 15). *The New York Times*, p. A24.

Riker, W. H. (1964). Some ambiguities in the notion of power. *American Political Science Review, 58*, 341–49.

Rogers, D. (1994, January 26). Two liberal champions leave House, bringing fresh Democrats to the fore. *The Wall Street Journal*, p. A5.

Rogers, D. (1995, July 11). House GOP leaders move to wipe out national service, education projects. *The Wall Street Journal*, p. B4.

Rosenbaum, D. E. (1996, April 26). Ammunition for the Fall. *The New York Times*, pp. A1, A12.

Rosenzweig, R. M. (1982). *The research universities and their patrons*. Berkeley: University of California Press.

Ross, E. D. (1942). *Democracy's college: The land-grant movement in the formative stage*. Ames: Iowa State College Press.

Rorty, R. (1987). Method, social science and social hope. In M. T. Gibbons (Ed.), *Interpreting politics* (pp. 241–59). New York: New York University Press.

Rudolph, F. (1990). *The American college and university*. Athens: University of Georgia Press.

St. John, E. P., & Noell, J. (1989). The impact of financial aid on access: An analysis of progress with special consideration of minority access. *Research in Higher Education, 30*(2), 563–82.

Sanchez, R. (1995, January 10). Goodling vows a fresh look at education. *The Washington Post*, p. A15.

Sanchez, R. (1995, January 31). National service corps caught in the cross-fire. *The Washington Post*, p. A1, A6.

Sanchez, R. (1995, March 24). National service program shows profile to stall cuts. *The Washington Post*, p. A21.

Saunders, Jr., C. B. (1991, April 3). The broadest changes in student aid in 25 years could be part of the Education Amendments of 1992. *The Chronicle of Higher Education*, pp. B1, B2.

Schattschneider, E. E. (1970). *The semi-sovereign people*. New York: Holt, Rinehart and Winston.

Schonberger, B. (1991, May 8). Student lobbyists "set the tone of priorities" for new higher education act. *The Chronicle of Higher Education*, pp. A1, A22.

Schuster, J. H. (1982). Out of the frying pan: The politics of education in a new era. *Phi Delta Kappan, 63*, 583–91.

Segal, E. (1994). Toward the reality of national service. In J. F. Jennings (Ed.), *National issues in education: Community service and student loans* (pp. 3–11). Bloomington, Ind.: Phi Delta Kappa International.

Senate panel adopts plan for direct student loans. (1993, June 11). *The Wall Street Journal*, p. A5

Separate regulation of colleges, proprietary schools to be proposed. (1995, September 8). *The Chronicle of Higher Education*, p. A46

Simon, H. (1957). *Models of man*. New York: Wiley.

Slaughter, S. (1990). *The higher learning and high technology: Dynamics of higher education policy formation*. Albany: State University of New York Press.

Stanfield, R. L. (1982). Student aid lobby learns new tricks to fight Reagan's spending cutbacks. *National Journal, 14,* 1261–64.

Stanfield, R. L. (1995, June 17). Economic and educational opportunities. *National Journal*, pp. 1487–90.

Sundquist, J. L. (1968). *Politics and policy: The Eisenhower, Kennedy, and Johnson years*. Washington, D.C.: Brookings Institution.

Thomas, N. C. (1975). *Education in national politics*. New York: David McKay Company.

Vobejda, B. (1989, August 16). Trade schools, colleges in tug of war. *The Washington Post*, A19.

Waldman, S. (1995, March/April). Sallie Mae fights back: The brutal politics of student-loan reform. *Lingua Franca: The review of academic life,* 34–42.

Waldman, S. (1995). *The bill: How the adventures of Clinton's national service bill reveal what is corrupt, comic, cynical—and noble—about Washington*. New York: Viking.

Wartenberg, T. E. (1992). Situated social power. In T. E. Wartenberg (Ed.), *Rethinking power* (pp. 79–101). Albany: State University of New York Press.

Wartzman, R. (1995, January 17). Gingrich differs with Clinton on AmeriCorps. *The Wall Street Journal*, p. A18.

Washington update. (1991, September 18). *The Chronicle of Higher Education,* A36.

Ways & Means Committee. (1991, June 12). *The Chronicle of Higher Education,* A19.

Ways & Means Committee. (1992, February 12). *The Chronicle of Higher Education,* A23.

Wells, R. M. (1995, July 22). National service gets little support. *Congressional Quarterly*, p. 2182.

Wells, R. M. (1995, December 9). Sharp ideological divisions mark student loan battle. *Congressional Quarterly*, pp. 3740–41.

Wells, R. M., & Tin, A. (1995, May 27). GOP plan would close doors of department in a year. *Congressional Quarterly*, p. 1512.

Wells, R. M., & Nitschke, L. (1995, September 30). Panels' plans would increase loans costs for students. *Congressional Quarterly*, pp. 3008–9.

White, B. (1993). The Bush administration's proposals for reauthorization of the Higher Education Act. In J. F. Jennings (Ed.), *National issues in education: The past is prologue* (pp. 73–87). Bloomington, Ind.: Phi Delta Kappa International.

Wilson, J. T. (1982). *Higher education and the Washington scene: 1982.* Chicago: University of Chicago Press.

Wolanin, T. R., & Gladieux, L. E. (1975). A charter for federal policy toward postsecondary education: The Education Amendments of 1972. *Journal of Law and Education, 4,* 301–24.

Wolanin, T. R., & Gladieux, L. E. (1975). The political culture of a policy arena. In M. Holden, Jr. & D. L. Dresang (Eds.), *What government does* (pp. 177–207). Beverly Hills, Calif.: Sage.

Wolanin, T. R. (1976). The national higher education associations: Political resources and style. *Phi Delta Kappan, 58,* 181–84.

Wolanin, T. R. (1990). Making higher education's case in Washington. In S. H. Barnes (Ed.), *Points of view on American higher education* (pp. 228–31). Lewiston, N.Y.: Edward Mellen Press.

Wolanin, T. R. (1993). Reauthorizing the Higher Education Act: Federal policy making for postsecondary education. In J. F. Jennings (Ed.), *National issues in education: The past is prologue* (pp. 89–105). Bloomington, Ind.: Phi Delta Kappa International.

Yarrington, R. (1983). Higher education: Two public relations case studies. *Public Relations Review, 12,* 396–419.

Zapler, M. (1994, September 21). President Clinton swears in 15,000 for the national service program. *The Chronicle of Higher Education*, p. A38.

Zook, J. (1993, February 17). Clinton administration may start direct lending to students by next year. *The Chronicle of Higher Education*, p. A18.

Zook, J. (1993, August 11). House-Senate comprise gives White House most of what it wanted on direct lending. *The Chronicle of Higher Education*, pp. A23–24.

Zook, J. (1994, February 2). Key chairman to retire. *The Chronicle of Higher Education*, pp. A21, A24.

Zook, J. (1994, May 18). U.S. announces next group of colleges to join direct lending. *The Chronicle of Higher Education*, p. A26.

Zook, J. (1994, June 8). Negotiators haggle over details of direct lending. *The Chronicle of Higher Education*, p. A20.

Zook, J. (1994, July 13). Loan-guarantee agencies adopt a range of strategies to cope with the era of direct lending to students. *The Chronicle of Higher Education*, p. A23–24.

Zook, J. (1994, October 26). U.S. plans to let those with guaranteed loans refinance their debts in direct-lending program. *The Chronicle of Higher Education*, p. 38.

Zook, J. (1994, November 2). Clinton extols direct lending and unveils a new name for it. *The Chronicle of Higher Education*, p. A53.

Zook, J. (1994, December 7). As more colleges sign up for direct lending, GOP lawmakers express reservations. *The Chronicle of Higher Education*, p. A32.

Zook, J. (1995, January 20). Plans in Congress to limit direct-lending program fail to curb enthusiasm of financial-aid officers. *The Chronicle of Higher Education*, p. A26.

Zook, J. (1995, February 10). Subcommittee chairman advocates "limited" role US role in education. *The Chronicle of Higher Education*, p. A33.

Zook, J. (1995, March 3). House panel slashes more than $240 million in federal student aid, other college programs. *The Chronicle of Higher Education*, p. A29.

Zook, J. (1995, April 7). Congressional review renews debate about direct lending. *The Chronicle of Higher Education*, p. A29.

Zook, J. (1995, May 19). Backers of direct lending question loan-guarantee. *The Chronicle of Higher Education*, pp. A34–35.

Zook, J. (1995, May 26). The battle over subsidies. *The Chronicle of Higher Education*, pp. A23, A27.

Zook, J. (1995, June 9). Lobbying for survival, TRIO programs point to success stories. *The Chronicle of Higher Education*, p. A26.

Zook, J. (1995, June 16). National-service program hurt by politicking over its future. *The Chronicle of Higher Education*, p. A29.

Zook, J. (1995, July 21). Lawmakers press Education Dept. on alleged intimidation of student-aid critics. *The Chronicle of Higher Education*, p. A24

Zook, J. (1995, July 28). House's budget for education restricts direct-loan program. *The Chronicle of Higher Education*, p. A35.

Zook, J. (1995, August 11). House votes to end national-service program: Clinton vows to veto bill. *The Chronicle of Higher Education*, p. A25.

Zook, J. (1995, August 18). Both sides cite numbers in debate over direct lending. *The Chronicle of Higher Education*, p. A27.

Zuckman, J. (1991, April 13). Alexander and Senators differ on who gets college aid. *Congressional Quarterly*, pp. 919–20.

Zuckman, J. (1991, October 12). Panel approves Pell Grant plan, but tougher tests are ahead. *Congressional Quarterly*, pp. 2958–59.

Zuckman, J. (1993, May 8). Panel favors Clinton's plan for direct student loans. *Congressional Quarterly*, pp.1152–53.

Zuckman, J. (1993, June 19). National service goes to floor in both chambers. *Congressional Quarterly*, p.1577.

Zuckman, J. (1993, July 24). Will national service funding cut into student aid? *Congressional Quarterly*, pp. 1959–60.

Zuckman, J. (1993, July 31). National service impasse ends; Conference to come. *Congressional Quarterly*, pp. 2055–56.

Zuckman, J. (1993, July 31). Accord reached on direct student loans, more compromises in works. *Congressional Quarterly*, pp. 2059–60.

Zuckman, J. (1993, August 7). Pared funding speeds passage of national service. *Congressional Quarterly*, pp. 2160–61.

Zuckman, J. (1993, August 14). Both sides hope to be no. 1 in dual loan system test. *Congressional Quarterly*, pp. 1152–53.

Zuckman, J. (1993, September 11). Senate clears national service despite GOP objections. *Congressional Quarterly*, p. 2397.

INDEX